The Collector's Encyclopedia of Toys and Dolls

The Collector's Encyclopedia of Toys and Dolls

edited by Lydia Darbyshire

CHARTWELL
BOOKS, INC.

A QUINTET BOOK

Published by Chartwell Books Inc.,
A Division of Book Sales Inc.,
110 Enterprise Avenue,
Secaucus, New Jersey 07094

ISBN 1-55521-667-6

This book was designed and produced by
Quintet Publishing Limited
6 Blundell Street, London N7

Art Director: Peter Bridgewater
Designer: Dave Johnson
Project Editor: Lydia Darbyshire
Editor: Lindsay Porter

Typeset in Great Britain by
Central Southern Typesetters, Eastbourne
Manufactured in Singapore by
Tien Wah Press (Pte) Ltd

Some of the material in this book
appeared in previous publications

Contents

Toys, unlike many other antiques, have an almost universal appeal. Everyone has owned at least a few playthings in childhood and

Introduction

experienced the joy of acquisition that is very similar to the excitement the adult collector feels when buying a rare model car or an exceptionally fine French

automaton. While a piece of jade or a Meissen dessert service may appeal to only a few people, antique toys arrest the attention of the urbane and the unsophisticated alike. Because of this high level of interest, prices have spiralled and collectors compete for especially good pieces.

In character, toy collectors range from the tough, mechanically minded, who look for metal toys and quantify the rarity of trains or buy mint-condition, diecast models to be hoarded away in their boxes, to those who only purchase toys that can be used as decorative antiques, and they are inevitably attracted to dolls and automata, those exquisitely constructed mechanical figures that were originally made for display.

A

Made *c.*1902 by Bing, this rare, hand-painted model of the Spider car is among the earliest items available to collectors of motor vehicles. The car is 13in (32cm) long and has real leather seats and rubber tyres. Bing also made a steam-powered version.

A

Each week, across Europe and the United States, there are busy shows, fairs and swap-meets, where enthusiasts can sort through a vast assortment of merchandise or sell their own surplus items. Most of the large salerooms now run regular auctions of toys and those auctions are often further divided into specialist areas such as soldiers, dolls, diecasts and tinplate toys. In most antique markets and centres there are a few toy dealers, although decorative pieces such as dolls and automata are also found in the stock of general dealers. In the US and Australia, a number of specialists publish mail-order lists of their stock, so that collectors in the most remote places are constantly offered fresh items.

A

Manufactured in the 1960s, these Mignot figures representing soldiers and a horse-drawn gun and supply cart from the Confederate Army during the American Civil War were produced using moulds that had been made *c.*1900. The figures are 54mm tall.

B

This splendid example of a French miniature car – the P2 Alfa Romeo – was introduced by the Paris-based company C.I.J. (Compagnie Industrielle du Jouet) in 1925. The tyres with shaped tread identify this example as one of the second series. It has been repainted in silver.

C

A group of toys made by some of the leading manufacturers of late 19th- and early 20th-century toys: a battleship, made *c.*1902 by Gebrüder Bing of Nuremberg; a gauge 0 locomotive, tender and rolling stock by Märklin of Göppingen; and a boxed set of a colour party of toy soldiers by Britains of London.

A

The most expensive toys are the automata, especially those made in France by such famous firms as Decamps, Lambert or Bontems, all of which worked in Paris. These companies created tableaux and mechanized figures that imitated or parodied contemporary life, so that we find monkeys dressed in the costume of society elegants and beautiful bisque-headed ladies who preen themselves in dainty mirrors or appear to play the piano. Such figures are very expensive to produce and were made, not for children, but as luxury novelty gifts for adults. An automaton often took pride of place in the drawing room or boudoir and was set in motion as a special treat for visitors. Much simpler versions were made as

B

toys, such as babies that appear to cry when their prams are pulled along or birds that flap their wings and lay eggs; but even these can now be quite expensive.

Because of the inherent quality of automata there is little surprise when individual pieces sell for record prices; but when a doll or tin toy sells for thousands, surprise is always expressed, since many of the objects were originally mass-produced and cheap. Dolls have always been popular with collectors, but in recent years the prices paid for examples at the top range of the market – Bru, Jumeau, Lenci or Kämmer & Reinhardt, for instance – have risen steeply, and now collectors are looking at other areas: modern dolls, celluloid and vinyl dolls and fabric dolls now all find keen buyers. Tinplate toys have emerged as a respectable collecting field since the 1960s, and thereafter prices for the better pieces moved steadily upwards, though they have levelled off recently. The most popular items reflect contemporary transport, especially cars and delivery vehicles, and a well-preserved tourer by Carette or a splendid battleship (complete with lifeboats) by the other

great German firm, Bing, always finds an eager buyer. Such manufacturers produced good quality models, heavily constructed to withstand years of play, and although the paintwork is often damaged, the basic toy frequently remains in working order.

Another German maker, Lehmann, created more amusing, but ephemeral pieces, such as a clown attempting to control a wayward donkey or a bride battering her new husband – the type of piece that a pavement vendor could display to city gentlemen on the look-out for a colourful toy for a son or godchild. Lehmann clockwork toys were made from fairly thin, very brightly lithographed tinplate, and they now offer an attractive collecting field, as a large number have survived. Penny toys were another popular line for street sellers – tiny models of horses, carriages, cars and trains. They now hold great appeal because so many of them can be displayed in a small space.

As early tinplate has become more expensive, people have turned in growing numbers to the more recent diecast toys that were produced in much greater variety for the more affluent children of the post

A

war period. These accurate models, most highly valued when they are still in their original boxes, are now so tightly priced and categorized that collecting them has become as formal a business as collecting stamps or coins, with regular price lists and narrow classifications. So many have survived that it is easy to become hooked, and since they can still occasionally be found in a jumble or garage sale, the chance of discovering a rarity is always just around the corner.

As early toys have become harder to find, a reproduction and 'collectors' edition', market has developed. Some of the firms which cater for that market do, indeed, reproduce the products they created many years ago; others issue limited editions of toys in a modern idiom, such as cars or London buses. As many of these

A

A

A

The massive self-propelled gun and the army staff car were made by Britains. The Dinky Guy Weetabix van (top) attracts attention because of the scarcity of the transfers; Dinky used the same basic van with a range of different names.

toys sell cheaply, they offer to people who do not wish to spend a great deal of money the chance to become part of the collecting fraternity. On the other hand, limited editions, particularly diecasts, sometimes escalate rapidly in value, so that is is also possible, with a good eye, to buy as an investment.

In this book, the main collecting areas are discussed and advice is given on how to avoid expensive mistakes, how to care for old toys and how to spot the work of some of the most famous makers. When first produced, most toys were made for pleasure. Above all, collecting should be enjoyable, concerned not so much with investment as with the appreciation of a maker's artistry.

B

HOW TO COLLECT

For many collectors of toys the aim is to acquire mint, preferably boxed items. Unfortunately, this ideal can rarely be achieved, and most collectors have to compromise.

As we will see, the range of toys available to collectors is immense, and one of the first decisions that a collector makes is not only what type of toy is to form the basis of the collection but also what particular area within a collecting field. Interest may have been aroused by a toy kept from childhood or in-

herited from a parent or grandparent; perhaps there is a family association with a particular manufacturer or place. The next decision will have to be the size of the ultimate collection. This may depend on financial considerations, time or storage space. It may depend, too, on the type of toy to be collected, for a collection of early German boats is obviously going to be much smaller than a collection of Britains infantry.

Whatever area you choose, before you spend any money, visit as many museums that contain displays of toys as possible, and look at the stock of dealers at toy fairs and swapmeets. Read as much as you can on the subject; some of the books and journals are listed at the end of this

book. Joining a specialist collectors' club will keep you in touch with other like-minded people and will be a useful way of buying or exchanging surplus figures later on if you are in the fortunate position of acquiring duplicates (which is likely if you are going to concentrate on toy soldiers or diecast vehicles).

When, at last, you buy, collect what appeals to you, even if it seems to be against the mainstream. You should spend as much as you can afford, however, to ensure that the toys you buy are in as good condition as possible. Occasionally, you may come across a damaged, restored or even repainted piece that is extremely rare or that you need to complete a particular display. It is acceptable to

B

A fine, live-steam model of a liner made by Bing c.1912. Flying the French flag, the ship is still in good condition and shows only minor flaking of the paintwork.

buy such a piece as a stop-gap until a perfect example comes your way, or the figure may be so rare that only damaged examples are likely to be offered for sale. As long as the damaged piece is priced accordingly, it will, in time, rise in value.

Toy collecting is now an established part of the antiques scene, and specialist fairs, swap-meets and auctions are held regularly throughout Europe and the US. The better auction houses produce catalogues that are useful reference books, include estimates of prices likely to be realized (or, that the auction house would like to be realized, which may be a slightly different matter). On the whole, however, these catalogues provide new collectors with a useful guide to the prices he or she is likely to have to pay.

Country and provincial sales are more of a problem. Lots are often catalogued by new recruits to the auction rooms, and buyers must take advantage of the viewing and not rely on descriptions in the catalogue. Even though in some countries buyers can reclaim their money if they can prove that lots have been inaccurately dated in the catalogue, this can be a long and difficult process. New collectors should buy at reputable auctions until they have gained some experience.

Before buying at auction, decide just how much you can afford to spend, remembering to include in your maximum sum both the buyer's premium and the VAT that will be due. The hammer price is not the price you will have to pay. When the lot in which you are interested comes up, aim to get in on the second bid. If the bidding goes beyond your limit, shake your head firmly and look down.

Similar caution should be exercised when buying from dealers. Most do look after the interests of their customers, but there are, unfortunately, some unscrupulous people who will take advantage of a new collector and try to pass on old, uninteresting stock or over-painted or restored pieces. Specialist sellers are always glad to welcome serious

new collectors, and they will generally provide invaluable advice and assistance. It is sensible to tell a dealer of the purpose and scope of your collection so that he or she can look out for pieces for it. In general, collectors are on safer ground if they buy from a dealer than from an auction house. Always make sure you obtain a detailed, dated invoice that includes a description of the condition of the piece. You should also make sure that the dealer will, from time to time, be prepared to let you return pieces, either as part of a trade or because your area of collecting changes. Some dealers will not do this because they have many items on commission or because they do not like recognizable pieces re-appearing in their stock. A refusal to take pieces back does not automatically mean that a dealer is unscrupulous.

A rare gauge 2, clockwork-powered *King Edward* locomotive with a six-wheeled tender in the livery of the London & North-Western Railway. It was made by Gebrüder Bing c.1902, and although the locomotive's leading bogie is missing, it is still an exciting, desirable piece.

This Smoking Monkey automaton was made by Gustave Vichy, said by some to be the king of automaton makers, c.1860. The monkey holds a lorgnette in one hand and an ivory cheroot holder in the other.

enthusiast, a motor car with good, original paintwork and fine external condition is preferable by far to one that runs beautifully but is badly chipped or dented.

For anyone beginning to collect toys, it is essential to be made aware of any repairs or replacement parts. Recently, because of the great skill of some restorers, it has become fashionable for dealers to claim that a re-paint or restoration by a highly regarded restorer is almost as good as an original finish – a claim that is obviously untrue, since nothing can compare with the soft patina of age. While it is proper to restore a toy that has lost almost all of its original paintwork, this course should be a last resort; originality is always preferable.

Replacement parts in non-ferrous metals or even plastic substances are also common, and the new collector needs to examine all sections of an expensive toy with great care before purchase. Most reputable dealers will supply buyers with a detailed bill stating condition, age and manufacturer. Those hunting in street markets, car boot or garage sales are completely on their own and it is there that highly priced fakes and

'marriages' are most likely to be encountered. What might seem to be the bargain of all time often turns out to be a clever mock-up, using parts from differing periods and even from completely different items. Established dealers, collectors' clubs and some auction rooms are all willing to assist new collectors who want to buy sensibly as an investment. They are aware that expensive mistakes can put people off collecting. So it is in their interest to give a degree of protection until the buyer has confidence in his own judgement.

Many antique toys are now purchased from mailing lists or auction catalogues, in which some general terms are used to describe condition. 'Very good' indicates that the piece is without any blemishes or dents, though it might be slightly faded or have the patina of age. 'Good' means that the piece is in reasonable, but not superb, condition. 'Play-worn' is an all-embracing term that can include anything from a slightly chipped toy to one that has lost all its paint and some parts as well! The latter category is more suitable for the restorer or a collector seeking spare parts to repair another item. As restoration can be very expensive,

B

UNDER-STANDING THE MARKET

When purchasing recently made tinplate toys such as robots or aircraft, it is advisable to make sure that they are still in working order, as much of their appeal depends on their complete performance with lights, sound and movement. It often surprises non-specialists to discover that collectors of vintage tinplate items are not concerned whether a toy is in full working order. To the

C

A Monkey Piano Player made in the early years of the 20th century when Vichy had been taken over by Triboulet. The musical movement contained in the base of the piece plays two airs, and the figure's jaws, eyelids, head and arms move when the mechanism is activated.

C

it is better for the novice to avoid items in very bad condition; they are very difficult to re-sell and repairs can cost more than the price of a perfect example. The phrase 'mint and boxed' is occasionally used for tin toys, but is more often reserved for diecast models of a more recent date. Perfection is necessary before a piece can legitimately be so described.

If a toy is purchased with some documentation, such as original receipts or a photograph of it with the first owner, these should be safely stored. Original boxes, even if in very poor condition, should also be kept, since they often help to establish the date or manufacturer. Toys in attractive boxes, such as those used by Lehmann or Martin, are especially desirable, and the original packaging adds to the value.

A

LOOKING AFTER YOUR ACQUIS- ITIONS

Manufacturers who created toys did so with the aim of encouraging children to play with them. The toys were attractively finished; they often had novelty actions; or they could be built up into convincing layouts and sets to represent railway systems or armies. These characteristics, designed to appeal to children, are now the feat- ures that contribute to their success as objects to be collected by adults. Originally made to be played with, toys today can be displayed in inter- esting and imaginative ways in even comparatively small homes.

However, even a medium-sized collection of toys needs considerable thought if it is to be displayed to best advantage, and if your collection includes boxes and the original pack- ing, you will have to contemplate making, or having made, some special shelves or cabinets. In the 1960s and 1970s plain, shallow, glass cases, with plate-glass shelves, were popular, and these complemented the decor of the Scandinavian style found in many homes at the time. Such cases are still one of the best ways of displaying ranks of soldiers or groups of diecast vehicles, and they have the advantage that they can be moved and re- arranged with comparative ease.

Open shelving should be avoided, for it affords the pieces no protection from harmful dust. How- ever, the cost of glass-fronted cabinets may prove prohibitive, and for smaller items, units may be successfully made from deep picture frames, although these will generally be too small for all but one or two groups of toys to be displayed satisfactorily. The recent trend of using old cabinets from chemists' and tobacconists' shops provides a suitable 'period' feel for the many toys, but such cabinets are both large and costly. Oak cabinets should be avoided for toy soldiers as the wood appears to induce lead rot in solid and hollow-cast figures.

If toys are to be displayed in a living room, it is important to keep them in the darkest part of the room and away from direct sunlight, which will fade the paintwork or colouring. Muslin curtains that filter damaging ultraviolet rays can be used, although these need to be of the museum-approved type. Even comparatively cheap toys deserve protection, as every true collector works to avoid any deterioration while a toy is in his or her care.

All toys will require an occasional dusting, and this should be done with a very soft cloth or brush. Do not use any cleaning substances or soap and water – the former will scratch away the surface, the latter will cause metal toys to rust. If a metal toy is very dirty, wipe it gently with a little machine oil applied with a soft cloth. It may take a long time to clean the surface, but this is the only way to ensure that no damage is caused. It is tempting to polish or wax a toy once it has been cleaned, but this should always be resisted, as a little of the polish will remain on the surface and eventually alter the appearance of the toy. An antique toy should not look as if it has just left the factory. If it does, it has probably been over-cleaned or over-restored.

Obviously, different types of toys have different storage requirements, but some of the main points to bear in mind are mentioned below. Acid-free tissue paper and cardboard boxes, deep enough to allow the lids to sag a little, are most satisfactory. Your aim must always be to keep your acquisitions safe from attack by acid and humidity, but the different materials from which toys are made have slightly different requirements.

LEAD AND LEAD ALLOYS

Lead rot or lead disease can cause whole battalions of toy soldier to crumble away. It happens when impurities in the lead cause it to oxydize, and it appears as roughish grey patches. It is often seen in figures that have been stored in damp places for any length of time, but fortunately it does not seem to spread to figures that are unaffected, and removing infected figures from a damp environment to suitable storage conditions stops the deterioration. When buying figures, look at the base, which is where lead rot is usually first seen. It also tends to affect parts of figures that are not painted, and ensuring that the paintwork of your figures is in good condition will help to protect them. Store your metal figures in a clean, dry environment, adding drying crystals to the cabinet if you suspect damp. Oil is, of course, to be preferred to water if any figure requires more thorough cleaning than the removal of dust.

TINPLATE

One of the commonest problems with tinplate toys is the dents that have been caused while the toy was played with. Although it is often possible to smooth dents out by using the back of a wooden spoon, the metal will probably have stretched slightly, and it will be impossible to restore the toy to its original shape. To avoid further damage, always wrap up your toys in several layers of newspaper or in bubble-wrap if you have to transport them.

Like figures made from lead and lead alloys, toys made of tinplate must be kept in a dry atmosphere – never keep a tin toy in a kitchen or bathroom. Once the metal has rusted externally nothing can be done to restore the toy. Internal rust can be

A

An early display box of a type first introduced by Britains in 1906 of the five regiments of the cavalry of the British Army. The set eventually became set 129, and it contained 14 figures each of the 2nd Life Guards, the 1st Dragoon Guards, the 2nd Dragoons (the Royal Scots Greys), the 11th Hussars and the 12th Lancers. Although acquiring an original, complete set is an ambition for many toy soldier collectors, many toy soldier enthusiasts make up sets such as this from other, incomplete sets and by repairing and repainting damaged pieces.

B

Britains set 26, the Boer Infantry, together with its splendid box, which adds greatly to the set's value and interest. The set was first issued in 1897 and continued to be made by Britains until 1913. The eight figures are at the slope in the original set; in 1906 Britains changed to on guard figures and to figures bearing shoulder arms, so it is possible to date such sets fairly accurately.

treated by gentle brushing with a soft wire brush or wire wool, and it is important to prevent the rust becoming established for it will gradually eat through the metal and destroy the lithographed decoration. Mechanisms that are rusty can be treated with small amounts of proprietary rust removers, which should deal with both rust and accumulated dirt. However, gaining access to the mechanism often means taking the toy to pieces. If you are determined to do this, bear in mind that not only will you have to open the tinplate clips that hold the toy together, you will have to bend them again to close them, which will inevitably weaken them – and you may not be the first person to try to get to the mechanism.

Repairing a clockwork mechanism is not a difficult task, but if you replace an original spring with a weaker one, the toy's efficiency will be reduced, while using a stronger spring can damage gears and lead to further, more complicated repairs. If a spring breaks near one or the other end, it can be reconnected without noticeably affecting the toy's performance, although shortening a spring by too much will diminish the power and shorten the duration of the action. Springs of the 'piano wire' variety, which are wound on to cylinders, tend to be sturdy and rarely break. The toys in which such springs were fitted were, in any case, cheaply made, and attempting to repair them may prove to be more trouble than it is worth.

Battery-operated tin toys often suffer from corrosion of the battery compartments, caused by original owners failing to remove the batteries when the toy was put away. If your collection includes battery-operated toys, always remember to remove the batteries whenever the toys are in store. Repairing loose connections can be a simple soldering task if they are easily accessible. However, it may be necessary to undo delicate tinplate tabs to reach the battery connections or even to remove the fabric used to clothe some automata and mechanical figures. In these circumstances, it may be wiser to leave well alone.

Do not store your tinplate toys in direct sunlight. They (like other toys) will fade. Similarly, keeping your toys in cases that are illuminated electrically can cause problems, not so much from the light but from the heat generated by the bulbs. Make sure that show cases are adequately ventilated.

COMPOSITION

Cardboard boxes and acid-free tissue paper are again the best way to store composition figures. Composition is especially prone to damage from damp, which can cause the wire armature to rust, and to excessive dryness, which can cause the composition itself to crack and shrink. You should also give your figures sufficient room to 'breathe' and not cram them together into boxes.

WAX

Wax figures should be kept in cabinets away from strong lights. Inspect the bodies of wax dolls from time to time, especially at the area at which the shoulder is attached to the body. The glue will harden with age and the calico may rot as the hardened glue contracts. Never attempt to clean the face of a wax or wax over papier mâché doll with water. A little cold cream may be use – but try

A

A bisque-head doll with a composition body by Heinrich Handwerck of Waltershausen, Germany, a company that was founded in 1886. The doll is 19in (48cm) tall.

an area that is not visible. Never store wax figures in plastic bags, as the condensation will affect the texture of the doll. White, natural materials – silk or fine cotton – are the safest fabrics to place next to a wax doll.

WOOD

Dolls made of wood and some sorts of composition should, as with wax dolls, never be moistened. The laquer used to varnish the doll will be water-based and you may even get down to the gesso layer underneath. Check wooden torsos for woodworm.

PAPER AND CARD

Soldiers made from these fragile materials should be stored in portfolios or plan chests so that they can be kept quite flat. They should also be protected from bright light, for ultraviolet will quickly fade paint and ink. Interleaf each sheet with acid-free tissue paper so that there is no chance of the ink from one sheet staining another. Never roll paper or card; it may tear or split.

BISQUE

It is possible to wash the faces of china and porcelain dolls, but take care not to let the water soak into the body.

PLASTIC

Far from being the unbreakable material that it was claimed when it first appeared on the toy scene, plastic figures, especially some of the early examples, should be stored as carefully as those made from apparently more fragile materials. Some of the early plastics contained a high proportion of chalk, which causes them to become dry and brittle; figures made from this snap very easily. Accessories made from some of the softer plastics seem to revert to messy lumps of melting matter. Most plastic figures are probably perfectly stable, but it is sensible to treat them carefully nevertheless.

CELLULOID

The first 'plastic' material to be produced, celluloid was originally manufactured from pulverized tissue paper, which was converted into nitrocellulose by the addition of nitric and sulphuric acids and combined with camphor, pigments, fillers and alcohol. The recipe for this highly inflammable substance was refined over the years, and most celluloid dolls were produced by the Rheinische Gummi- und Celluloid-Fabrik of Mannheim. In 1897 Rheinische Gummi was advertising its products as: 'unbreakable, washable dolls' heads of finest modelling and very light weight … colour-proof, washable and swimming dolls with movable arms in seldom seen beautiful colours and shapes.' It is, however, important to remember that celluloid is not unbreakable, and celluloid dolls should be handled with the same care and delicacy as their bisque counterparts. Strong light, especially sunlight, should be avoided, as not only will the skin colouring fade but the celluloid will become brittle. Moreover, although the vast majority of celluloid dolls were produced in Mannheim, other doll-making companies experimented with the substance. Kämmer & Reinhardt, for example, added colourings of carmine and carmine cinnabar by brushing the 'make-up' on to specially roughened areas of the dolls' faces, which were then coated with a transparent mat varnish that took away the rather fatty glaze of the celluloid. Needless to say, this colouring is not washable. If a celluloid doll is extremely dirty and you are not certain that it is made of washable celluloid, try rubbing an affected area with a little cold cream on a soft cloth, ideally choosing part of the doll's face or body that is hidden by clothes or hair to experiment on.

FABRIC

The greatest enemies of fabric dolls and soft toys are moths. Many people find the smell of mothballs unbearable, but there are modern equivalents, and it is sensible to store all cloth dolls with an insecticide. Washing fabric dolls, whether they are rag dolls (that is, made of linen, calico, cotton or muslin) or whether they are made of felt, stockinet or velvet is not practicable. Although some success may be achieved by using one of the proprietary dry cleaning fluids that are available as a spray and leave a white powder that can be shaken out, expert advice should be sought if a fabric doll is seriously discoloured and dirty. The materials used for stuffing fabric dolls varied. Some were stuffed with other types of cloth, while others were stuffed with sawdust, kapok and, recently, foam chips. If you acquire a fabric doll or soft toy and are worried that the stuffing may be harbouring insect pests, wrap the doll carefully in polythene and put it in your freezer for two weeks.

REPAIR AND RESTORATION

Hollow-cast toy soldiers are one of the few areas of collecting where it is perfectly permissible to repair, restore and repaint damaged figures. If your aim is to build up a regiment or a ceremonial display, you may have to buy damaged figures of especially rare sets. Indeed, this is part of the attraction of the hobby for many people. Specialist shops and journals cater for all aspects of the modellers' needs, and researching into uniforms and colours adds an extra dimension to any collection. The repair and restoration of toy soldiers in other materials and made by other methods should be undertaken only as a last resort, for composition and wooden figures will never look the same again and may well lose some of their resale value.

When you are collecting all other types of toy, repair and restoration should be left to the expert. Most collectors prefer a non-operational or damaged toy to one that has been mended – and possible irreparably damaged – by an amateur.

A

Many French toys exhibit considerable ingenuity of contruction. This fire-fighting set, Les Pompiers, has a steam-operated fire pump, a wheeled escape ladder and metal crew, all of which are painted rather than having lithographed decoration. The engine is 7½in (19cm) long, and the set was made *c*.1900.

B

Before motor cars became universally popular with tin toy manufacturers, fairground amusements made apt subjects. This highly decorated ferris wheel was made in Germany in the late 19th century, and such toys are greatly sought after and therefore difficult to find. Ferris wheels, which are also known as Russian carousels, were occasionally designed to be powered from stationary steam engines, although many were simply turned by hand. The degree of decoration can add to the value of toys like this.

A

A

CHAPTER

1

Dolls have existed from the earliest times. Whether it was

for religious, symbolic, votive or talismanic reasons, man

has long made images in his

Dolls

own likeness. The most

ancient civilizations –

Egyptian, Greek and Roman – made dolls; an Egypto-

Roman rag doll, dating from the 3rd or 4th century AD, was

A

This bisque-head, open-mouth doll bears the impressed mark *Made in Germany 129*, which suggests that she was made by J.D. Kestner of Walterhausen, a company that, in the first two decades of the 20th century, marked its dolls only with the mould number. The pate is of plaster, which is also typical of Kestner dolls. She stands 20in (50cm) tall and wears her original wig. The jointed body is of composition.

found with other simple toys in a child's grave, and terracotta figures, thought to have been dolls, have been found in graves of Ancient Greece. There are documentary and pictorial records of dolls as the playthings of the titled and wealthy in the courts of medieval Europe. And, as the 18th and 19th centuries saw more relaxed attitudes to children, dolls as the playthings of both boys and girls became increasingly common among all social classes.

In their long history, dolls have been made of many materials and in many different styles. Wood and rag dolls are among the earliest to have been made, the materials being cheap and accessible to all. As dolls began to be made commercially, more sophisticated materials including wax and porcelain were used, and the manufacture of dolls became an important industry, notably in Germany in the 19th and 20th centuries, but also in France, Britain and, especially after World War I, in the USA.

Antique dolls are now among the most popular of all collectables. Specialist sales are held regularly throughout Europe and the USA, and prices realized continue to climb. Despite the steadily rising prices, however, the number of collectors shows no sign of diminishing – indeed, the rise in prices that has been evident at recent sales may be the result of more and more collectors chasing a relatively stable number of dolls. These higher prices make it essential that novice collectors have a sound understanding of the types of doll that are available, the materials from which they have been made, the manufacturers and methods of manufacture and, of course, the rarity or otherwise of various styles or makes of doll.

The following pages are designed to assist aspiring collectors avoid making costly mistakes. Doll collecting is a rewarding and exciting hobby; it can also be a time-consuming and frustrating one. When you begin to research your new interest you will find much contradictory and inconclusive evidence. Doll factories did not usually keep archives, and records of what they produced were rarely kept by the companies: as living memory died, so the details were lost. Much information is to be found only in patent registers, and searching through these can reveal how and when dolls and doll mechanisms were made. The factory marks that are sometimes found on dolls' heads and torsos have been the subject of much research and have been laboriously recorded by collectors. Sometimes it is possible to suggest a date of manufacture by knowing when a company operated from a particular address; sometimes an old newspaper was stuffed inside a doll's head when it was first made, and this may be the only evidence of date and place of manufacture; sometimes it is possible to date and attribute a doll by comparing it with another, marked example. Often, however, dolls are unmarked and apparently unattributable, and it is then that experience and judgement are necessary.

A

The past few years have seen the publication of many books on dolls – some on individual manufacturers, others on types of doll – and some of these are listed at the end of this book. It is wiser for novice collectors to begin with some of the general, encyclopedic books before turning to detailed and in-depth studies of individual manufacturers. Many of the books now available contain beautiful colour illustrations of a whole range of dolls, but it is important to read the text and the captions carefully, not just to skim through the pages, admiring the plates. Nor should you disdain some of the older books that may still be found in libraries and second-hand bookshops. All books on dolls will contain valuable information, and you should build up a library of your own to which you can refer again and again.

As you read you will come across several words and phrases that are used by doll collectors to describe certain kinds of doll, a list is given on pages 98–9 and, you will find it helpful to understand these terms, which are used by authors, auction houses and dealers alike.

C

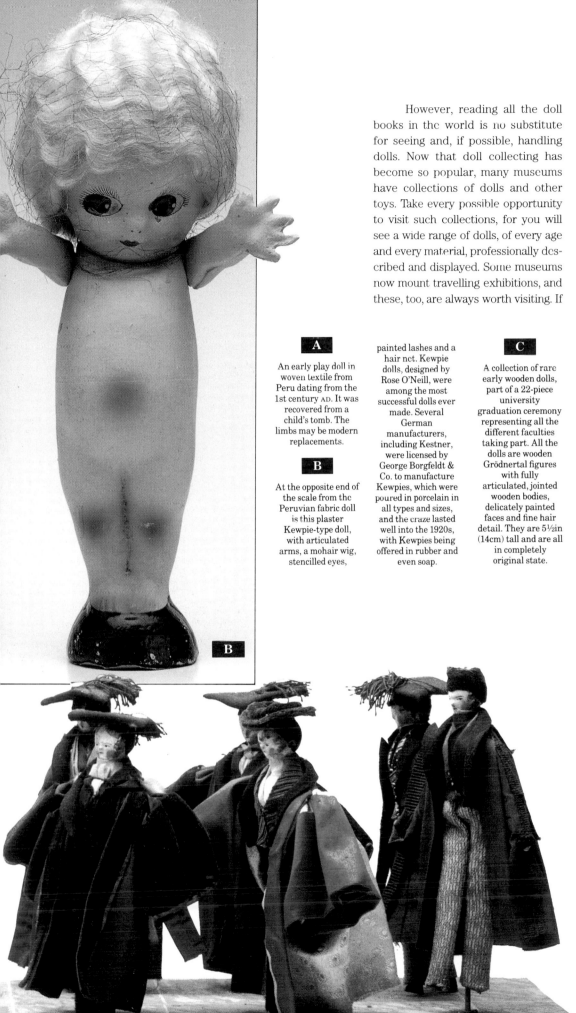

However, reading all the doll books in the world is no substitute for seeing and, if possible, handling dolls. Now that doll collecting has become so popular, many museums have collections of dolls and other toys. Take every possible opportunity to visit such collections, for you will see a wide range of dolls, of every age and every material, professionally described and displayed. Some museums now mount travelling exhibitions, and these, too, are always worth visiting. If

you attend auction previews, even though you have no intention of buying, take the opportunity to handle as many dolls as possible. Keep the auction catalogue close to hand and compare the description with the actual doll. Remember, though, that dolls are fragile, and if you break one, no matter what the circumstances, you will almost certainly have to pay for it.

As we saw in the introduction, novice collectors may be nervous of buying from dealers. Only experienced and long-established doll collectors however, have the knowledge necessary to buy from any source offering a doll for sale, but it is a fact that most established collectors often choose to buy from dealers. Novice collectors turn to other sources, presumably in the hope of picking up a bargain. They may well be lucky but are more likely to be disappointed. Auctions, for example, can prove hazardous for the unwary. A novice collector may well find him- or herself bidding against another novice, each pushing up the bidding, unaware that the 'opposition' has no more idea of the true worth of the doll than he or she has. Sometimes you may find yourself bidding against a dealer who has been commissioned to obtain an item at almost any price, and, of course, you may be bidding against several dealers, who make their living from buying and selling dolls and will be unlikely to look favourably on a collector buying a doll cheaply. There is also the danger that a doll you examined during the preview period and that appeared to be perfect was subsequently mishandled and damaged by another potential purchaser. Nevertheless, buying at auction, provided you are aware of the possible pitfalls, can be an exciting experience, and, as you gain confidence and experience, you will enjoy adding to your collection in this way.

However you acquire your dolls – at auction, from a reputable dealer, from an antique shop or from another collector – it is your responsibility to examine the dolls as thoroughly and

A

An early play doll in woven textile from Peru dating from the 1st century AD. It was recovered from a child's tomb. The limbs may be modern replacements.

B

At the opposite end of the scale from the Peruvian fabric doll is this plaster Kewpie-type doll, with articulated arms, a mohair wig, stencilled eyes, painted lashes and a hair net. Kewpie dolls, designed by Rose O'Neill, were among the most successful dolls ever made. Several German manufacturers, including Kestner, were licensed by George Borgfeldt & Co. to manufacture Kewpies, which were poured in porcelain in all types and sizes, and the craze lasted well into the 1920s, with Kewpies being offered in rubber and even soap.

C

A collection of rare early wooden dolls, part of a 22-piece university graduation ceremony representing all the different faculties taking part. All the dolls are wooden Grödnertal figures with fully articulated, jointed wooden bodies, delicately painted faces and fine hair detail. They are 5½in (14cm) tall and are all in completely original state.

carefully as possible. You should not rely on any faults being pointed out to you. Start with the head – usually the most valuable part of the doll. Most dolls' heads are bisque, and you should try to examine both the inside and outside to look for both firing flaws and hairline cracks, to which bisque is extremely prone. You will find an infra-red wand invaluable if the wig and pate are removed, although of course, this may not always be possible. As you handle more and more dolls and talk to other collectors you will learn what you should look out for and the kind of questions you should ask. Are the hands the same colour as the head? Are the ears applied or moulded? Do any visible firing faults or flecks of kiln dust in the glaze detract from the overall appearance of the doll? Is there any flaking around the ears? What is the condition of the painting? If the doll has an open mouth, are the teeth original or replacements and are they in good condition? How are the eyes fixed? If they are 'sleeping' eyes, is the mechanism original and in good order? Look at the shoulder-plate and neck. Are there signs of flaking or chipping? Experience and commonsense will suggest other details to look for. Are the clothes so tightly stitched on that you cannot examine the doll's body? Has a modern, synthetic thread been used? There may, of course, be a perfectly reasonable explanation, but it is also possible that the clothes are intended to disguise a modern body attached to an old head. Work through your list. You are considering buying the doll and you have every right to examine it as thoroughly as you can. You must, however, exercise care. Never force a wig away from a doll's head; never try to pull the kid of a body away from a shoulder-plate if it has been glued in position. If you damage a doll you will have to pay for it, no matter how the damage was caused.

Some general advice on buying at auction from dealers and from markets or swap-meets is given on pages 12–13. Remember, however,

always buy what appeals to you; you are going to have to live with your purchase (or, more likely as doll collecting becomes a passion, your purchases) and you will be the curator of your own private museum, with a duty to look after and preserve your collection for the enjoyment of future collectors. When you make your first purchase or acquire your first doll, you are joining a worldwide family of collectors and enthusiasts, most of whom will be glad to share their knowledge and experiences with you. Buy and enjoy.

WOODEN DOLLS

Wood was used as a material for doll making because it was inexpensive. In the 17th and 18th centuries the main areas for wood carving were the Grödnertal in the Austrian Tyrol, and in Bavaria and Thuringia in Germany Obviously these densely wooded areas provided the ideal conditions for an industry based on wood carving, and it is not difficult to understand why such an activity thrived in this period. Wooden dolls were also carved in France and Britain. In a British will of 1548 a wooden-headed doll covered with plaster is mentioned, and the manufacture of wooden baby dolls on a lathe is documented as early as 1733 in England.

St Ulrich, the main town in the Grödnertal in Austria, was the centre of a toy industry that had existed since the early 18th century. The region was deeply religious, heavily wooded and remote, and it is easy to see how the early carved figures in the churches – presipios – became the models for locally made dolls. There would have been a natural progression from carved religious figures to children's dolls to be sold in the markets. The people of the area

led an isolated life high in the Alps, snowed up in winter, with no other work, until the mid-19th century, when access to the area became easier. Apart from dolls, carved animals of ash, pear and boxwood, turned on a lathe, were produced.

As far as the manufacture of wooden dolls is concerned we know only what we see: no patents existed and a great deal of modern detective work has resulted only in limited knowledge about who made the dolls and in what quantities. From a knowledge of the period's social history and economics as well as from articles and family histories we can begin to build a picture of these dolls, which have been such a mystery to us for so long.

We do know that before 1800 German dolls were known as *Docken* (or sometimes *Tocken*). These rather primitive toys were turned in one piece of wood and fashioned in the same proportions as an adult. At first they had no arms and were unpainted,

A

Later they were painted, and later still they were given arms – two wooden chips glued to the sides. Some of them were given head-dresses, sometimes in the form of crowns, and some were made with simple mechanisms that enabled them to move their arms when pulled along by a piece of string. Records suggest that such dolls were being exported from Sonneberg as early as 1780, and that they were also made at Oberammergau, Berchtesgaden and in the Erzgebirge in Saxony, as well as in the Grödnertal.

An article written in 1875 des-cribes how wooden dolls were painted by outworkers who earned a farthing a dozen, out of which paint and size had to be bought. If they worked full time, they could paint several hundred dozen a week, which seems an enormous output. Whole families, particularly in the isolated areas such as Grödnertal, would be engaged in this work, some carving the dolls and others painting them. The guilds were very strong at the time – the contin-ental guilds being stronger than the British – and there was strict demarc-ation between carvers and painters.

A different stage in the painting would be undertaken each day, to allow drying time in between. When finished, the dolls were sold by ped-lars who would travel the length and breadth of the land, and indeed other lands, selling their wares. The pedlars would visit Bohemia or Saxony to obtain their dolls, thus encouraging foreign trade and a thriving industry.

These carvers may have belonged to a school of artisans who learned from a single master crafts-man and then, having developed techniques for using certain materials, followed the local tradition. Or they may have been individual craftsmen, working independently throughout the country from lathes in their own tiny workrooms and in their own particular styles, which, coincident-ally, had numerous similarities.

QUEEN ANNE DOLLS AND QUEEN ANNE TYPES

Among the most soughtafter wooden dolls are the so-called Queen Anne dolls or Queen Anne type dolls. In fact, some of these pre-date Queen Anne (who ruled between 1702 and 1714), and others were made well into the 19th century. They are associated with Britain, and although examples are found in the USA, they were probably taken there by early settlers.

These dolls' bodies were turned on a lathe, and they had hand-carved heads and painted, or black, pupil-less, enamelled eyes; sometimes the eyes are blue. The head and body were carved from one piece of wood to form a stump, and the head was fin-ished with gesso and varnish before the face was delicately painted. The fingers and hands were finely carved, covered with gesso and attached to the body with cloth and a pin. The legs were carved and jointed and set into grooves at the base of the torso; they often had well-defined calves

A

A wooden Queen Anne type doll, 21in (53cm) tall and dating from the early 19th century, with black, pupil-less eyes and 'stitched' eyebrows. The gesso-covered head is in good condition, with its tiny painted mouth and rouged cheeks. The stump-type, one-piece body has jointed, painted wooden limbs. The base of the wig is nailed to the head.

B

A wooden Queen Anne type doll dating from c.1850. The doll has a gesso-covered head, black, pupil-less, enamel eyes, small painted lips and highly rouged cheeks. The wooden limbs are jointed, with the lower portions painted white and green. The wig is of real hair.

and ankles. The eyebrows on the earlier dolls were the so-called 'stitched' variety, produced by a series of little black dots. The dolls were made with a high breast form, presumably to give a better line to the clothes of the period. The torso was left unfinished. The wig was tacked or nailed on to the head, and sometimes a beauty spot was evident on the cheek.

The styles changed through the decades. It may have been a case of detail giving way in the face of mass-production, or it may have been simply a change of technique that altered their look. The later dolls are less realistic than the earlier ones and appear to lack the craftsmanship. Their faces are of moulded plaster on a wooden stump, which would have been cheaper than the laborious hand carving of the earlier dolls.

PEG WOODENS OR DUTCH DOLLS

The so called peg wooden or Dutch doll was not, in fact, Dutch, nor was it derived from the word Deutsch. In fact, it came from Austria. At the beginning of the 19th century dolls had elongated bodies, spoon-like, gesso-covered hands, jointed hips and knees, gesso-covered lower legs and painted slippers, usually of orange or deep pink. These dolls are also known as penny woodens and *Nuremburg filles,* and they come from the Bavarian and Austrian Tyrol. The carving of the head and body is usually refined, and the face painting is subtle, suggesting that they were carefully and skilfully made rather than quickly turned out, cheap playthings. The painting of the hair is also exceptional, with a multitude of tiny painted curls providing a frame for the face. The dolls come in a whole range of sizes from 6in (15cm) up to 24in (60cm). Some exceptionally small examples exist, and some were made with a carved comb on the head and this was usually painted yellow. The name tuck comb woodens has been given by US collectors to this type of doll, which was manufactured for about 50 years, making dating difficult.

By the end of the 19th century Dutch dolls had taken on an entirely different character. The delicate face painting and structure of the earlier dolls were gone. To meet the needs of mass-production and a wider buying public, a doll was developed with a solid head. The painting was extremely crude, with black hair, dots for features and red blobs for cheeks. The head and body were still formed from a single piece of wood, but the torso was much shorter than that of the earlier dolls; the arms and legs were rudimentary, the hands being without detail and spoon-shaped, and the arms articulated at the elbow.

PEDLAR DOLLS

Turning peg wooden dolls into pedlar dolls with tiny trays or baskets displaying a multitude of wares for sale was a popular pastime in the Victorian era. An original collection of such dolls can form a fascinating social record of the life and times of a particular doll, as pedlars carried all kinds of wares from cottons, pots and pans and sewing equipment, to pictures, ornaments and religious items. Sometimes, the pedlar trays are not contemporary with the doll.

A

A

These early dolls are known as Lord and Lady Clapham, and they are, perhaps, the most famous of all English-made wooden dolls. They are documented as having been owned by a single family – descendants of the diarist Samuel Pepys, who moved to Clapham in London towards the end of his life. The dolls are unique among late 17th-century examples, and they are in pristine condition. In 1974 they came up for auction and were acquired by the Victoria & Albert Museum, London, where they may still be seen. They are seated here in English-made carved beech and elmwood armchairs with leaf-carved toprails and turned supports, legs and stretchers. The chairs are 21in (53cm) high.

B

A late peg wooden doll, 22in (55cm) tall, with crude face painting, a fully jointed body and crudely painted lower arms and legs, which end in stumps. The clothing is not original to the doll.

A

A

A papier mâché
shoulder-plate doll
with the type of head
that was made in
Sonneberg in the
1840s. The black
'Napoleonic' curls are
painted, and the
French body is of
pink kid.

B

A papier mâché
shoulder-head doll
with bent
composition arms and
legs. The cloth body is
stuffed with
horsehair. Stitched
under her dress the
doll has a note from
the original owner,
who called the doll
Rose Ann.

The factories making these dolls needed to be near paper mills to have easy access to their raw materials, and this led to the establishment of certain areas of manufacture. Papier mâché dolls came primarily from Britain, Germany and the USA and, to a lesser extent, from France. Nuremburg, in south Germany, had a paper mill in the 14th century, as did Sonneberg somewhat later. Rye flour used in the process came from the valleys beneath the wooded mountains, and this region, with its easy access to both paper pulp and flour, would have been naturally suitable for the development of the papier mâché doll industry.

Paper pulp has obvious advantages over clay: it is lighter, does not break as easily, can be dried in the open air instead of a furnace and takes a wider variety of finishes. Japanning – a hard lacquer – was one embellishment of papier mâché, while wax was the favoured finish among English doll manufacturers. The heads were often made and sold on their own so that home-made cloth bodies could be attached to them. Often these were simply stuffed cloth, and the variety of standards in these home-made bodies gives rise to a certain inconsistency. Sometimes the arms are of leather, sometimes of cloth; many are crudely stump-shaped. The heads were simply glued on to the body at the shoulder-plate.

Papier mâché is a substance that can be produced quite easily in a small workshop or even at home, and there are several interesting examples of papier mâché dolls that have been made by gifted amateur doll makers.

The dolls' heads were first modelled by a 'doll artist', and these skilled workers have left us a wonderful record of historic hair fashions with elaborate coiffures, ringlets and braids. Unfortunately the names of these talented doll artists are usually undocumented.

The mould makers, who probably worked in their own homes, made the moulds from the modelled forms. The moulds were often made

PAPIER MACHE DOLLS

Papier mâché – literally 'chewed' paper – is apparently a term with English origins and not, as most people might imagine, French. There were many methods and formulae for its composition, but all were based on raw paper pulp moistened with water. To this a filler such as flour, meal, sand, clay, whiting or chalk was added, and a binder was used to hold the substances together; this was usually an animal glue or a gelatinous material like starch paste

or gum arabic. It was a cheap, strong substance.

Some manufacturers of papier mâché dolls added resins, oils and repellants to make the dolls less desirable to rodents, and some added deodorizers to minimize the odours of the glue. Each manufacturer strove to keep his particular formula secret.

Papier mâché can be made of any vegetable or animal fibre. Unless a head can be analysed it is almost impossible to know exactly which additives were used, but German manufacturers generally employed watered-down animal glue.

When one considers papier mâché dolls and the nature of the market they served, it is obvious that they could not be expensively made.

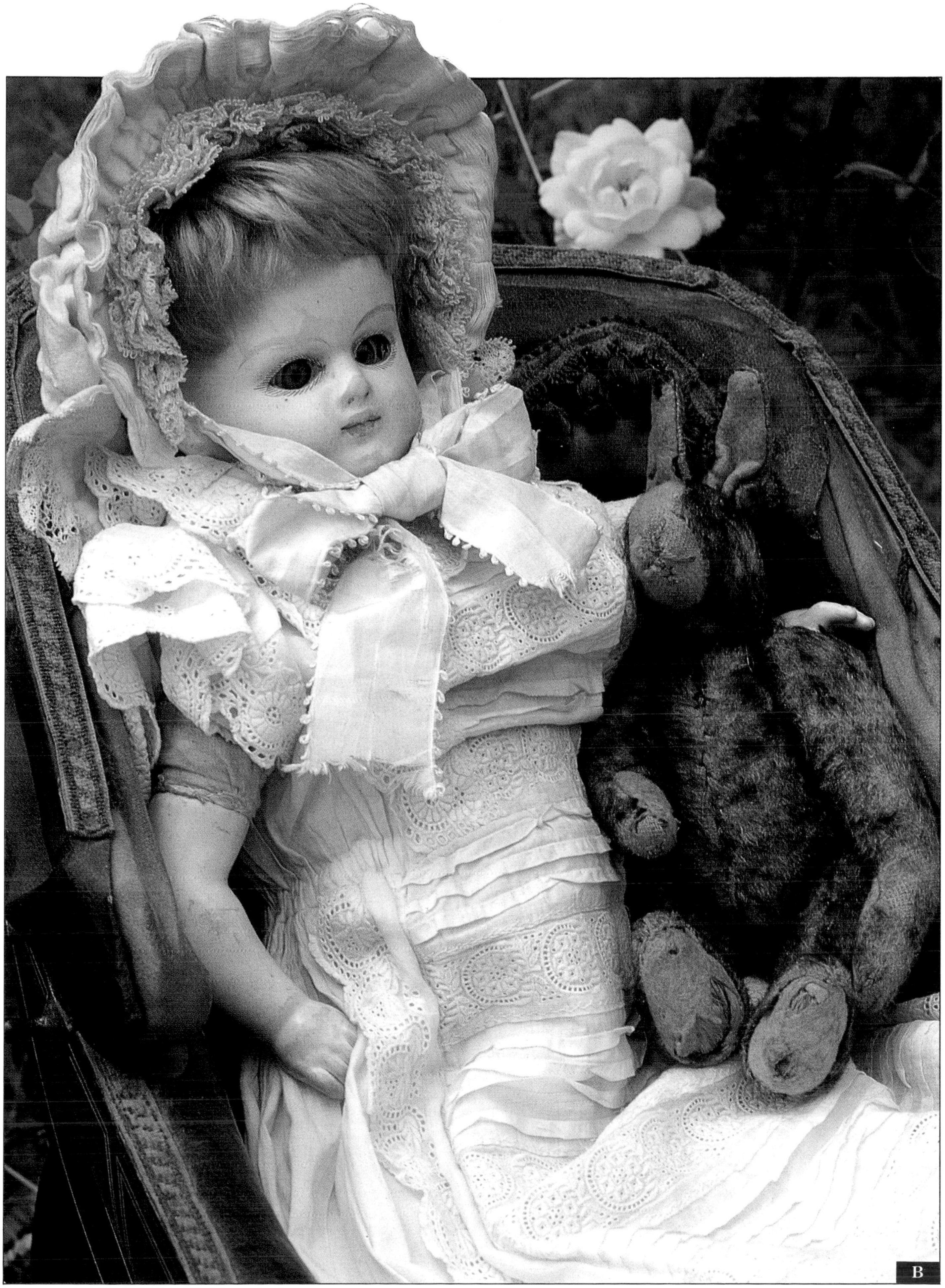

B

A

in several parts, and the lines on some heads will sometimes indicate how many individual parts were used. The papier mâché mixture would be pressed into the mould and allowed to dry. One-piece moulds would sometimes be used, especially for small heads. They were usually made of plaster of Paris or gypsum, and various places on the head – the seams, the nose and so on – would have to be reinforced. Linen or muslin was used as a reinforcing material, and after the head was completed it had to be dressed for painting. Filler and an undercoat would be used to dress the heads in this way, and chalk, clay, gesso, gypsum or plaster, in various thicknesses, were most common.

The skills of the finishers were all important as it was upon the effects they produced that the whole doll would ultimately be judged (with the exception of the clothing). The finisher gave the doll its skin pigments, eyes, eyebrow definitions, lip and hair colouring, as well as any extra decoration that might be included. Finally, a protective coat of glue wash or varnish would be applied. The glue wash was somewhat unsuccessful, as we see now with the French pink kid-bodied papier mâché dolls, in which the shine almost always appears to have been washed off.

There is much documentary evidence on the manufacture of papier mâché dolls' heads in the early 19th century by factories in the Sonneberg and Nuremburg districts of south Germany, and the majority of heads will have come from these areas.

GEORGIAN WAX-OVER PAPIER MACHE DOLLS

In the first quarter of the 19th century Georgian wax-overs, as they are sometimes called, were being produced in Britain. These are generally regarded as wax rather than papier mâché dolls, but they had papier mâché cores. The faces are flat and smiling, and the heads are often not quite smooth, perhaps through warping as a result of not being carefully pressed or dried. It is difficult to give any other explanation for their crude form. In spite of this, their serene charm is unique. The portrait-type dolls depicted famous personalities of the period, whose hair-styles may be familiar to us today from contemporary paintings, and the hair-styles on the moulded-hair dolls often help to date them.

M & S SUPERIOR DOLLS

The words *M & S Superior* have been found on paper labels on composition heads produced during the 1880s and 1890s. The initials are believed to refer to the firm of Müller & Strasburger of Sonneberg, which is thought to have been the first doll manufacturer in Sonneberg to have used papier mâché. The dolls are similar in style to Greiner dolls, with moulded hair, and tend to be blonde. The high glaze on these dolls, which was meant to be a 'superior' finish was, in fact, thick and brittle and subject to scratching. These dolls have not survived as well as the Greiners, and their faces always seem to be damaged. Furthermore, the glaze has yellowed with age, becoming less realistic and less attractive than the finish on the Greiner dolls.

MILLINERS' MODELS AND HIGH COIFFURE DOLLS

The name milliners' models is given by some collectors to papier mâché heads with kid bodies and non-articulated wooden limbs. However, there is no evidence to suggest that they were milliners' dolls, and, in any case, the elaborate coiffures on many of them would have precluded the donning of a sample hat. In addition, the bodies are rigid, making the pulling on and off of clothes extremely difficult, if not impossible. It is even doubtful whether these dolls were used to exhibit samples of the latest fashions as has been suggested. However, when describing unmarked dolls whose manufacturer is unknown the collector needs a means of identifying them to others, and very many of the type names given to dolls have arisen, sometimes long ago, in response to this need. The little milliners' models range in size from about 6in (15cm) to 20in (50cm), and the high styles of coiffures date from between 1810 and 1820.

As the 19th century progressed, innovations were made and one of these was the swivel-neck doll. It was not altogether successful in papier mâché because the material could not withstand the inevitable wear on the socket. By the last quarter of the century, many famous doll-making names were on the scene: Mlle Rohmer, the French doll maker, Heubach, Fleischmann & Bloedcl, Heinrich Handwerke, Kämmer & Reinhardt, Kestner, Schilling, Simon & Halbig and many others. Most of these had their origins in the manufacture of papier mâché heads. Experiments with the substance in the late 19th century led to the development of papier mâché that could be poured, rather than pressed, into moulds, but few of these later dolls were of the moulded hair variety: most had wigs and resembled the bisque dolls in style.

B

A

WAX DOLLS

Wax has been used in Europe since the Middle Ages as an artistic medium – funeral effigies and floral displays were often made of wax – and in 15th-century Italy it was used to make life-size portraits of notable people. Beeswax, which was used for the making of church candles, was used in devout areas of Italy and southern Germany to make votive offerings, and the figures for Christmas *crèche* scenes and religious figures were also often made of wax.

The art of making realistic wax portrait models seems to have been perfected in Italy, and during the 18th century there were many travelling waxworks, displaying figures in the style later to become associated with Madame Tussaud in London. Several famous wax modellers worked in London in the 18th century, and it is interesting to note that women were successfully involved in the work from early times. At a time when the quality and delicacy of the carved and turned wooden dolls that had been made in the early 18th century had begun to deteriorate, it seems likely that the techniques of inserting hair and eyes into life-size wax figures and of dressing them in elaborate and ornamented costumes were trans-

ferred to the making of dolls for the children of wealthy families.

Wax dolls are certainly among the most beautiful dolls that are available to collectors. The substance gives a rich, translucent skin tone of a quality that cannot be equalled even by the finest bisque. It is, however, a soft and inherently fragile material, and many examples have not survived. Before the early 19th century wax dolls were sometimes eaten by mice attracted by the beeswax; other dolls melted when left too close to the fire; some wax dolls probably just got sat on. Contrary to popular opinion, wax dolls will not melt simply by being left in a warm room. If they are left in direct sunlight, however, the colour pigments will fade and the wax

A

An English poured
wax doll with poured
wax limbs. Standing
17in (43cm) tall, she
is of the late Pierotti
type with hair,
eyelashes and
eyebrows inserted
into the wax. The
stuffed body bears the
Hamleys Toy Shop
stamp, and the doll is
in mint condition.
She is dressed in her
original white cotton
dress, underwear and
straw bonnet.

B

A wax over papier
mâché shoulder-head
doll with fixed blue
eyes. The limbs are
also wax over papier
mâché, and the doll
stands 29in (74cm)
high. The wig is
mohair, and the
clothes are original to
the doll, which was
probably made in
France c.1870.

This rare poured wax lady doll, which is 24in (60cm) tall, was made in the 1920s. The poured wax limbs have rigid arms and movable legs; the shoes are moulded.

This wax over papier mâché shoulder-head, slit-head doll is 19in (48cm) tall.

C

An exquisite example of a poured-wax head doll. Note the superb modelling of the eyes.

that has been exposed to the light may become quite white while the limbs that were hidden by clothing will have retained their colour.

At first, pure beeswax was used. Later, the beeswax was mixed with other waxes, including carnauba, which comes from the Brazilian wax palm and which is very hard and shiny at normal temperatures but has a very high melting point, 194°F (90°C). Paraffin was also used, especially when the wax was to be used for poured or wax-over heads, as were other additives, including colouring agents. Manufacturers kept their own recipes carefully guarded secrets, and it is now impossible to tell exactly what proportions and even exactly which ingredients were used. It is, in any case, unnecessary for today's collectors to know the precise recipes used for the purposes of identifying individual manufacturers.

SOLID HEADS

There are three types of wax dolls' heads – solid, poured and wax over composition or papier mâché. In the 18th and 19th centuries, good quality dolls had solid wax heads, wax limbs and stuffed fabric bodies. Solid heads can, of course, be made simply by carving the features from a solid block of wax, but more often a sculpture would be made from which a mould would be taken. The mould would be warmed and the molten wax poured in, white lead and carmine having been added as colouring agents. Hair could be moulded and facial features indicated, but on the whole such heads tend to be rather flat and featureless. Eyes are often nothing more than glass beads stuck on by a lump of molten wax, and the hair is painted rather than being moulded.

B

C

POURED WAX HEADS

As the name suggests, these dolls' heads were also made by pouring molten wax into a warmed mould. However, before the wax had completely set, any excess was poured off, to leave a shell lining the mould. Some manufacturers repeated the process two or three times to achieve the required thickness. When the wax was set, the mould was removed and the eye holes cut for the insertion of glass eyes (which were attached by molten wax inside the head cavity). Generally, eye lids and brows were moulded individually at this stage, and eyelashes and hair would be added. The head would be dusted with potato starch, powdered alabaster or pumice to give a smooth complexion, and the cheeks were tinted with rouge and the lips and nostrils touched with vermilion. Holes were made in the shoulder-plate so that the head could be attached to a stuffed cloth body. The lower arms and lower legs were fashioned and attached to the body in the same way.

This was the method of doll production favoured by some of the greatest manufacturers working in Britain in the 19th century, Pierotti, Montanari, Marsh, Meech and Peck. Most poured wax dolls are unmarked, and collectors refer to 'Pierotti-type' dolls or 'Montanari-type' dolls, as it is impossible accurately to attribute the dolls to an individual maker. In some rare cases a Montanari doll may be found bearing a signature in brownish ink on the lower-left-hand corner of the torso. Also rare are the marked dolls by Pierotti; occasionally the name is found scratched roughly on the back of the doll's head. Often the only identification on a doll is the name of the toy shop – Peacock, Aldis, Cremer, Hamley or Morrel – stamped on the front of the body, although this, of course, does not reveal the maker's name.

The wax used for poured wax dolls varies in colour from a very hot pink through various flesh tones to pale pink. Only the very early, almost pure beeswax dolls have a tell-tale yellowish tinge. Unfortunately, over the years dolls with a heavy dusting of pumice may have turned a dirty-looking grey colour as the layer of pumice has solidified and discoloured. Removing this layer is a task for an expert and should never be undertaken by a novice collector as the wax may be irreparably damaged.

WAX-OVER

Wax is an expensive material, and when the mass-production of dolls began to get underway in the mid-19th century ways had to be found to reduce manufacturing costs, and one method adopted was to make a core of papier mâché or composition and dip it into, or paint it with, molten wax. Such dolls are known as wax-overs or dipped-wax dolls. The colour was either added to the base and covered with white wax or it was added to the wax itself; the method used can usually be determined by inspecting the edge of the shoulder-plate where the wax is thinnest. Glass eyes were added in the

same way as for wax heads, although they were generally glued with plaster rather than wax, and, because the core made the heads sturdier than poured wax heads, sleeping eyes, either on a wire or with a lead weight, could be used. The glass eyes used in wax dolls made before 1850 were without pupils and were very dark, almost black in colour. The examples with sleeping eyes have a wire, which opened and shut the eyes, coming out of the body at the waistline. Such eyes were introduced c.1825. Eyebrow details were usually painted on to the papier mâché before the wax was added.

The early wax-over dolls often have a slit in the top of the head – they are therefore often known as slit-head dolls – through which the hair was inserted and glued down before being arranged in ringlets. Some are found with a hole cut at the back of the head, through which, presumably, the eyes were secured. This is covered by a papier mâché pate. The pate is then waxed over and the hair attached to it.

The bodies, legs and feet of slit-head dolls are crudely stuffed, the feet often turning inwards to give a pigeon-toed effect; the arms are often of leather. Curiously, the dolls with brown leather arms usually have only three fingers on each hand, while those with white kid arms have the full complement of five.

Wax-over dolls are often found with extremely crazed faces. This is caused by the expansion and contraction of the wax and the underlying material at different times. Although this is unsightly, it is quite normal and should not cause concern unless a piece of wax actually comes away, when expert advice should be sought immediately.

A

A wax over papier mâché shoulder-head doll that is in mint condition. She was probably made by Fritz Bartenstein of Hüttensteinach c.1880.

Wax dolls were also made in France, and in the mid-19th century Sonneberg in Germany was famous for them. These heads were usually reinforced with plaster. Fritz Bartenstein (1839–1913) of Hüttensteinach, Germany, was a well-known maker of wax dolls. He is particularly famous for his double-faced doll, one face laughing, the other crying, which was patented in 1880. The head could be turned by the movement of a string, and one of the faces would be hidden by a hood. There is a similar type of doll shown on page 63. Bartenstein also made a two-faced doll in wax over papier mâché, with the face moving horizontally under a metal cap. The body is of cardboard, and sometimes bears the Bartenstein stamp in purple ink.

Other early wax over papier mâché dolls include the so-called 'pumpkin head' dolls, with fancy, moulded hairstyles, stuffed bodies, wooden limbs and either painted feet or painted red or green boots; they have black pupil-less eyes. Also from this area are the charming little wax over papier mâché 'bonnet head' dolls with moulded hats, often with three plumes in the front.

By 1904, very few wax dolls were being made in Sonneberg, and Britain was the only country where they continued to be popular. The German companies Kestner and Kämmer & Reinhardt also made wax dolls, and the famous Kämmer & Reinhardt Mein Liebling (My Darling) doll was also made in wax. By 1920, wax dolls were being used popularly for display and costume purposes. In 1925 in Paris Mme T. Lazarski made display dolls similar to the British examples. Wax dolls were also made by the leading manufacturers as display mannequins for shop windows.

Four china shoulder-heads with black painted hair. From left to right: a shoulder-head, 4in (10cm) high, with two sew holes, a 'low-brow' hair-style, blue painted eyes and a red eyelid line, dating from 1890; a 4in (10cm) high shoulder-head with three sew holes and an unusual hair-style, which is taken back behind the ears, dating from 1880; a 5in (13cm) high shoulder-head with three sew holes and 24 moulded ringlets around the head in an otherwise simple hair-style, with well-defined face painting, highly rouged cheeks and a red eyelid line, dating from 1860–70; and finally, a 4in (10cm) high shoulder-head with two sew holes, 10 moulded ringlets and heavily rouged cheeks, dating from 1860–70.

B

An early pink lustre china shoulder-head, 6in (15cm) tall. The brown moulded ringlets hang straight down and have been finely detailed. It is unmarked but probably dates from c.1840.

CERAMIC DOLLS

Three types of ceramic are used to make dolls' heads – porcelain or china, Parian (white bisque) and bisque (unglazed porcelain).

CHINA

The common name for glazed porcelain is china, and this substance was used by German, French and Danish manufacturers to produce dolls' heads. China-headed dolls, made from hard-paste porcelain, with their high glaze and fascinating hair-styles are an exciting area of collecting, providing great social history interest and wide variety for the collector.

As with papier mâché dolls heads were often sold alone for the bodies to be made by mothers or nursemaids. China heads on their own are quite commonly found and are now extremely collectable. Most chinas are unmarked – the word 'chinas' is a collector's abbreviation for china-headed dolls – and if one is found with a mark this is regarded as a real bonus.

Chinas were produced from around 1830 and represented men, women and children in glazed porcelain. Production continued well into the 1900s, and yet knowledge of chinas is scant, which makes dating tantalizingly difficult.

As the chinas could be purchased as heads only the bodies would have been made at home, and many heads are found on very crude bodies, varying in shape according to the skills of the hands that made them. Other chinas are found on commercially made peg wooden, jointed bodies with china limbs jointed at elbows and knees. These tend to be among the rarest bodies on chinas. Some chinas are found on commercially made, rigid leather bodies with leather arms and hands – they are so stiff that most cannot be arranged in a seated position – and these are often the bodies found on the earlier dolls. Commercial cloth bodies may also be found on some dolls, and these have china arms with well-defined fingers and china legs with painted black boots and garter ribbons with bows usually

A

painted in pink. Not all boots are painted black – they have been found in a variety of colours, including orange and purple lustre. The collector who has found a good china head and who wishes to make it into a doll can make her (or his) own, at least until an old body can be found.

Most heads were made by pouring liquid clay into moulds. Another method was to press rolled-out clay into moulds. Poured heads are fairly smooth inside, while pressed heads are uneven. Some chinas are referred to by collectors as 'pink lustre' heads, and these deeply coloured examples are most desirable. The so-called pink lustre is a pink enamel glaze, obtained by applying a film of gold over the rose colour of the head. Generally the deeper lustres are earlier, the later ones tending to be paler. There are, of course, exceptions to every rule, and pink lustre was made until the 1900s. The heads were attached to the cloth bodies by gluing, by stitching through the sew holes (the holes made by the manufacturer at the lower edge of the shoulder-plate) or by nailing through the sew holes. These holes are generally considered to be an indication of the age of the doll, and most collectors are of the opinion that chinas with three sew holes at the base are among the earlier examples. However, some chinas have three holes in the front and two at the back, which confounds this theory, but there may have been a need for three sew holes because of the slope at the base of the shoulder-plate. Some early dolls have also been found with four sew

B

holes. It should be pointed out that once a mould was made, it probably remained in continuous use over a long period if it was a popular seller – for example, a particular doll, first made in 1850, might still have been in production in 1865, which is another reason why accurate dating is so difficult.

GERMAN AND DANISH CHINAS

Some of the renowned porcelain factories of the first half of the 19th century such as Meissen, Royal Copenhagen and Königliche Porzellan Manufaktur (KPM) in Berlin made china-head dolls, and there were many other manufacturers, mostly producing unmarked examples. The quality of modelling, painting and craftsmanship in these early dolls is

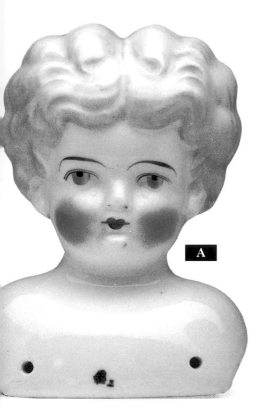

A

A pair of blond-haired china shoulder-heads. The 'low-brow' hair-style on the left is the more commonly seen style, with wavy hair low on the forehead. The shoulder-head is 6in (15cm) high. The face has been well painted, and there is a red line above the eyes. There are three sew holes, and the piece dates from 1890–1900. On the right is a china shoulder-head 4¾in (12cm) high, with two sew holes. The face is child-like with the ears partly showing, a style that was often used on boy or man dolls. It dates from the 1880s.

outstanding. They usually had brown or black painted hair, painted eyes and a pink lustre to the china, which gives a warmth to the skin tones. Later chinas had glass eyes and bald-headed chinas, on which wigs could be set, were developed between 1845 and 1860. The top of the head was painted with a black spot like the papier mâché dolls of similar period, although what this denoted is not known. Collectors call them 'black spot' chinas. Early chinas usually had sloping shoulders with fine and deep hair moulding; pinkish or reddish cheek tones add still more charm to these dolls. An extremely rare early type consists of a china head on a jointed peg wooden body with china arms and legs.

FROZEN CHARLOTTES OR FROZEN CHARLEYS

These dolls of glazed china throughout are also known as bathing dolls. They were made from *c*.1850 to World War I and usually have extended, immobile arms with clenched fists and painted hair-styles. They came in a variety of sizes, from miniature to about 20in (50cm). Some had short black or blond brush-stroke hair, while others had moulded hair styled as for a little girl. Examples are found with moulded clothes, although these are very rare, and some have moulded boots in varying designs or moulded bonnets. The china of these Frozen Charlotte dolls is either white or pink-toned. As with other chinas, these have been reproduced, the reproductions tending to be flawless. Many of the old dolls seem to have specks of black kiln dust baked into the porcelain and scattered over their bodies, and this can be a clue as to authenticity. Long experience in handling dolls is the best safeguard against reproductions and fakes; the novice collector should take advice.

HAIR-STYLES

Many people collect chinas for their different hair-styles, and there is an almost limitless variety, including braided coronets, snoods, centre partings, exposed ears with a bun at the back (like the young Queen Victoria), a 'spaniel ears' style, which flares at the sides, and the 'painted wagon' style with centre parting and 13 curls around the face ending at the neck. Sometimes the doll's hair line has a straight edge, which is a little hard-looking, while others have fine brush strokes framing the face, which give a more delicate look. Some styles are low on the back of the neck, and others are painted high on the nape. Obviously it is difficult for the collector to identify unmarked dolls, and it is not even known how or if they were marked at the time of manufacture. Collectors over the years have given names to different hair-styles, such as the snood head china known as Mary Todd Lincoln. No documentation exists to

B

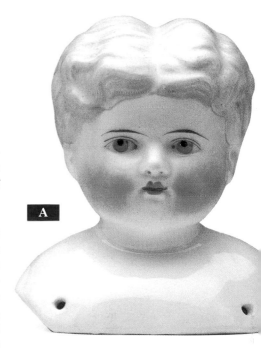

B

A pink lustre china shoulder-head doll, which is 26in (66cm) tall. The body is in the Lacmann style, with long legs, red leather arms and well-detailed hands. The head has soft curls over the ears, and the eyes are lined in red. The shoulders slope steeply, and the shoulder-head has three sew holes at front and back. The doll, which dates from 1860, wears her original dress.

prove whether this was in fact a portrait of the lady, but her name has been associated with this type of china for many years.

ORNAMENTALS

The ornamental chinas with exotic features were clearly an attempt by the manufacturer to woo customers. Nothing has been left untried. Trims of every kind were moulded on the heads – bows, feathers, flowers, bands, snoods and every kind of hair ornament. Different colours were used for this, gold being greatly favoured. Sometimes a black-haired china would have a gold moulded net over the hair, or a blond-haired doll would have a black moulded snood. China heads in many different forms and with various hair designs were used on Autoperipatetikos bodies. One particular style of doll with a low snood is known by collectors as Empress Eugénie.

Such wide ranges of chinas exist that one can only assume that they were very popular. Their durability must have made them attractive, for although they were breakable they could be washed and did not scratch or lose their colour.

CHINAS AFTER 1860

As the century progressed, the style and form of chinas changed. The most marked difference was in hair colouring: while dark brown and black hair had always been made, there was a sudden profusion of blonds. It is interesting to speculate why this would have been. Were the manufacturers attempting to increase their range by introducing new styles, or were they trying to appeal to a completely different market?

Variations of blond, from honey and strawberry to dark oatmeal,

A

appeared, and at the same time there was a discernible difference in the look of the chinas. They became more child-like, with chubby checks and short necks; boys and men were depicted with side partings. The quality of the manufacture, including the fine face painting, remained the same in spite of these changes. Hair-styles tended to be short and bobbed, and the so-called 'curly top' chinas, with curls all over the head and falling down over the forehead, began to appear. There was the Dolly Madison style with the moulded bow; the so-called Highland Mary with a fringe; the Princess Alexandra with a snood (this doll is the same as the Empress Eugénie, and differs only in that the Empress always has pierced ears and the Princess does not). Another style is known as the Currier and Ives with the head band moulded and brought very far forward on the head. Very similar to this is the 'spill curl', in which the head band is further back on the head. Among the well-known German doll makers that made chinas were Cüno and Otto Dressel, Kestner, Kling and Heubach.

A

Countess Dagmar, a Parian shoulder-head doll, stands 17in (43cm) tall. Her hair is finely modelled, and she has blue painted eyes with red dots and a red upper line. She has a moulded blouse, a stuffed fabric body and bisque arms and legs, with black painted boots with red laces and blue painted garters.

A

By the 1900s, the age of the china had passed, to be replaced by other kinds of dolls. The quality had been lost, definition was poor. Even among collectors in Europe, the popularity of chinas waned a few years ago because of a spate of reproductions, while in the US they were less favoured than fine quality bisque dolls. This kept the price of chinas unrealistically low. Although their popularity and price have now increased, they are still attractive to the collector.

PARIAN DOLLS

The United Federation of Doll Clubs (UFDC) in the USA defines Parian as unglazed porcelain (fine white bisque) without tinting. The word Parian comes from Paros in Greece, where white marble was found, and 'Parian ware' was the term given to entirely white, marble-like items, such as figures, and the substance was soon adopted by porcelain manufacturers for use in doll making: the so-called 'Parian' dolls were made between 1850 and 1880.

Parians are often assumed to be German and are thought to have been made in the Dresden potteries as well as in other parts of Germany. They usually have golden hair. Documentary evidence, in the form of manuals or catalogues relating to dolls being made at Dresden, has never been found. It is hard to believe that dolls were not considered worthy of note and therefore not included in sales catalogues since the quality of design, modelling and workmanship are so obviously high. A little information has recently come to light, which confirms the origins of these Dresden heads.

Some Parian manufacturers put makers' marks on their wares. C.F. Kling & Co. of Ohrdruf, Thuringia, was founded in 1834 as a porcelain factory and began to make dolls and dolls' heads c.1870, continuing until the 1940s. Kling made china and bisque heads, bathing dolls and nanking dolls. Some of the all-porcelain dolls are marked some of their blond shoulder heads with a *K* inside a bell. Among the numbers found with the bell symbol are *148 0, 186.5, 189 3* and *123 2*. Simon & Halbig of Gräfenhain, Thuringia, also made Parian dolls' heads with moulded blond hair and fine quality painting. These are usually marked *S*H* with the numerical size in the middle. Dernheim, Koch & Fischer of Gräfenroda, Thuringia, which operated from 1860 to 1900, marked its wares *DKF*. It made Parian heads, notably one of fine quality with the Dresden flower decoration, each petal standing out separately.

B

B

A rare Parian shoulder-head doll, the so-called Princess Augusta Victoria doll, which has beautifully moulded, elaborately styled hair, pierced ears and a moulded ruffled collar with a modelled cross. She was made in 1870.

When Parian dolls are marked the mark will probably be inside or on the back of the shoulder-plate. Like china heads, Parian heads are found without bodies and were probably sold in a similar way for homemade bodies to be attached to them. Interestingly, some china and Parian dolls appear to have been made from the same moulds, but the Parians tend to look more realistic than the chinas with their high glaze, because skin tones and textures are more finely portrayed in this medium.

The face painting on Parian dolls is generally of excellent quality and definition and the eyes, which are generally painted, are usually blue. Brown-eyed Parians are considered rarer and were evidently less popular in their day. Glass-eyed dolls are also found occasionally. Generally speaking, with the exception of the extremely early dolls, rare examples often denote a less popular line, with fewer of the type originally being made. Obviously dolls that were popular were made in greater numbers, and these are the ones that we find in quantity today. Oddly enough, the dolls that were less popular yesterday and that are now hard to find have become the more treasured and expensive collectors' items.

Parian heads are found on as wide a range of bodies as are chinas. Sometimes they are on the homemade creations of the household nursery, while the commercially made bodies are of cloth and generally have Parian limbs. More rarely, they also have cloth legs and leather arms.

As with chinas, collectors needed to devise a way of identifying the usually unmarked Parian dolls, so they gave them names, some of which are shared with chinas. Dolly Madison (1870–80), Countess Dagmar, with both blond and black hair (1870), Empress Eugénie, Princess Alexandra, Alice in Wonderland, Jenny Lind (1870), Highland Mary, Mary Todd Lincoln and Adelina Patti are among the best known.

However, certain heads are found only on Parians, as if they were produced either by a different manufacturer or the design lent itself more readily to Parian. Generally speaking, there are far more elaborately decorated Parian dolls in existence than china. Parian versions of Empress Eugénie are sometimes referred to as Lucy. This wonderful head with its silver-white feather and purple lustre tassel has an exquisitely moulded, firmly structured face.

Glass eyes are also to be found on Parian dolls and are the most highly sought after of the type, commanding high prices. Some of the most prized Parians have elaborately moulded frills on their shoulder plates and exquisite hair ornamentation. Another doll not found in china is the so-called blue scarf doll. This is said to represent the Empress Louise of Prussia at Schönbrunn Palace. These dolls have been reproduced by Emma Clear of the USA between 1940 and 1950 and are marked with her name and the year.

Miss Liberty is a seldom seen example; she has a lustre crown and streamers, blond or brown hair, painted or glass eyes and moulded earrings or pierced ears. Princess Augusta Victoria (1870) is another Parian not found in china. She has a moulded hair band, high curls, moulded, ruffled collar and modelled cross. The so-called flat top is an interesting doll, found both in Parian and in china. Dating from 1840–50, she has a flat top to her head and rows of little sausage curls coming down around it – a most unrealistic hairstyle. Flat tops are found with either painted or glass eyes. Amelia Bloomer is a most interesting and seldom seen Parian, with painted eyes and short, cropped hair. It is not known if this Parian was actually meant to be a portrait of the famous lady herself or just a similar type. Amelia Bloomer (1818–94) was a pioneer of women's rights in the USA, which may be why the doll is portrayed with short cropped hair.

There are also a number of stone bisque dolls with a wide assortment of hats, bonnets and bows which are unique to the Parian type; one in particular has a moulded fur hat and collar. Stone bisque is a coarse white bisque of poorer quality than most Parians because it is made from less finely ground clay. Interesting features are often found on these dolls, however, and this is their attraction.

A

The left-hand doll, which is pushing a toy pram dating from the 1860s, has a Parian head and lower arms and legs with painted and moulded boots. The moulded blond hair is in an intricately curled and waved style. The doll was made in Germany. The right-hand doll, seated in an early three-wheeled pram, is an English-made, poured wax doll, with wax lower arms and legs.

B

A rare Parian shoulder-head doll, 13in (33cm) tall, with moulded blond hair and painted eyes. The head is turned to one side. This doll is the chubby-cheeked type of child-like Parian dolls. The body is stuffed, but the arms and legs are Parian, and the legs end in moulded, purple lustre decorated bootees. She is in her original box.

A

BISQUE DOLLS

A

The left-hand doll is a pale bisque shoulder-plate doll with closed mouth. The face has been delicately painted, and the head has a solid dome, Belton-type head. The doll is apparently unmarked, although there may be a mark under the early kid body. The arms are bisque, and the feet are kid and have stitched toes. She wears an original two-piece dress and matching bonnet. The right-hand doll is a good quality bisque, closed-mouth shoulder-plate doll, 20in (50cm) tall. Dressed as a young man, the doll has a solid dome, Belton-type head, turned to one side. The head is unmarked. The early kid body is gusseted, and the arms are bisque. The suit, shirt, waistcoat and top hat are original. The doll may be an early Kestner.

B

Simon & Halbig made this bisque-head, open-mouth oriental character doll. The head is marked *S H 1129 Dep 10* and is delicately coloured. The doll, which has a jointed composition body, wears her superb original clothing.

C

This beautiful French bisque doll bears the incised mark *Bru Jne 9* on her head; the shoulder-plate is also incised. She has brown eyes, a delicately painted face and the original blond mohair wig. She has a swivel neck, kid body, bisque lower arms and wooden lower legs.

The third, and for many collectors, the most important type of ceramic dolls are those with bisque heads and limbs. Bisque is made from the same substance as china, but it is unglazed. After an initial firing at a very high temperature the facial painting is carried out, and the bisque is then fired again, this time at a lower temperature. Such painting is sometimes known as 'fired in bisque'.

Bisque was the material most favoured by the great French and German doll makers, and it remained a favourite material for the creation of dolls' heads from the mid-19th century until the 1930s. Bisque proved to be an extraordinarily versatile material, and the second half of the 19th century saw a tremendous range of designs and treatments of dolls, which were created to represent women, children and babies, men and boys. The heads were modified from the previously used shoulder-head or swivel neck to socket and flange necks. Eyes were painted, then glass, later sleeping or 'googly'. It is, in fact, only in recent years that bisque has been superseded as a material for dolls by vinyl.

French bisque dolls are rather different in style from the German ones and have more delicate, understated countenances. Huret, Rohmer, D'Autremont and Barrois are among the famous names of French doll patentees between 1850 and 1860. These dolls are, in fact, fashion dolls in appearance and are the forerunners of the dolls conventionally called French fashion dolls. Their commercially-made bodies are of many different materials – leather, leather and wood, gutta-percha or tin – and were often marked on the body by the manufacturer. Hurets and Rohmers are particularly sought after by collectors. They differ greatly in design from the German chinas: they have cutaway heads to enable glass eyes to be inserted, and cork pates over which the wigs were fixed.

A

A

This excellent example of a boudoir doll is 41in (104cm) tall. She has a painted stockinet face, which is in almost mint condition, with stencilled eyes. The body is cloth and the limbs are jointed at knees and elbows. The doll has a tiny waist and large bust. The exquisite clothes – underwear, satin dress with diamanté and lace trims, bonnet with an organza floral decoration and flowers and high-heeled shoes – are all original.

B

A ballerina doll made of plush fabric; she is 23in (58cm) tall. The moulded face is painted in the style of the 1920s, with exotic eye shadowing and rouged cheeks. She is wearing her original net tutu, and her pointed toes are in felt ballet shoes.

B

FABRIC DOLLS

From a child's point of view, the warmth and cuddliness of cloth dolls makes them especially attractive. Cloth, or rag, dolls have been with us since the earliest times: they have been found in the ancient tombs of Peru and Egypt.

A rag doll was always an affordable toy. It could be either home made or commercially produced and was within reach of both rich and poor. Some cloth dolls were made purely as playthings, others were produced for promotional purposes. Promotional dolls are a collecting field in themselves and include such dolls as Rastus, Cream of Wheat Chef (1922), the two-piece rag dolls for Kelloggs, Goldilocks and the Mama Bear (1917–18), which were designed by Lela Fellom, and the Aunt Jemima doll (1923–25).

Certain companies' names spring to mind when considering cloth dolls, among them Käthe Kruse and Lenci, both with an inspiring history of manufacture and still in business today. Such names as Steiff, Chad Valley, Deans Rag Book Company and Nora Wellings were also in the forefront. Besides these well-known firms' products, there are numerous cloth dolls and advertising dolls from anonymous companies.

KÄTHE KRUSE

Kathe Kruse was born in 1883 in Breslau, Silesia. She had a large family and a great love of children and since she was an artist and her husband a sculptor, she used her own children as models for her very realistic dolls, the first of which were made for them. Her early commissioned dolls were made in Berlin (from 1910) and the later ones in Bavaria.

To make the dolls, the head was first sculpted and a mould taken. The shape of the head was made from stiffened muslin, which was sprayed with fixative and painted. In the early dolls the muslin was visible.

Sometimes the painting on these dolls has been chipped off or worn away, but unless it is extremely bad, it is best left alone. Overpainting is usually rated against a doll in terms of value. A doll in poor facial condition is priced accordingly. Since the Käthe Kruse firm is still in operation it is possible to send dolls back to the factory for repair and renovation, but repair means different things to different people, and the collector is recommended to proceed with extreme caution before taking any decisions regarding restoration. Paint chips, facial scratches and rubbed noses are common, but such wear is acceptable and should be left alone. After all, these dolls were toys, designed to be loved and played with, and a few signs of wear should not cause anxiety. A toy in mint condition, on the other hand, may denote one that was unsold or unsuccessful, inasmuch as it was not played with.

The early Käthe Kruse dolls have appealingly sad faces, and it is said that she made them like that to reflect the sadness of World War I. These dolls were not cheap to begin with, and they command good prices today, particularly the earlier ones. During World War I and after, the materials used in manufacture changed, and the factory began producing shop mannequins: these large dolls have become costly and are extremely collectable.

A

A group of Lenci dolls. The large blond doll on the left dates from 1930. She has a black Lenci stamp on the left foot, a pressed felt face and eyes looking to the right. Nearly 17in (43cm) tall, she is wearing her original cream net dress. The tall doll in the centre at the back also dates from 1930. She is 25in (64cm) tall, and has a swivel head, open-closed mouth and simulated teeth, and a long black mohair wig in a snood.

On the right of the group is an 18in (46cm) tall doll whose eyes are looking to one side. She has a black mohair wig and swivel hips. The small doll at right front is 9in (23cm) tall. She has a *Lenci Torino* label and a *Bresse* label. She holds a felt cockerel. To her left is a doll with a label that reads: *Bambola Italia Lenci Torino Made in Italy*. She is 9½in (24cm) tall and carries a mohair-covered duck with an orange beak and feet.

The dolls are signed Käthe Kruse on the left foot and are marked with a serial number. This was a coded control number system from which the age of the doll can be ascertained if it has not worn off. Between 1945 and 1951 the right foot bore the stamp *Made in Germany US Zone*. At first, Käthe Kruse dolls were made under contract by Kämmer & Reinhardt, but these examples, in production for only a year or so, are rare.

Until 1928 Käthe Kruse dolls had loosely sewn-on heads; the turned head was first produced in 1929. From 1910 until 1929 they all had painted hair, after which real hair wigs were introduced and became very popular, although the painted hair examples still continued. The eyes were almost always painted, and all dolls had closed mouths. One dating clue is that dolls made before 1930 had very wide hips; after that date they were narrower.

It is interesting to note that from 1910 until 1956 only five different doll head types were produced, with slight variations as well as different numbers and names. The first head was merely called no. I. Second was *Schlenkerchen* (The Little Dawdler) – Doll II *Träumerchen* (The Little Dreamer) and *Du Mein* (You mine). Dolls V and VI were next (Dolls III and IV did not exist). *Deutches Kind* (German Child) was Doll VIII and *Hämpelchen* was Doll XII. After the 1957 model Hanne

A

Kruse dolls came into existence. Käthe Kruse dolls were also produced in celluloid. The firm's financial crisis of 1950 led to the production of synthetic doll heads. Old style heads were also produced and also magnesit heads, made from a cement-like substance.

Käthe Kruse died in 1968 at the age of 85, but her memory lives on in her creations, and her dolls continue to be made in West Germany in Donauwörth.

LENCI

Lenci dolls are to Italy what Käthe Kruse dolls are to Germany. Similarly, they began early, and continue production today. 'Lenci' was the pet name of Elena, the wife of Enrico di Scavini of Turin who made felt dolls of extremely high quality and design. They were first registered under the Lenci trademark in 1922. The dolls appeal to people of all ages, and early examples are highly valued by collectors.

Lenci dolls are characterized by their all-felt heads and bodies with articulated limbs, painted features and exquisitely designed felt clothes. The faces were moulded with great realism and child-like expression, with chubby cheeks. Sometimes the clothes are of patchwork, with felt floral trims. Some of the child dolls have cross expressions; some are girl or lady dolls, their faces painted with two-tone lips; their eyes often have two white dots added; some have real hair wigs and others mohair. It is popularly believed that the Lenci hands have the two middle fingers stitched together but this is erroneous: some are like this but others have only stitched finger definition. Because of the commercial success of Lenci dolls there were many copies at the time. True Lencis are marked in numerous ways – with ink stamps, card tags, ribbon labels and metal tags – the earliest being the metal tag. After 1938, cardboard tags were used. The firm produced a great variety of dolls including a complete series of foreign costume dolls, a range of ethnic and sporting dolls, miniatures and mascots, as well as the well loved child dolls.

Lenci dolls were always quite expensive and certain serial numbers of doll attract a higher price than others due to general appeal. Condition and original clothing, as always, are determining factors in price: these dolls were particularly known for their colourful felt clothes. Unfortunately, they are subject to moth and other infestations, and signs of insect damage should not be ignored. Dolls can be treated for such problems and careful repair to holes undertaken but this is difficult and the inclusion of an infested doll in a healthy collection could have serious results. The most prized Lenci dolls are those made between 1920 and 1930.

STEIFF DOLLS

Fraülein Margarete Steiff, Giengen, Württemburg, is best known for stuffed toy animals of superior quality. Although she died in 1909, the firm continued in the family and is still going today. Her dolls were of felt, plush and velvet and were characterized by a seam down the centre of the face (which gives a rather odd appearance) and a button in the ears. Felt head dolls were first made in 1894. Most were character dolls, which have become extremely hard to find. Some have specially balanced feet enabling them to stand up without support.

A

CELLULOID DOLLS

Celluloid was originally a patent name, but it has now become accepted as the word used for the pre-plastic material from which some 'unbreakable' dolls were made, although, in fact, it was quite brittle and very breakable. In 1869 the Hyatt brothers, who were working in the USA, patented a nitro-cellulose and camphor substance which they called 'celluloid', which can be considered as the first synthetic material. In fact, the substance had been created earlier in the UK. The invention of celluloid had a revolutionary effect on the average household, and ivory and wooden items such as combs and tooth-brushes now gave way to moulded celluloid ones. Sheets of celluloid could be moulded and compressed under heat and finely detailed dolls' heads could be produced.

It is a common misconception that celluloid dolls are late in date. The Rheinische Gummi- und Cellu-loid-Fabrik Co. in Germany was pro-ducing dolls in 1873, and its tortoise or *Schildkröte* trademark, without the diamond, was registered in 1889. Many of these dolls are, therefore, earlier than is often supposed. In 1899, the same firm used the tortoise in the diamond with the words *Schutz-marke* (trademark) beneath.

Until the last few years, cellu-loid was considered the poor relation of the doll world, but nowadays cellu-loid dolls are avidly collected, partic-ularly by Germans. By the early years of this century many firms were manufacturing toys in celluloid, and its non-peeling, non-flaking proper-ties were very attractive. However, there were as many disadvantages as there were advantages in the material, and these eventually led to its decline and to the production of what we now know as plastic. Celluloid proved to be fragile and flammable; if it was

too thin it would squash; if it was too thick it would crack; it would become bleached and brittle in the sunlight. However, with all these problems it is surprising how many examples one still finds of dolls intact and in remarkably good condition. It is likely that cracked and damaged examples found their way to rubbish tips and perished, unlike their bisque counter-parts, some of which lay buried for nearly 100 years, to be dug up again

A

This French celluloid doll, which is 21in (53cm) tall, is marked on both head and back with the eagle's head trademark of Petitcolin of Paris, Etain and Lilas. It is also marked *France 57½*. Petitcolin was established in 1914, and the moulded-hair-style of this doll suggests that it was made in the 1920s

B

A French celluloid doll, whose head was made in the last quarter of the 19th century. The head is attached to a swivel neck. The body and costume are of a later date than the head.

B

from Victorian rubbish tips and re-loved in the 1970s and 1980s. The popularity of the celluloid doll declined in the 1920s and had largely disappearing by the 1930s.

One of the most exciting things about collecting celluloid dolls, apart from the fact that inexpensive examples are still relatively easy to find, is that many renowned doll manufacturing companies in both Germany and the USA made celluloid versions of their bisque-headed dolls; these bear the same mould numbers and are obviously much less expensive than their bisque look-alikes. They are, on the other hand, more sought-after than the basic celluloid baby doll and command higher prices. They are often on the same quality bodies as the bisque heads. It is also probable that during the years in which the dolls' hospitals existed, many dolls had broken bisque heads replaced by celluloid which was cheaper and less fragile.

Among others, celluloid heads have been found with the marks of Armand Marseille, Kestner, Jumeau and Kämmer & Reinhardt; some of the better mould numbers of the Kämmer & Reinhardt characters are made of celluloid and are quite rare. Grace Storey Putnam's Bye-Lo baby has also been found in celluloid. Before World War II the Japanese made a great variety of celluloid dolls, and celluloid Kewpies and mechanical dolls from the USA were also produced. The German firm of Käthe Kruse made celluloid dolls as well as a whole new range of costume dolls; König & Wernicke of Waltershausen made celluloid dolls in 1912, as did Bruno Schmidt in 1900. Although the finest celluloid dolls are from the well-known doll manufacturers in France, Germany and the USA, they have been made all over the world.

Among the French celluloid dolls, the most commonly found marks are SNF in a diamond (Société Nobel Française, registered in 1939 and in 1960) and SIC in a diamond (Société Industrielle de Celluloid), and the eagle symbol and the word *France* (made by Petitcolin in 1902–25). The early celluloids very much resembled the pale flesh tones of the bisque dolls, while later examples developed stronger colouring.

By far the rarest of the celluloid dolls is the celluloid resin of the French fashion-type, swivel-head doll, usually found on a leather body. Nothing is clearly known or documented about these dolls and they may even have been made in the USA. The only certainty is that they are almost never found. Some celluloid dolls have real hair wigs while others have moulded hair in contemporary styles which give a more accurate historical reference.

Celluloid heads are to be found on all-celluloid bent limb baby bodies, on jointed composition bodies, on leather bodies with U-joint thighs, straight-limb toddler bodies or fixed limbs. Eyes may be painted, made of glass or even celluloid. Some celluloid dolls are very crude while others are as fine in quality as the bisque dolls.

GERMAN DOLLS

Germany was the most prolific doll-making country in the world, and it is from here that doll collectors have received their greatest legacy. The great German doll-making companies made every conceivable type of doll in a wealth of designs and materials and in great profusion. The sheer quantity produced has assured Germany's place at the forefront of the world market; although German dolls are less rare and less expensive than French examples, the quality of the

A

On the left is an open-mouth character baby doll, whose head bears the mark *996 A & M*. It is 9in (23cm) tall and has a bent-limb composition body. The clothes are original. The doll on the right is by Kestner. It has intaglio eyes, painted brush-stroke hair and a bent-limb, baby body. It bears the mark *142*.

B

This Armand Marseille doll has an unusual face. It is marked *AM 12 Dep Made in Germany*, but it resembles faces of dolls by Heinrich Handwerck. The doll's original clothing consists of a green woollen coat and straw bonnet, and she is pushing a toy baker's delivery cart.

A

bisque and face painting is equal to the French examples, and their lower price is simply a reflection of the high numbers that are available to collectors.

The golden age of the German doll spanned roughly 75 years from the mid 19th century to the first quarter of the 20th century. During this time the Germans came to dominate the world doll market through the enormous variety of their wares and their competitive price structure. German doll making was eventually destroyed by the world economic recession in the inter-war years, World War II and the subsequent development of cheap synthetics in a throw-away age.

The vast majority of the German doll-makers were located in the southeastern province of Thuringia. These included – with their start-up dates in parentheses – Adolf Wislizenus (1851), Alt, Beck & Gottschalck (1854), Gebrüder Krauss (1863), Edmund Ulrich Steiner (1864; Steiner later moved to the United States), Louis Wolf & Co. (1870), Bähr & Pröschild (1871), Franz Schmidt & Co. (1890), Kley & Hahn (1859), Emil Bauersachs (1882), C.M. Bergmann (1889), Bruno Schmidt (1900) and König & Wernicke (1912).

Consequently, the town of Waltershausen gained such a reputation that wholesalers and retailers advertised 'Waltershausen dolls' as a reference to the high quality of the product. Sonneburg led the reputation of being the centre for all grades of doll making. The doll makers of Thuringia produced dolls not only from forestry products such as wood and papier mâché, but also from bisque and porcelain.

Because so many famous companies were located in Thuringia (now in the German Democratic Republic), there was obviously a healthy exchange of ideas, craftsmanship and even craftsmen. Furthermore, members of the doll-making families married each other, temporarily merging the companies, although there must also have been great rivalries.

The Thuringian lead in this field was not sudden, but grew from the labours of the early German doll makers who established traditions of workmanship. Carvers in wood, modellers, papier mâché craftsmen and generations of cottage industry workers had built up a thriving doll and toy manufacturing tradition in south Germany. The natural resources were there in abundance – wood for carving, fine china clay, wood pulp, a dense population providing cheap labour force and a good transportation network, the importance of which should not be overlooked. To give some idea of the size and scale of manufacture, in 1870 the firm of Fleischmann in Sonneberg, Thuringia, was said to be employing some 32,000 workers, including outworkers.

huge numbers of dolls were made by Marseille, they are the most frequently encountered by modern collectors.

Marseille was born in Russia in 1856 and later settled near Sonneberg where he started business as a porcelain manufacturer. By 1890, he was producing bisque heads and began, with his son Armand Marseille Jr, to supply heads to George Borgfeldt, Louis Wolf, Charles Bergmann and others. Armand Marseille Jr married the daughter of Ernst Heubach, a doll maker who began manufacturing in 1887. The Marseille company, like many others, suffered during World War I when dolls were not exported from Germany, the USA or the rest of Europe. However, by 1920 they were in production again and remained so until about 1926.

B

ARMAND MARSEILLE

Armand Marseille of Köppelsdorf and Neuhaus is probably the first doll manufacturer's name which the new collector will learn, for Marseille dolls have always been regarded as some of the least expensive of the German dolls and therefore the most likely purchases for the new collector. Armand Marseille's company was the most prolific of the doll makers and his quality of production was consistently excellent. Because of the laws of supply and demand, the most commonly found dolls are among the least expensive and because such

A

This fine quality open-mouth bisque-head doll was made by Kämmer & Reinhardt, and the head is marked *K * R 117n*. Mould number 117n indicates that the doll was in the Mein neuer Liebling (My New Darling) series, which was made until the 1930s. The doll is 22in (56cm) tall.

The first of Marseille's anchor trademarks was registered in 1893; this showed the anchor, flanked by the initials *A.M.*, in a circle. When the mark incorporated with the letter *W*. it indicated that the dolls' heads had been made exclusively by Marseille for Louis Wolf, a Sonneberg company with branches in Boston and New York City that distributed both German and American dolls in the US and commissioned special designs from several German manufacturers. In 1910 Marseille introduced a stylized anchor incorporating his initials, while the more formal anchor with the initials on either side of the upright was introduced *c.* 1920.

Marseille made bisque heads both for his own company and for many other doll manufacturers, including Bergmann, Borgfeldt, Cuno & Otto Dressell and Otto Gans. Such heads are often marked with the initials *A.M.* incorporated into the other companies' marks. Dating heads by Marseille is extremely difficult as the same moulds were used not only for several years but for different materials. Those bearing the initials *D.R.G.M.* were made after 1909, while those marked *D.R.M.R.* were produced after 1910. However, expert advice should be sought about exact dates, although the initials *A.M.* are always recognizable. Confusion arises because some of the four-figure numbers – 1890, 1892 to 1903, 1905 and 1909 – actually refer to years, while other four-figure numbers are mould numbers, which were introduced between 1895 and 1899. Some three-figure numbers were introduced in 1910, 1911, 1913, 1925 and 1926, but there does not appear to have been any systematic approach to the introduction of numbers – the 500 series seems to have been introduced in 1910, for example, while the 400 series was first used in 1926. Much research has been carried out into the dates of first use of all Marseille's marks and also into the different materials used in particular moulds. However, it is important to remember that many moulds were used for several years; a doll bearing the impressed mark *1890* might have been made in the 1900s or even later.

In addition to the mould number, many of the bisque heads made by Marseille for its character dolls and dolly-faced babies bore the incised name of the style of the doll – Fany (introduced in 1912), Baby Phyllis (1925), My Dream Baby (1925), for instance – and it seems that dolls' heads with girls' names were manufactured exclusively for the US market.

SIMON & HALBIG

Simon & Halbig of Gräfenhain, Thuringia, was probably one of the first companies to develop greatly in size, and it made a profuse variety of dolls' heads in Parian and papier mâché. However, it did not make doll's bodies. Bodies were purchased from other companies, and although they may be of Simon & Halbig design and produced especially for that company, they were not actually made by Simon & Halbig, apart from the all-bisque dolls for which it did make the bodies. In fact, J. D. Kestner of Waltershausen, Thuringia, was perhaps the only German company to make both its own doll heads and bodies.

It also adds to the confusion of new collectors to know that Simon & Halbig made heads for some of the renowned French factories of the period, including Jumeau, Daspres and Roullet & Decamps. It is similar to the situation today when a cheaper item may be made in Hong Kong for a UK brand name; so it was then with the French companies, which sometimes had cheaper dolls' heads made for them in Germany for assembly in France on French bodies and with French clothes.

Simon & Halbig mould numbers and marks are generally incised on the back of the dolls' head, on the back of the shoulder-plate or on the front of the shoulder-plate. Research has shown that some mould numbers were reserved for different versions of the same mould, while other series of numbers were used for particular types of doll – for example, the 400 series was used for porcelain dolls and the 800 series for all-bisque and bathing dolls. Simon & Halbig shoulder-head dolls are among the

A

A

earliest dolls available to collectors, but dating is difficult as, like Marseille, Simon & Halbig used the same moulds for several years and also used the same mould numbers for different sizes, sometimes on the heads it produced for other manufacturers.

KESTNER

Johannes Daniel Kestner Jr from Waltershausen advertised papier mâché dolls with leather bodies in 1823, although he is reputed to have started production as early as 1805. These dolls were probably the early milliners' models whose origins are obscure. He also made buttons, clothing and fine quality goods; he used a crown as his trade mark. Kestner should probably be regarded as the

father of the Waltershausen doll industry: he was certainly the first in the area. His firm was probably the only company to produce both heads and bodies, and a Kestner doll can, therefore, be regarded as a whole product of the firm and not a marriage between a head made by one firm and a body made by another. In the 1850s Kestner made china-head and wax-over-papier mâché dolls, but as these are unmarked, they cannot be identified. After Johannes Kestner died in 1859 the company bought a porcelain factory and produced Parian heads and later the bisque heads that we usually associate with Kestner. However, the Parian heads were also unmarked and are therefore not definitely identifiable. Fortunately the later, exquisite dolls, produced from the 1880s, 1890s and onwards were marked. Kestner's grandson Adolph took over the firm in 1872 and ran it until his death in 1918, after which the company rode out World War I and the Depression, finally merging with Kämmer & Reinhardt in 1930. The company was held in extremely high esteem.

HEUBACH

Gebrüder Heubach, of Lichte, Thuringia, which was founded in 1820, was one of the earlier doll-manufacturing companies in Germany. This firm is primarily noted for its character dolls, piano babies, figurines and all-bisque dolls. Many had moulded hair and intaglio eyes and were of good quality, although the standard of the bodies varied. The intaglio painted eyes had moulded details, including a raised white dot. In most cases, the pupil and iris were indented to give a deeper look, and this gave the Heubach eyes a realism and range of expression impossible with glass eyes. Moulded hair may have been adopted for cheapness or it may have been a throwback to the moulded-haired Parians. Gebrüder Heubach dolls are usually marked with a rising

sun or *Heubach* in a square. Some collectors confuse Gebrüder Heubach with Ernst Heubach, whose firm was founded in 1887. The Ernst Heubach dolls are generally marked *Heubach, Köppelsdorf, EH* or *HK*, sometimes with a horse-shoe trade mark. Four- and five-digit numbers seem to have been used for Gebrüder Heubach but the earlier dolls, before the company began to make character dolls, are something of a mystery because the numbering is inconsistent, often unaccompanied by a symbol and sometime in such an obscure position on the doll's body that it cannot be located – for instance, under a shoulder where the body would hide it. It is known that Heubach produced dolly-faced dolls before the character dolls that were such a distinctive feature of its output.

KAMMER & REINHARDT

The firm of Kämmer & Rienhardt of Waltershausen is a famous name in the doll-collecting field and is best known for its character dolls.

A

A Kämmer & Reinhardt doll with a celluloid head and a composition body. She was made between 1905 and 1927 and wears her original checked pinafore dress.

B

Gebrüder Heubach made this bisque-head boy toddler doll, which bears the company's rising sun trademark and the mark *8 Germany*.

B

These are perhaps the *crème de la crème* of the German doll industry, certainly in terms of price, rarity and collectability. The firm began *c.*1886. Ernst Kämmer was an experienced doll maker but it is not known who made the Kämmer & Reinhardt heads at that time. Certainly Simon & Halbig made them after 1902 when Ernst Kämmer died. Kämmer & Reinhardt developed new stringing methods for doll's bodies. Any improvement had to be patented, because, with so much competition, ideas would be copied immediately if an invention was not patented. It is from this wealth of patent material that we have gleaned so much of our doll information. Kämmer claimed to be the first to

six-sided star was adopted as a symbol by the Kämmer & Reinhardt factory. Simon & Halbig heads were also produced for mechanical dolls, novelty items and bisque-faced dolls, and this was probably the first firm to use coloured bisque for black dolls and Burmese dolls with slanted eyes. Chinese and red Indian dolls were also produced with appropriate bisque colouring.

Heinrich Handwerck's factory was founded in 1876 in Gotha, near Waltershausen. Max Handwerck may have been Heinrich's son, and his factory was founded in 1900 for the manufacture of ball-jointed dolls' bodies and dolls' heads. Although it was taken over by Kämmer & Reinhardt, it was always run separately. Most of the heads used were manufactured by Simon & Halbig, however, and it is thought that most of the mould numbers ending in 9 are, in fact, Simon & Halbig dolls.

Franz Reinhardt was the businessman of the company and after Kämmer died he became much more adventurous and aggressive in his approach. He purchased the Heinrich Handwerck factory in 1902 after the death of Heinrich; this company had been producing dolls' bodies. The Kämmer & Reinhardt dolls made before 1901 were modelled by Kämmer, and after his death they were produced by Simon & Halbig. Indeed the famous Kämmer & Reinhardt character dolls (see pages 62–3) were almost certainly made by Simon & Halbig. Reinhardt expanded and by 1932 his firm had become the leading doll company in Waltershausen, surpassing Kestner. The firm also produced composition, rubber and celluloid dolls made by the Rheinische Gummi- und Celluloid-Fabrik Co. with the turtle trade mark. The firm is thought to have introduced the bent-limb baby body – a five-piece body – in about 1909. This innovative company also made unusual eye mechanisms and other life like features, and introduced changes in dolls' anatomies to reflect changing fashions in clothes as well as to make the dolls appear more like real babies.

C

A bisque-head mulatto doll with an open mouth and sleeping eyes. The head is marked *S & H K * R*. The doll is 22in (56cm) tall and has an articulated, black composition body.

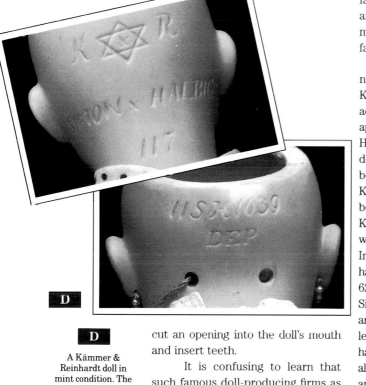

D

C

D

A Kämmer & Reinhardt doll in mint condition. The closed-mouth bisque head is marked *K * R Simon & Halbig 117*, as may be seen in the close up of the back of the head. Mould number 117 was used for the company's Mein Liebling (My Darling) series. The doll is 25in (64cm) tall and has her original dress, underwear, socks and shoes.

cut an opening into the doll's mouth and insert teeth.

It is confusing to learn that such famous doll-producing firms as Franz and Bruno Schmidt, Heinrich Handwerck, Kämmer & Reinhardt, Bergmann, König & Wernicke, Kley & Hahn and Catterfelder-Puppenfabrik, to name a few, did not make their own doll heads. By about 1927 Kämmer & Reinhardt had taken over production of the Simon & Halbig heads. Heads can often be found with both Kämmer & Reinhardt and the Simon & Halbig marks on them: the

D

MINOR GERMAN MANUFACTURERS

Franz Schmidt of Gengenthal near Waltershausen came on the doll scene around 1890, making dolls' bodies and parts. Simon & Halbig made heads from his own design and heads are sometimes found with both firms' trademarks. Some of his heads have pierced nostrils or actual holes in the nose: this is said to be his own device and was introduced about 1912. He also made wood, composition and celluloid dolls, and he claimed to be the first to manufacture character dolls with sleeping eyes. The first character dolls by Kämmer & Reinhardt had painted eyes.

The firm of Adolf Wislizenus of Waltershausen was one of the earliest companies, dating back to about 1851. He made composition and papier mâché dolls and looked to Simon & Halbig for the production of bisque heads. His heads are marked *A.W.*, *A.W.W.*, *A.W. Special* and *Old Glory*.

A few doll makers were located in neighbouring Bavaria, which was also heavily wooded and has good china clay deposits. One of the best known is Schoenau & Hoffmeister of Burgrub, which began operations in 1901 as a porcelain factory. The company adopted a five-pointed star trademark. It manufactured open- and closed-mouth dolls, some in regional or 'exotic' costumes.

CHARACTER DOLLS

The leading doll makers of Germany pioneered the manufacture of the character doll. The first such dolls were made by Kämmer & Reinhardt, which was said to have been inspired by seeing an exhibition of the dolls by Marion Kaulitz, a 'progressive' designer based in Munich. The decision to make a range of realistic-looking dolls was a move away from the dolly-faced tradition, towards toys with which children could actually identify. It was realized that babies did not usually have very

A

Kestner's mould number 243 is usually seen as an oriental baby as here. The doll is 13in (33cm) tall and has an open mouth and blue glass eyes. It was made c.1914 and bears the impressed mark *F10 243 JDK*. It is wearing its original Chinese outfit, stitched in metal threads in blues, greens and purples.

A

pretty faces and that they looked more like little old men. At first these dolls had an indifferent reception, but suddenly their popularity rocketed and the firm had difficulty in meeting the demand. The 1908 slump in the doll world became the boom of 1909. Character dolls had arrived.

Those produced by Kämmer & Reinhardt were to become the *crème de la crème* of the German doll industry. Kämmer & Reinhardt character dolls were numbered starting with mould 100. This was superseded by 101, which took the form of a boy or a girl affectionately named Peter or Marie; this model was made with both painted and glass eyes. In 1910 Reinhardt's own nephew was used as a model for the boy and girl moulds number 114, called Hans and Gretchen. This also comes, although rarely, as a head and shoulder-plate with a kid body. Some of the model numbers appear to be missing and one can only assume that a few samples were made but never put into production; for example, 108, 111 and 113 have not come to light so far. One of those to be found is model number 115, which has moulded hair, glass eyes, closed mouth and a toddler body. Another example, 115a, has a wig, glass eyes, closed mouth and is the original mould for a Käthe Kruse and a Schoenhut doll. Mould 116 is an older version of 100, the so-called Kaiser Baby, a boy with open mouth, teeth and a tongue, and painted and moulded hair. This is only a nickname given by collectors to this mould and has nothing to do with the Kaiser as a child; it is thought to be a model of the son of the artist who first sculpted the bust, and the Kaiser was born in 1859 and the Kaiser Baby first made as late as 1908, it is not likely that this particular baby would have been used so many years after his birth. Such are the confusions of the doll world. The next mould is the extremely beautiful 117 in open- and closed-mouth versions. The 117a open mouth has teeth, and gives the impression of being an older child, while the 117n, yet another version, has open mouth, teeth and flirting eyes. (The *n* stands for *neu* – i.e., new models.)

That there was some liaison between Kämmer & Reinhardt, Käthe Kruse and Schoenhut is almost certain, but it is possible that ideas were simply copied. At any rate, the 115 and 115a models look exceptionally like Käthe Kruse dolls, and Käthe Kruse modelled her dolls on her own children. Moulds 118–120 have not been found. Mould 121 is a baby or toddler with open mouth, teeth and tongue; 122 a baby or toddler; 123 a

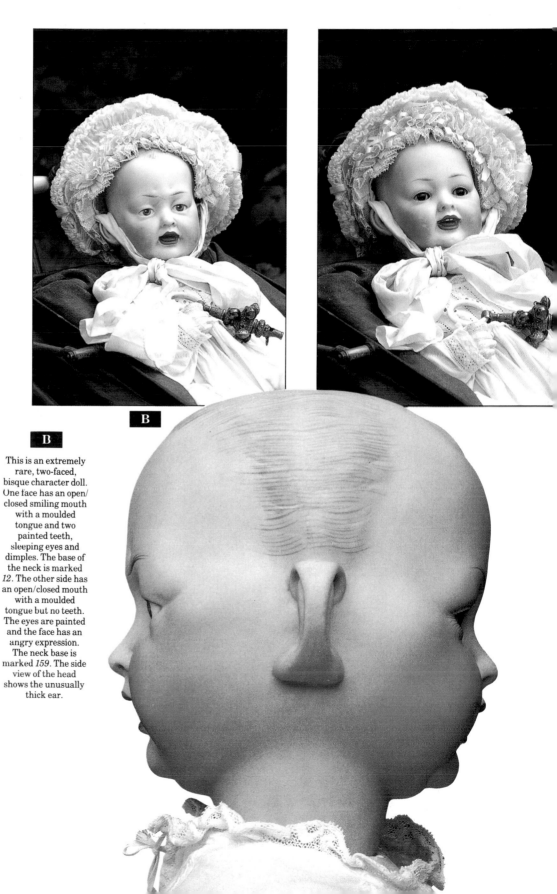

B

B

This is an extremely rare, two-faced, bisque character doll. One face has an open/closed smiling mouth with a moulded tongue and two painted teeth, sleeping eyes and dimples. The base of the neck is marked *12*. The other side has an open/closed mouth with a moulded tongue but no teeth. The eyes are painted and the face has an angry expression. The neck base is marked *159*. The side view of the head shows the unusually thick ear.

A

A

This bisque shoulder-plate, closed-mouth doll is 14in (36cm) tall. The leather body has bisque arms. The paperweight eyes are blue, and the head bears the indistinct number *139*, suggesting that it may be an early Kestner destined for the French market.

B

The bisque shoulder-head of this open-mouth doll is incised *S & H 1079 Dep Germany*. Simon & Halbig's mould number 1079 was first made in 1892. The doll is 23in (58cm) tall and has a kid body and wood and composition limbs. The pink lace dress, matching hat and mohair wig are original to the doll.

Funny Face boy with closed mouth, smiling with flirty eyes; 125 has not been located; 126 is a baby or toddler with open mouth and may be mechanical or with flirting eyes; 127 is a painted-haired baby or toddler boy in bisque; 128–130 have not yet been found. This list shows what an imaginative and innovative company Kämmer & Reinhardt was and how worthy of the highest accolades.

Among other makers was the firm of Kestner, whose identifying mould numbers are confusing; sometimes they are accompanied by the initials *J.D.K.* and sometimes not. Generally speaking, the character mould numbers are in a series from 178 to 190 (with the exception of 188, which has not been found) and a 200 series. They have open mouths, closed mouths and open/closed (which means that the mouth appears to be open, with parted lips, but the bisque aperture has not been cut). One of the most sought-after Kestner characters is mould 243, the oriental baby.

Armand Marseille made character dolls with moulded hair, painted eyes and closed mouths with numbers such as 500, 550, 590 and 600. The most famous was the 351 open-mouth, or 341 closed-mouth, Dream Baby in various sizes.

Simon & Halbig also made open- and closed- mouth characters with both painted and glass eyes, with a wide assortment of character numbers, for example 150–153, 1279, 1294, 1299 and some 1300 series numbers.

Gebrüder Heubach also made many character dolls. Its numbering system appears to be erratic: those with five-digit numbers would seem to have been the last dolls made, but the 'googlies', which are known to be of a later date, have four-digit numbers. Sometimes the numbers are not impressed properly, so care must be taken when interpreting a number. Some dolls have only the rising sun mark, and others the square, incised mark. There seems to be no consistency, and one imagines that the confusion must also have affected the manufacturers themselves.

All in all, there was a wealth of character interpretations and the collector certainly has wide scope, even within the products of the Heubach company alone.

B

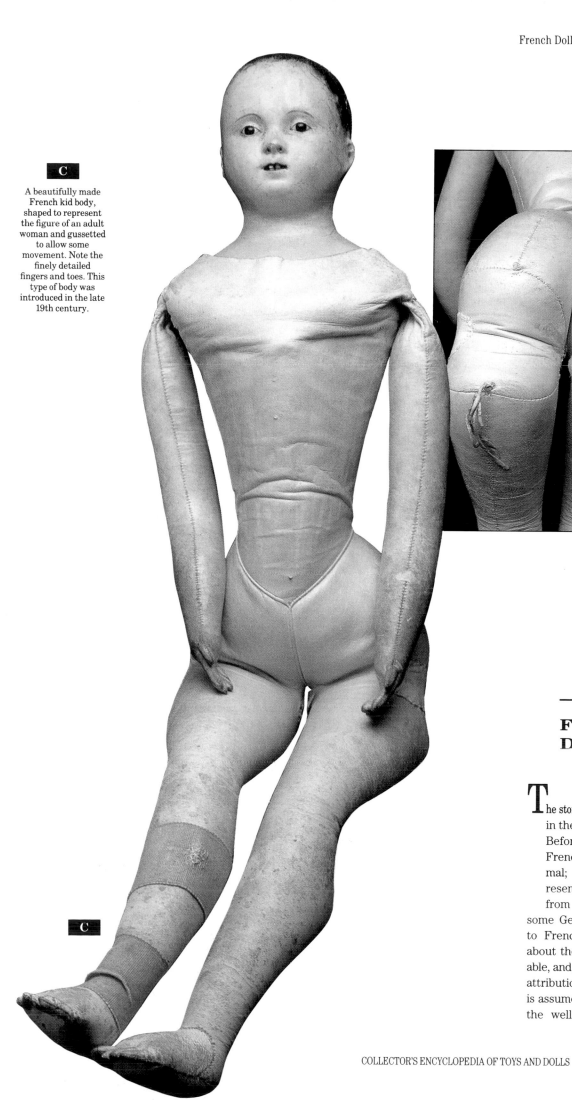

C

A beautifully made French kid body, shaped to represent the figure of an adult woman and gussetted to allow some movement. Note the finely detailed fingers and toes. This type of body was introduced in the late 19th century.

C

FRENCH DOLLS

The story of the French doll really begins in the middle of the 19th century. Before that, the influence of the French doll industry was minimal; some papier mâché dolls, resembling the Sonneberg dolls from Germany, were made and some German heads were attached to French bodies, but information about them is disjointed and unreliable, and, as the heads are unmarked, attribution is difficult. Sometimes it is assumed that a head that is not of the well-known and authenticated

A

This bisque-head, closed-mouth French doll is 26in (66cm) tall. The head is incised *F.G. 10* in a cartouche. Gaultier was operating in Paris between 1860 and 1916. It is known to have produced bisque dolls' heads and doll parts, and Gaultier was awarded a silver medal at the Paris Exhibition of 1878. Dolls' heads and shoulder-plates bearing the initials *F.G.* are often attributed to Gaultier. This doll has fixed blue eyes and chubby cheeks. The jointed body is composition, and the wrists are not articulated. The wig is not original to the doll.

German variety, must be either French, or a German head designed for the French market. Generally, there is little evidence to support this.

French dolls in their day were for the pampered rich and, with their exquisite costumes lavishly made in humble back streets by independent outworkers, they have kept their exalted position at the top end of the doll-collecting world to this day. It is this quality, detail and lavishness of costume for which French dolls were perhaps best known; in effect they were complete replicas of the fashions of the day, and today they are highly prized by collectors if they still have their original clothes. It seems astonishing that in 1855 a doll complete with nine-piece layette could be purchased for 1 franc 19 centimes.

JUMEAU

At the roots of development of the French doll industry was the firm of Jumeau, which gave the impetus to the early French doll industry. Much valuable information has been put together from studies of contemporary exhibition reports and commercial directories without which our knowledge would be sparse. The firm was founded in 1842 by Pierre François Jumeau, who was in partnership with a M. Belton for a short time; little is known of Belton. Early shoulder-plate dolls with leather bodies and domed bisque heads are sometimes known as Belton-type heads, although Jumeau claimed that his patent for bébé dolls had been taken out as early as 1840. The Jumeau factory address appears to have been 18 rue Mauconseil, Paris, until 1867. Emile Jumeau, the younger son of Pierre François, took over the business in 1875 and further developed it. He obtained some heads from Germany, evidently because they were cheap, and even bought wax heads from England. His early dolls are marked *E.J.* for Emile Jumeau and collectors refer to them as *E.J.*s. In 1873, the firm expanded to factory premises, large by the standards of the time, in the doll-making area of Montreuil near Paris, but large numbers of outworkers were still used. The building actually

B

This is a very rare, life-sized French shop mannequin, which, although unmarked, may be by Bru. It has fixed blue eyes and a closed mouth, and the face is delicately painted. The wig and clothes are original.

C

A bisque closed-mouth French bébé with brown eyes. The head is marked *Déposé tête Jumeau* and there are tick marks and an incised *9*. The wig and clothing are original to the doll.

C

A

These three fashion dolls all have bisque swivel heads. The doll on the left was made by Jumeau *c*.1870; it is 15in (38cm) tall and is impressed with the numeral *1*. The doll in the centre bears the impressed mark *F.G.6* on both the head and the shoulder-plate. It is 22½in (57cm) tall and was made *c*.1880. The right-hand doll, which is 14½in (37cm) tall, is marked *L déposé 1D* on the shoulder plate. It has proved impossible to identify a doll maker who might have used such a cipher; three contenders have been suggested – Léon Desty, who was recorded as a doll maker in Paris in 1869, Mlle Léontine Delbosque, who appears in the directories for 1876 to 1889 as a doll maker and L. Doléac, who made dressed and undressed dolls between 1881 and 1906. Dolls incised *L.D.* are rare.

exists to this day, but is now owned by a plastics concern. Outworkers were mainly used to design and create the wonderful clothes. Jumeau employed orphans and prisoners – the cheapest available labour force – in an attempt to cut costs; the competition from the cheaper imported German dolls was a constant threat. The quality of the German dolls was excellent, and the German bodies have endured rather better than the French in many cases. The gesso covering on the French bodies tends to be much more brittle and has a tendency to lift off, particularly on the fingers. Pierre François was conservative in his ideas and the success and progress of the Jumeau factory was a direct result of Emile's endeavours. The term bébé first appears to have been used around 1859 and was in general use by 1870. It was introduced to distinguish those dolls with child-like faces from the dolls representing fashion models, which had the faces of adult women and which are usually referred to as Parisiennes or, simply, as fashion dolls.

PARISIENNES OR
FASHION DOLLS

Authenticating and dating the early Jumeau heads is extremely difficult since they are unmarked. Parisiennes were developed around the 1860s and were a true creation of their elegant and affluent time. Much as the Princess of Wales inspires fashions today, the Empress Eugénie inspired many of the luxurious fashions seen on Parisiennes whose original clothing has survived. Often the costume is worn and threadbare, but the collector is urged to let repair, rather than replacement, be the general rule. The Parisiennes, with their bustles and fine dresses of silk, taffeta wool and lace, are a wonderful record of the elegance and extravagance of a bygone time. Parisienne heads were generally attached to a gusseted, stuffed leather body. The limbs are of leather, wood or porcelain. Cheaper heads were made in one piece with the shoulder-plate, and in these the eyes would sometimes be painted. The wigs were usually of animal fur.

B

This French open-mouth doll, which is 27in (69cm) tall, is marked *Bru Jne 11*. Her lips are slightly parted and are painted in two colours.

B

Heads are generally unmarked, and those with painted eyes are often attributed to Huret or Rohmer, although some were undoubtedly made by Jumeau. It can be frustrating for the collector not to be able to identify so many of the Parisiennes. If they are marked, the dolls of the mid-1860s will bear a *J*.

BÉBÉ JUMEAU

The bébés, as mentioned, were the child-like dolls. Their charm was that they could be articulated; early examples have fixed wrists and ball-jointed bodies with separate ball joints at shoulder, elbow, thigh and knee. They were hugely popular and sales soared. In 1881 85,000 dolls were said to have been sold. By 1889 the firm of Jumeau claimed to have 1,000 employees and to be selling 300,000 dolls per week. The very early dolls were unmarked and are referred to as almond-eyed, first period Jumeau or portrait Jumeau. Also from the early period we have the Jumeau triste or, the long face Jumeau, as

A

This character doll bears the incised mark *S.F.B.J. 236* on its open/closed mouth, bisque head. This is the so-called Laughing Jumeau, and it has two moulded teeth and a jointed toddler body. It is 22in (56cm) tall.

B

This delightful long face Jumeau triste is wearing a hand-made original costume, although the large bow at the back may have been added later.

A

American collectors call it. These heads are never marked and the bodies bear the *Jumeau Medaille d'Or Paris* stamp in blue. The later closed-mouth Jumeau dolls are sometimes marked in red *Déposé Tête Jumeau Breveté S.G.D.G.*, sometimes with red and black ticks and check marks, together with a size mark. Others are unmarked except for the size mark, or they bear the ticks and checks together with the size mark. These may also have the oval body label *Bébé Jumeau Diplôme d'Honneur*. The *B.L.* mark possibly stands for *Bébé Louvre*, being a doll made by Jumeau exclusively for the Magasins du Louvre department store between 1880 and 1890. By 1888 the open-mouthed bébé Jumeau had been introduced. it was more expensive, but nevertheless enthusiastically received. Oddly enough, today the closed-mouth version is twice the

C

This French character doll with sleeping blue eyes has a bisque head marked *S.F.B.J. 251*. Dressed as a sailor boy, the doll is 20in (50cm) tall.

B

A

A

Le Parisien was patented by Steiner in 1892. This bisque-head, open-mouth doll, which is 24in (60cm) tall, is marked *A 15 Paris* and, in red, *Le Parisien* (see below). She has fixed blue eyes, a jointed composition body and a key-wound mechanism which activates her legs to walk. The face painting is good, and she has pierced ears and her original purple carton pate.

B

This doll, which is marked *A. 11 T.*, has mismatched brows. The mouth has a light line between the lips, and the wig is similar to old Bru wigs. The mark *A.T.* has been attributed to A. Thuillier, a Paris doll manufacturer of bébés and dolly-faced dolls on jointed wooden, kid or composition bodies, who was active between 1875 and 1890.

B

price of the open-mouth type. Some of the open-mouthed dolls are marked with the early closed-mouth red stamp, and all bear the size, while others have a simple *Tête Jumeau* stamp in red, and as many again have no mark except the size.

BRU JNE. & CIE

Of all the French companies of the period, that founded by Leon Casimir Bru in 1866 is at the forefront for quality and innovative design.

The firm was continued by his son, Casimir Bru Jeune. Bru dolls have pink or white kid bodies and articulated porcelain or wooden limbs. Bru made heads of porcelain, rubber or hardened paste, two-faced dolls and a nursing bébé calle Bébé Têteur. The heads on the leather bodies were swivel-necked with bust-shaped breast plates. Early Bru dolls were marked with an incised half crescent and dot or a circle and dot. These dolls are now among the most prized in any collection and command high prices. Their faces have a whimsical

charm surpassed by none and, together with Thuillier (A.T.) dolls, they stand in the ranks of the top-priced dolls. Later Brus had open mouths and composition bodies. Paul Girard was Casimir Bru's successor in the firm and his dolls were marked *P.G.*

In addition to its reputation as one of the finest manufacturers of bisque fashion dolls, Bru was a pioneer in the development of mechanical dolls. In 1881 it registered a patent for Bébé Gourmand, and in 1891 Bébé Petit Pas (Baby Small Step) was patented.

A

C

This beautiful A mould, bisque-head Steiner has a closed mouth and original clothes.

JULES NICHOLAS STEINER

Steiners are among the best-loved French dolls, particularly the A mould Steiners with their sweet, expressive faces. The firm acquired the May Frères dolls business in 1897 and specialized in talking mechanical bébés: in 1890 it patented the Bébé Premier Pas, a doll with an open mouth, two rows of teeth and a wind-up, kid body. This was unmarked and had a domed head as well as a talking mechanism. Steiner won many awards for his dolls. Steiners marked with the A and the size

are referred to as A moulds and those with a C and the size as C moulds. The name *Bourgrin* is found on many of these heads. Some are marked *Le Petit Parisien Bébé* (The Little Parisian Baby). D mould and an FA and FC series are also recorded.

Steiner, which is also known as Société Steiner, claimed to have invented the bébé, and while the truth of this may be questioned, there is no doubt that many of the earliest bébés were manufactured by Steiner. The company's founder, Jules Nicholas Steiner, was a clockmaker by trade, which may explain the number of mechanical dolls produced, many

of the company's dolls having walking or talking mechanisms – some dolls had both. In 1892 Steiner was succeeded by A. Lafosse; in 1902 Lafosse was succeeded by Jules Mettais who was, in turn, succeeded by E. Daspres in 1906. Because of the various owners, the company's marks tend to vary widely. Some of the mechanical dolls are marked only on the mechanism itself, while some dolls' heads are marked *J. Steiner* or simply *Ste.* In 1889 the trademark incorporating a child-doll holding a flag was registered, and this was sometimes used as a stamp on dolls' bodies.

GAULTHIER

Fernand Gaulthier was a maker of fine quality bisque-headed fashion dolls on leather or composition bodies between 1860 and 1916. Swivel-neck shoulder-plate heads were set on French fashion bodies with kid or bisque arms. They were often marked on the shoulder-plate with the initials *F.G.* and the size. The early girl-doll heads on composition bodies are marked *F.G.* with the size at the top of the head, while the later mark is the *F.G.* in a scroll. Dolls were made with both closed and open mouths and were noted for their excellent quality and exceptional eyes, which are large and piercing. The girl dolls have a certain childlike quality, with chubby cheeks.

S.F.B.J.

German competition increased and difficult times came in the mid-1890s. In 1899, the French companies, including Jumeau, banded together under a new title, Société Française de Fabrication de Bébés et Jouets (French Manufacturers of Baby Dolls and Toys Company) – S.F.B.J. The group consisted of 10 associates and the original companies to join with Jumeau were Bru, Fleischmann & Bloedel, Pintel & Godchaux, Genty, Girard, Remignard, Gobert, Gaultier (then known as a porcelain manufacturer) and Rabery & Delphieu, Fleischmann & Bloedel was founded in 1873 by Salomon Fleischmann and Jean Bloedel in Sonneberg, and it quickly became an important supplier of dolls to the French market, producing walking, talking, nodding and even kissing dolls. In 1890 the trademark *Eden Doll* was registered for all the company's doll products, and in 1899 it registered Bébé Triomphe. Simon & Halbig made bisque heads, marked *Dep,* especially for Fleischmann & Bloedel's French exports, and because of the importance of the French market, Fleischmann & Bloedel became a founder member of the S.F.B.J., although it eventually closed in 1926. Ad. Bouchet and P.H. Schmitz also quickly joined the S.F.B.J., with Danel & Cie being added in 1911. The syndicate used some German-made doll parts, including

This extremely unusual French clown doll has an open-mouth bisque head, which is incised *Déposé fabrication française favorite No. 6* [the next word is illegible] *A.L. Cie, Limoges* and, in red, *Déposé la Géorgienne*. This is the mark of A. Lanternier & Cie, which was based in Limoges and made bisque heads between 1891 and *c.*1925. The company used several marks, and some of the heads appear to bear the signatures of Ed. Tasson or T.E. Maskon, but the identity of these people is unknown. The doll has a jointed composition body and probably wears its original clothing. It is 19in (48cm) tall.

B

An Albert Marque doll, 22in (55cm) tall, wearing its original wig and clothes. Such dolls are among the finest that a collector can own.

C

The bisque, closed-mouth French bébé doll was made by Jumeau and is marked *Déposé tête Jumeau S.G.D.G.* with an incised *11*. The eyes are brown and the body is jointed composition.

C

heads made by Simon & Halbig, which were imported into France between 1900 and 1914, but it also continued to make heads and bodies in the existing factories in France, using the old moulds. Most S.F.B.J. dolls have bisque heads on composition bodies.

Most of the leading French manufacturers were members of the syndicate, but they continued to produce dolls that had been introduced before 1899. Therefore, as late as 1921 Bébé Jumeau, Bébé Bru and Eden Bébé were still being manufactured and sold under their old names. Some earlier marks – the Jumeau bee, for example – were reused, and the S.F.B.J. trademark was registered in 1905.

MINOR FRENCH MANUFACTURERS

The achievements of companies such as Jumeau and Bru often obscure the output of some of the smaller French doll manufacturers, and it is possible for collectors to acquire comparatively cheaply dolls by lesser known makers that are just as beautifully made and desirable as those by the better known and more expensive companies.

Schmitt & Fils, which was based in Paris between 1863 and 1891, produced Bébé Schmitt, a jointed, indestructible doll with a bisque head, in 1879–90. Its trademark was two crossed keys within a shield. Another small Parisian company, Jullien, which was founded in 1863, originally made novelties, but after 1875 records indicate that several types of doll, including nanking and wooden dolls, together with musical figures or marottes, were being manufactured. In 1892 Jullien registered *L'Universal* as a trademark for a composition bébé.

Some highly regarded dolls bear the incised mark *A.T.* These have been attributed to A. Thuillier of Paris, which made bébés and dolly-faced dolls on jointed wooden, composition or kid bodies between 1875 and 1890. Petit & Dumontier of Paris claimed to make 'unbreakable' dolls and bébés between 1878 and 1890, and the incised mark *P + D* has been attributed to the company.

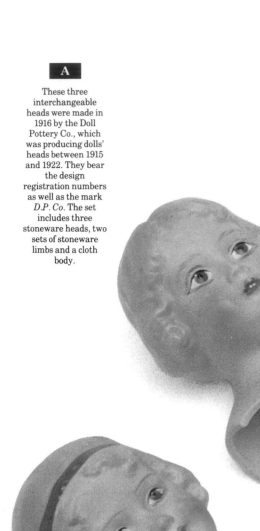

A

These three interchangeable heads were made in 1916 by the Doll Pottery Co., which was producing dolls' heads between 1915 and 1922. They bear the design registration numbers as well as the mark *D.P. Co.* The set includes three stoneware heads, two sets of stoneware limbs and a cloth body.

BRITISH DOLLS

With the ban on imports of German toys in the 1914–18 War period, English companies attempted to produce pottery-headed dolls for the home market. The industry was developed in a very short time, and the dolls were crude, of poor quality and generally unattractive. However, since they were produced for such a limited period, they are rare and probably worth collecting. Many British doll companies existed over the period, producing wood, wax, china or pottery and fabric dolls. They are too numerous for all to be mentioned in this book, but some of the most popular are discussed here.

PORCELAIN DOLLS

DIAMOND POTTERY CO. AND DOLL POTTERY CO.

The Diamond Pottery Co. Ltd, Stoke-on-Trent, was affiliated to a hard-paste porcelain company and most of the English china-headed

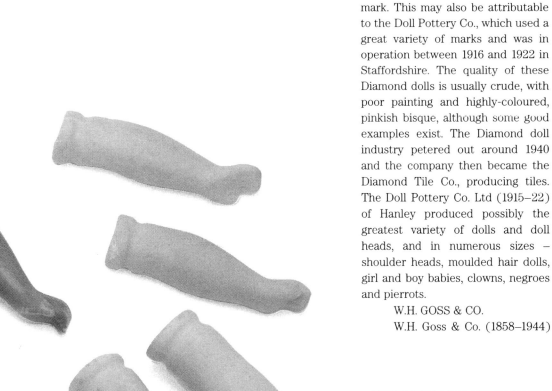

dolls to be found will have the *D.P.C.* mark. This may also be attributable to the Doll Pottery Co., which used a great variety of marks and was in operation between 1916 and 1922 in Staffordshire. The quality of these Diamond dolls is usually crude, with poor painting and highly-coloured, pinkish bisque, although some good examples exist. The Diamond doll industry petered out around 1940 and the company then became the Diamond Tile Co., producing tiles. The Doll Pottery Co. Ltd (1915–22) of Hanley produced possibly the greatest variety of dolls and doll heads, and in numerous sizes – shoulder heads, moulded hair dolls, girl and boy babies, clowns, negroes and pierrots.

W.H. GOSS & CO.

W.H. Goss & Co. (1858–1944) of Stoke-on-Trent, Staffordshire, produced limbs and heads with painted and glass eyes. These dolls are now extremely rare and although they appear somewhat crude and highly-coloured in comparison with the German and French dolls, they do command quite high prices. Goss is normally associated with commemorative china ware, and not dolls.

HANCOCK & SONS

Hancock & Sons (1857–1937) of Cauldon was, by 1917, producing over 70 different types of dolls' heads – open and closed mouth, moulded-haired and so on. As with the other English companies, face painting and detail was crude. There were many other English porcelain companies making dolls at this period, but few of their products are marked or identifiable.

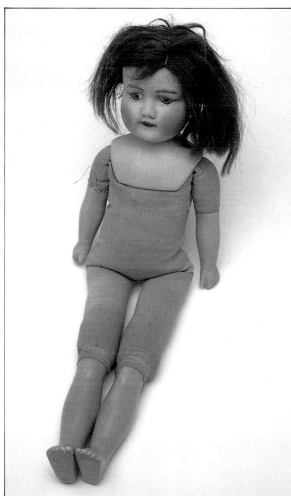

B

This Classic doll was made by Speights Ltd of Dewsbury, which made dolls between 1913 and 1924. The shoulder-head is stoneware, the body is cloth, and the limbs are composition. The mohair wig is of rather poor quality. The back of the shoulder-plate bears the mark *4 Classic England*.

WOODEN DOLLS

These are generally very early, and some fine examples exist, but they are nearly always priced beyond the reach of the novice collector. We have very little historical detail about the manufacture of wooden dolls, but they are likely to have been made by small craftsmen, perhaps furniture makers or turners, who would have had suitable tools for turning the wooden stumps. Few examples date from before the late 17th century. The most famous of all English wooden dolls are Lord and Lady Clapham, a pair documented as owned by a single family – descendants of Samuel Pepys, the diarist, who went to live in Clapham, London, towards the end of his life. The dolls are unique among late 17th-century examples and are in pristine condition. Lord Clapham's hat bears the label *T. Bourdillon Hosier & Hatter to His Majesty, 14 Russel Street, Covent Garden*. They came up for auction in 1974 and, after an export licence was refused to a Swiss collector, they were eventually purchased by the Victoria & Albert Museum, where they may now be seen.

WAX DOLLS

Among the most highly regarded of British dolls are the wax dolls made in the late 19th century, and several of the leading manufacturers worked in London.

CHARLES MARSH

Charles and his brother William made poured wax and wax over papier mâché dolls between 1878 and 1894. The wax the Marsh family used was usually tinted a pretty pink, and the dolls are characterized by a 'dolly' effect, with wide eyes and a straight 'look', although they appear to have been 'little girl' dolls rather than babies. They were strongly constructed. The dolls seem to have had a more clearly defined neck than was usual with other wax dolls, and the head was held in an erect posture. The hair, often mohair, was inserted in tufts with a centre parting. Marsh

paid particular attention to the moulding of the ears, and the hands often have divided fingers. Most Marsh dolls have a stamp, naming Charles Marsh as 'sole manufacturer' and C. Gooch as his distributor. The mark also indicated that Marsh 'cleaned and repaired' dolls.

HERBERT JOHN MEECH

Meech claimed that he was the doll maker to the royal family (probably Edward VII), and he was in business between 1865 and 1891. A maker of medium sized poured wax dolls, Meech also made busts for hairdressers. The wax he used was rather

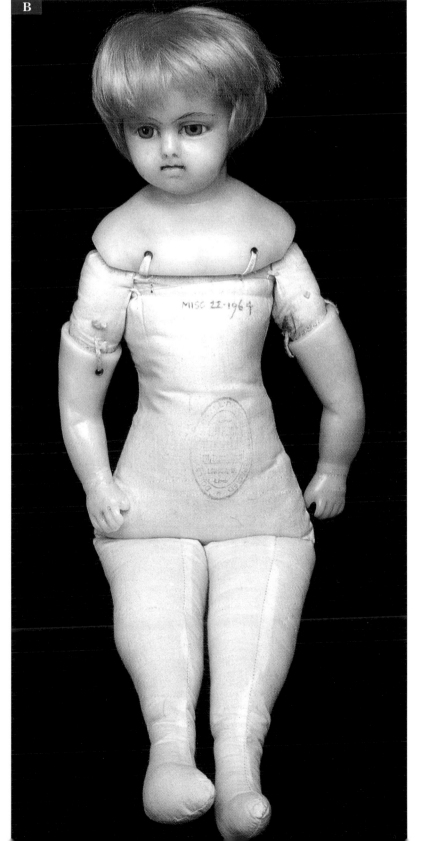

B

pale but of good quality and well modelled. The dolls seem to have some sort of 'family' resemblance: they have rather sulky, but strong, features, fine eyes and modelled lids, inserted eye lashes and thick eyebrows. Human hair was used. The lips are sculpted and tinted. The hands have closed fingers, dimpled knuckles and a marked 'life line' on one palm. The costuming and millinery of the dolls was particularly beautiful. The trademark *H.J. Meech Doll Maker* is found as a rubber stamp on the dolls' torsos.

MONTANARI

The most famous of the London makers was perhaps the Montanari family, which made large poured wax dolls and also exhibition figurines. Early dolls have inserted hair, usually in a slit, although special figures had hair inserted by a needle. Although the actual modelling of the dolls was probably done by Napoleon Montanari, Augusta dressed the dolls in expensive materials, including lace, fringes, seed pearls and ornaments. The dolls had rather heavy features and dark hair, with plump limbs that

had creases at wrist and elbow. The family was active from 1851 until the 1870s, and the dolls were clearly created for the children of wealthy families. Many of the dolls are unmarked, but some of the early dolls have the ink signature *Montanari* on the fabric at the base of the torso. The family is known to have used *Mty*, and the spelling *Montanary* has also been found.

Augusta died in 1864 and her son Richard Napoleon continued with the family business, making baby dolls with a wax or muslin mask framed by a lacy bonnet. It is possible that Richard Napoleon modelled dolls for Mrs Lucy Peck.

LUCY PECK

Mrs Lucy Peck made large, handsome dolls in poured wax. The elegant dolls represented the fashionable female figure and were finely dressed and coiffured. Some dolls have glass eyes with the old-fashioned wire opening apparatus. Mrs Peck claimed that she used the services of a famous wax modeller from the 1851 Great Exhibition: this may have been Richard Montanari or

A

This wax over papier mâché shoulder-plate doll dates from the first half of the 19th century. The body is stuffed with horsehair, and maroon leather arms have four fingers and a thumb. The pigeon-toed feet are stuffed. The mohair ringlets are glued to the head, which exhibits the crazing commonly seen on dolls of this type. The long pantaloons, the cotton dress with a blue silk trim and the lace and silk hat are original.

B

B

A doll by Charles Marsh dating from *c*.1880. The head is poured wax, with inserted mohair, and the glass eyes are blue. The doll, which is dressed as a bride, has a cloth body adapted to have a bust. There are two stamps on the body, one showing the Royal Warrant.

A

C

An unusual black-faced doll by Norah Wellings made of brown velvet with inserted glass eyes. The doll is 35in (89cm) tall and has a black mohair wig stitched to its head. The fingers are individually shaped, apart from the centre ones, which are stitched together. The necklace is of amber beads. Norah Wellings had originally worked as a designer for Chad Valley, and some of her dolls have obvious similarities to those of the Birmingham company. Miss Wellings worked from the Victoria Toy Works in Wellington Shropshire, between 1926 and 1959 with her brother Leonard, producing a range of soft toys and dolls.

a member of the Pierotti family. The range of dolls produced is so wide that it is possible that she employed someone to make the fashion figures while she concentrated on the play dolls. Mrs Peck was active in London between 1891 and 1921, and she sold dolls at her shop, The Doll's Home.

PIEROTTI

The Pierotti family made finely modelled wax dolls' heads from about 1789, and by 1850 the Pierottis were offering composition and papier mâché dolls as well. Pierotti heads were combined with stuffed bodies, also made by members of the family. They made small and large dolls and also produced figurines and life-size models and busts. The colouring was usually realistic, but some later dolls have a characteristic 'shrimp pink' tone. The family may be said to have invented the royal model baby. Their dolls have heads that are often turned slightly to one side and plump necks. Finger and toe nails were engraved, and the legs were moulded and shapely. The mark *Pierotti* was occasionally incised on the back of the neck, but more usually Pierotti dolls bear the stamp of the shops through which they were sold.

MADAME TUSSAUD

The name most people associate with wax figures is that of Madame Marie Tussaud (1760–1850), and many visitors have been to the famous London wax exhibition that bears her name and that she founded. Few of her actual works survive, however, most having been destroyed in a fire in 1925. Madame Tussaud was not so much a doll maker as a figure maker, and although she certainly made dolls, they are hardly ever found. She is best known for her portrait wax dolls, although there is evidence that she made wax babies.

FABRIC DOLLS

There were a great many manufacturers of English fabric dolls and the most significant names were inevitably the most prolific; it is their work that is likely to be found by the modern collector.

Boudoir dolls are not highly sought after commercially, but some very attractive examples can be found in the cheaper range of dolls. As always, condition determines value. Obviously the more elaborate the costume, the more costly the doll may be. Boudoir dolls, as the name suggests, were designed to adorn the boudoir or bedroom. They usually took the form of long-limbed women with fabric- or silk-covered and painted faces, often with hats and decorative costumes made by different designers. Such dolls were made between 1910 and 1938 by firms like Chad Valley and Dean's Rag Book Co.

CHAD VALLEY

Chad Valley Dolls, founded in 1823 and still going strong, was a Birmingham firm specializing in promotional dolls and toys of well-known characters and cartoons, such as Bonzo dog. It also made teddy bears and stuffed animals of high quality, and were toy makers to the royal family. In the 1920s they produced Mable Lucie Atwell dolls and Snow White and the Seven Dwarfs, in all of which the quality of workmanship showed. Sometimes their dolls are confused with Lenci dolls (see page 51), which command a higher price, the Chad Valley dolls still being in the lower end of the price range.

DEAN'S RAG BOOK CO. LTD

Dean & Son Ltd, London, and Dean's Rag Book Co., Ltd, its subsidiary, date back to 1840. This company has a long history of printing and publishing and is well known for its series of books in the shape of a doll. Since 1958 it has acted as sole agent for the Merrythought company and it also produces a series of national costume dolls. Dean's dolls are generally of good quality and detail – price, of course, is governed by condition – but they are in the lower end of the

A

Nora Wellings designed the dark blue velvet HMS Furious sailor for Chad Valley *c.*1935. These sailor dolls were sold as souvenirs on ocean-going liners, especially in the years immediately before World War II, when Chad Valley also made a series of soldier dolls.

A

price range for cloth dolls. They are to be recommended as an area for the new collector to explore. It is as well to remember that it can be worth while to purchase the latest products of companies such as this: today's new dolls are tomorrow's antiques.

Both Chad Valley and Dean's Rag Book Co. frequently used felt in their doll production (as did Lenci). Originally made from beaver or rabbit hair, and latterly from wool waste, felt could be steamed into shape, and it could be brightly coloured. Above all, it was hard wearing. Felt did, of course, suffer from moth damage and many fine examples have been spoilt in this way. A word of caution: if you buy a felt doll, examine it very carefully for infestation and tell-tale holes, as a newly added doll which is infested can spread the problem to other examples in your collection. Moth damage can usually be treated and the doll made safe.

NORAH WELLINGS

Nora Wellings Dolls (1926–59) was established by an ex-Chad Valley designer in Shropshire. She is perhaps best known for the little tourist sailor dolls made to sell on board ship. Apart from her felt dolls, Nora Wellings is perhaps most often associated with velvet dolls of very high quality. These are usually marked and are still relatively inexpensive by doll standards.

B

Pale green velvet was used by Dean's Rag Book Company to make this skater c.1930.

B

mann, Steuber, Gibson and Robinson. American heads were usually of composition, papier mâché or rag.

Jacob Lacmann was based in Philadelphia, where he made dolls' bodies from 1860 until about 1883, using heads by Ludwig Greiner and the Sonneberg company Cuno & Otto Dressel. Bodies have been found bearing the legend *J. Lacmann's Patent March 24th 1874* in an oval.

ERNST REINHARDT

In 1904 Ernst Reinhardt of Sonneberg took out a patent for 'dolls' eyes punched in two steps and connected by a bar' and for 'dolls' eyes with punched semi-spherical covers attached'. Four years later he patented a 'cover for dolls' eyes, the cover [being] painted and [having] artificial eyelashes'. It seems that these innovations were made while Rheinhardt operated a doll assembly factory. In 1909 he emigrated to America, settling at first in Philadelphia where he produced bisque-headed dolls with papier mâché bodies and wooden limbs. In 1917 Reinhardt established the short-lived Bisc [sic] Novelty Manufacturing Company in Ohio, and this was among the first companies to manufacture high quality bisque dolls' heads entirely of US materials. The company's marks acknowledged Reinhardt's contribution: *Reinhardt/ East Liverpool/Ohio* and also *Made in USA/Reinhardt*. Betweem 1918 and 1922, Reinhardt manufactured bisque dolls in several places in New Jersey; during this period dolls were marked *Perth Amboy, Mesa* and, in 1920, *Augusta*.

IZANNAH F. WALKER

Among the early American doll-making names is that of Mrs Izannah F. Walker of Rhode Island whose dolls are, to the inexperienced eye, somewhat like those of Martha Chase. They are made of stiffened stockinet with rather primitively painted features and painted hair, typified by corkscrew curls at the side of the head. Some have painted shoes. There is some evidence to suggest that her first dolls may have been made as early as 1840 although she did not obtain a patent until 1873. These dolls are very rare and command high prices. They are seldom, if ever, found in Europe. Izannah Walker died about 1888.

JOEL ELLIS

Joel Addison Hartley Ellis of Springfield, Vermont (1848–1925), is another of the early American doll makers. The early firm of Ellis, Britton & Eaton was succeeded by the Vermont Novelty Co., makers of unusual all-wooden, articulated dolls known as Joel Ellis dolls. The head and body were turned in one piece and, because the dolls resembled German artist's figures, they were known as mannikins. They had metal hands and feet and came in three different sizes:

AMERICAN DOLLS

In the early days, the United States imported most of its dolls. American dolls are not known to have been produced before the Civil War, but later in the 19th century New York, Philadelphia and New England became the principal doll making areas. Heads were often imported from Europe and added to American-made bodies; in addition, many of the doll makers in America such as Greiner had learned their skills in Europe. The best known makers of bodies were Jacob Lac-

A

12, 15, and 18in (30, 38 and 45cm). The heads were pressure moulded and hand painted and were either blond or brunette. These dolls are extremely rare and highly priced, and they are not generally found in Europe.

A. SCHOENHUT & CO.

A. Schoenhut & Co. of Philadelphia made some of the most noteworthy of American dolls. Albert Schoenhut was born in Germany in 1850 and emigrated to America when he was 17 years old. Within five years – by 1872 – he had founded his own company, which, for the first few decades made musical toys, including the first toy pianos. The company enjoyed a great success with its Humpty Dumpty Circus, which was patented in 1903. This was a group of circus performers, including a lion tamer, ringmaster and lady acrobat; all were identical apart from the clothes and paint. Schoenhut also made both jointed dolls and bent-limb

A

Part of Schoenhut's Humpty Dumpty Circus, the first figures of which were patented in 1903. The Circus initially included the clowns. A ring master, a lion tamer, an acrobat, a lady acrobat and a lady circus rider were added later. The figures had wooden or, later, bisque heads, and they were identically shaped, being differentiated only by the clothes and paintwork. Shoenhut also made Hobo and a Negro Dude (c.1904), a Chinaman acrobat (1906) and, in 1907, the popular Max and Moritz figures. There was also a vast array of animals to add to the Circus.

A

A

This Greiner doll has a papier mâché shoulder-plate. It is 24in (60cm) tall and has a stuffed body, painted, rather sad eyes, moulded and painted black hair, leather arms and stuffed legs. Tucked into her dress was a note reading: 'This doll belonged to Sarah Neemes, born in England June 16, 1828.' The doll was probably made in America, although it is impossible to suggest exactly when, as Greiner was known to have been making dolls from 1840, and Sarah Neemes emigrated to America in 1836.

B

In the early 20th century many US manufacturers used printed rag dolls to advertise their products. This uncut cloth Quaker Crackers doll was manufactured and copyrighted in 1930 by the Quaker Oats Company of Chicago, Illinois.

C

This home-made rag doll, which is 15in (38cm) tall, was produced in Philadelphia c.1810. Its method of construction shows how little such figures have changed through the centuries.

baby dolls, and until 1924 all the company's dolls were made of wood. In 1924 the company introduced cloth-bodied dolls with wooden heads, and after 1928 it also used composition for some of its dolls. Some of the wooden dolls were fully articulated and had carved, wooden heads, some with moulded hair and some with wigs. These dolls were strung with wire and make a characteristic 'twanging' noise when moved. The eyes were either painted or 'sleeping', and some of the faces resemble Kämmer & Reinhardt dolls. They are very appealing, and their durability has ensured that many have survived.

In 1913 Schoenhut introduced a range of dolls called Baby's Head, and a later group, dating from 1915, was called Miss Dolly Schoenhut. The company made a few wooden infant dolls resembling the popular Bye-Lo doll in 1925, but it went into bankruptcy during the Depression.

GREINER

Ludwig Greiner was a German doll maker who emigrated to the USA and opened a factory in Philadelphia. He was issued with the first US patent for a doll's head in the US, patent No 10770, dated 30 March 1858. Sometimes his heads bear a paper label with the patent date on it. However, it is known that Greiner was producing dolls in Philadelphia as early as 1840, and a Greiner doll has been found with a newspaper dated 1845 stuffed inside the head and obviously put there during manufacture.

The Greiner finishing glaze was very durable, and his dolls have come down to us in good condition. Greiner made only heads; the bodies were generally home-made, from crudely stuffed cloth, sometimes with leather arms. Commercially produced bodies could also be purchased, and these were available from Jacob Lacmann, also of Philadelphia, who was in business between 1860 and c.1883. Lacmann's bodies were made of cloth with leather arms and hands. The dolls had red or blue-striped socks and sewn leather boots in red, blue or yellow.

Greiner dolls are seldom, if ever, found outside the USA and clearly were not exported.

A similar type of doll is known as the pre-Greiner. These dolls obviously come into the same category as the Greiner dolls but pre-date the patent. The finish is finer and the glaze thinner, and the dolls have either blown glass or painted eyes. The earliest examples have moulded hair braided on each side at the front and wound under the ears to join a braided coil at the back of the head. These dolls date from 1837–40 and are clearly intended to represent Queen Victoria, who is often shown wearing this hair-style at the period.

It is often speculated that the so-called pre-Greiner dolls with glass eyes were imported heads and were never made by Greiner in the US, but it is also postulated that when Greiner emigrated to the United States, as an experienced doll maker, he would have taken with him quantities of blown glass eyes. When his stock was used up, he would have had difficulty replacing them in Philadelphia and would perhaps have switched, at least temporarily, to painted eyes. He must have found a way to make the glass eyes in the United States and began producing glass-eyed dolls even before he took out his patent.

It seems unlikely that the early, so-called pre-Greiner heads were imported into the United States. This would have added greatly to the cost of the finished product and made it over-priced. More probable is the theory that the so-called 'pre-Greiner' dolls were, in fact, some of Greiner's own early dolls.

Greiner's patent was extended to 1872, as is demonstrated by paper labels found in later heads. Greiner and pre-Greiner are terms that often confuse the novice collector but that can be useful, when clearly defined, in the search for knowledge.

After 1874 the company was known as Greiner Brothers, and in 1890 it was succeeded by Knell Brothers.

LOUIS AMBERG & SON

This company, which had offices in Cincinatti and New York City, was founded in 1878 as a doll importer and jobber. It began to manufacture its own composition dolls after 1903, although it continued to purchase many of its dolls from other American as well as European manufacturers. In the years preceding World War I Amberg produced an enormous range of dolls, and during the war it inaugurated two advertising slogans – 'American Dolls for Americans' and 'The American Standard' – both of which were used while supplies of dolls from Europe were interrupted. Amberg's extensive range included I Walk – I Talk – I Sleep (1903), Sunny Jim (1909), Bobby and Baby Beautiful Dolls (1910), Cry Baby Bunting (1911) and Baby Peggy, the Nation's Darling (1923).

AMERICAN CHARACTER DOLL CO.

The trademark *Petite* was used by the New York City company the American Character Doll Co. on a line of composition babies it produced in the early 1920s. The names given to the dolls included Teenie Weenie and Walkie, Talkie, Sleepie, and other infant and baby dolls, also in composition, continued to be made throughout the decade. The company also made wood-fibre composition dolls, which were called Aceedeedee Dolls.

ROSE O'NEILL

A native of Wilkes-Barre, Pennsylvania, Rose O'Neill first drew her whimsical line illustrations of the fairy-like Kewpies for the *Ladies Home Journal* in 1909. Their instant popularity resulted in what has been described as a 'tidal wave of dolls'. The dolls were designed by Joseph Kallus and began to appear in 1912. (Kallus, a successful designer, founded the Cameo Doll Co. in 1922 to manufacture composition and wooden dolls, including versions of the Kewpie and also Grace Storey Putnam's Baby Bye-Lo.) By the outbreak of World War I some 21 factories in Germany and the USA were manufacturing Kewpies to try to meet the demands of George Borgfeldt & Co., which had exclusive distribution rights after 1916. All-bisque Kewpies were made by Kestner, Gebrüder Voight, Hermann Voight and other porcelain factories. Celluloid versions were made by Karl Standfuss, while cloth Kewpies were made by Steiff. The Cameo Doll Co. among others, made composition Kewpies. Most Kewpies had Rose O'Neill's signature moulded on one foot, and heart-shaped or circular stickers were attached to the chests. Identifying the individual manufacturers is difficult, however, since the Cameo Doll Co. was the only company to use its own mark. Many unauthorized copies were also made.

GRACE STOREY PUTNAM

A similar success story to that of Rose O'Neill concerns Grace Storey Putnam (1922–25), of Oakland, California. In 1922 she designed the Bye-Lo Baby doll for George Borgfeldt & Co. She was, at the time, a teacher in an art college, and the Bye-Lo Baby was meant to represent a real three-day-old baby. It was in fact modelled on a black baby, hence its rather negroid appearance. Bye-Lo Baby dolls are to be found in all-bisque, wax and composition, and with celluloid hands; some have curiously shaped cloth bodies in several sizes designed by Georgene Averill. The heads were made in Germany for George Borgfeldt, to whom Putnam was under contract, by several manufacturers, including Hertel, Schwab & Co., Kestner and Kling. Grace Storey Putnam was under contract to Borgfeldt for 20 years and designed several other dolls, but it was for the Bye-Lo Baby – the 'Million Dollar Baby' – that she is remembered.

MADAME ALEXANDER

Madame Beatrice Alexander's dolls are perhaps the best loved of all American collectors' dolls. They are seldom, if ever, found in Europe and were never imported into England. Early examples fetch high prices. Madame Alexander's heritage was Russian, her father having been a doll maker from Odessa. She was his eldest daughter and she founded her own company in New York in 1923 producing rag-doll characters from Dickens. At first the dolls were made of rag with pressed mask-type faces, and the costumes were always exceptionally well made. Later, Madame Alexander dolls were made of plastics and vinyls, and the company is still creating and producing wonderful dolls.

RUBBER DOLLS

In 1839, Charles Goodyear developed a process for making rubber less brittle, which he patented in 1844, under the name vulcanization. The process involved treating rubber with sulphur, and is best known for its use in making car tyres. Charles' brother, Nelson, obtained a US patent for a rubber doll's head in 1851, which was extended to 1865. The rubber dolls were attached to stuffed cloth bodies, like the papier mâché heads. They had leather crowns for the attachment of wigs. Rubber dolls made by the famous Charles Goodyear company are marked *Goodyear* or *Goodyear's Pat. May 6, 1851. Ext. 1865.*

The New York Rubber Co. and Benjamin F. Lee were just two companies that made rubber dolls under licence from Goodyear. Dolls were sold through major department stores, such as Montgomery Ward and F.A.O. Schwarz.

Time has not been kind to the early rubber dolls; the paint chipped and the rubber perished. Later, the process was refined and rubber-and-composition dolls became popular. Later, only doll bodies were made from rubber.

A

Λ

Two vinyl dolls made by Madame Alexander. The dolls of Beatrice Alexander Behrman and the Alexander Doll Company are among the most popular of all dolls among US collectors. The blond doll's head is incised *3 Alexander 1979*, and it is known as Little Brother. These dolls come in pairs, and there is, naturally, also a Little Sister. The clothes are original to the doll. On the right is a 1974 model known as Baby Precious. She has vinyl limbs with well-defined moulding, a stuffed body, well-rooted hair and sleeping eyes. The clothes are original. One problem with identifying Madame Alexander dolls is that many of them do not bear any permanent marking, but were issued with only wrist tabs or cloth labels attached to their clothes.

CELLULOID DOLLS

Celluloid dolls were also produced in the USA. In New York John Wesley and Isiah Hyatt started manufacturing celluloid products in 1869, including some dolls. They developed the Embossing Company of New York in 1870 where they produced celluloid dolls' heads. In 1866 Franklin Darrow made raw-hide doll's heads which closely resembled papier mâché.

FABRIC DOLLS

Although Madame Alexander and Izannah F. Walker are possibly the best known of the US doll makers to use fabric, many other interesting and collectable fabric dolls have been made in America.

ARNOLD PRINT WORKS

This dress goods manufacturer was founded in North Adams, Massachusetts, in 1876. It was one of America's largest manufacturers of prints and dress fabrics and was quick to see the potential of printing figures on cotton and selling them by the yard to be cut out, seen and stuffed at home to create a range of cuddly, rather whimsical dolls and animals. Patents for printed cloth dolls and animals had been granted to Celia M. Smith and her sister-in-law, Charity Smith, of Ithaca, New York, in July and October 1892, and these were bought up by the Arnold Print Works. The patterns were printed in 'natural colours' on white cotton, and the company's mark, *Arnold Print Works. North Adams. Mass. Incorporated 1876*, was included on the cloth although not within the pattern itself. It was suggested that cardboard be put in the bottom of the figures when they were made so that they would stand securely. Celia Smith's creations, which were first produced in 1892–3, included Little Tabbies and Tabby Cat, Tatters and Little Tatters, Little Red Riding Hood, Topsy, Little Jocko, Little Bow-Wow, Our Soldier Boys, Bunny, Jocko, Floss (a sleeping dog), Hen and Chicks, Rooster and Owl, Columbia Sailor Boy, Pitti-Sing and Pickaninny. Most of these were printed on a complete yard of cloth, but some of the smaller figures were printed four to a half yard. Arnold Print Works also produced Palmer Cox's Brownies on cloth, and these became so popular that it is thought that Kodak's Brownie Camera was named after them. The Brownies, 12 small figures, appeared in 1892. They were printed on a yard of cloth and were meant to

A

A

A character doll representing an old woman by Bernard Ravca. The face contours are created by hand stitching and then hand painting. Originally Ravca's dolls wore paper tags, but these are easily lost, and the artist had many imitators, so collectors should always seek advice before purchasing a doll purporting to be by Ravca.

B

Grace Storey Putnam's By-Lo Baby was called the 'Million Dollar Baby' because of its enormous sales. Mrs Putnam created the doll in the early 1920s to resemble a three-day-old baby, and the result was an outstanding commercial success. Bisque heads were made by a number of German companies, including Alt, Beck & Gottschalck, Hertel, Schwab & Co., Kestner and Kling. The doll illustrated here bears on its head the incised mark *Grace S. Putnam Made in Germany 1360/30*. It is 13in (32cm) tall.

A

and stiffened, mask-face doll, and the facial features were printed on the fabric before it was pressed into shape. The heads were modelled nearly to shoulder level and were marked *Pat'd July 9th 1901* along the lower edge. A topsy-turvy doll in black and white, with a skirt covering the unwanted head, was made with the patented heads. By 1925 Bruckner's sons had taken over the business and registered a new line of rag dolls, which they called Dollypop Dolls.

A

Arnold Print Works of Adams, Massachusetts, produced sets of Palmer Cox's Brownies. Two sheets were printed, each containing the front and back of six characters.

be stuffed with bran or sawdust. They were about 7in (18cm) tall, and Cox's copyright was printed on the sole of the right foot. The set included John Bull, Canadian, Chinaman, Dude, German, Highlander, Indian, Irishman, Policeman, Sailor, Soldier and, of course, Uncle Sam. A large number of these were produced and, with patience, it is possible to assemble a complete set. The dolls were distributed by Selchow & Righter. Arnold Print Works continued to produce printed dolls until 1919.

ART FABRIC MILLS

Founded in 1899, rather later than Arnold Print Works, its major competitor, Art Fabric Mills was also a fabric manufacturer that turned to the production of colourful printed patterns for rag dolls. In 1900 Edgar G. Newell, the company's president, patented a Life Size Doll, which could be dressed in the cast-off clothes of real children. The trademark *Life Size* was patented on 13 February 1900, and the legend *Pat. Feb 13th 1900* appears on the sole of one foot and *Art Fabric Mills New York* on the other. The company also sold, through its main distributor Selchow & Righter, a Cry Baby pin-cushion and smaller figures known as Topsy

Dolls, which were sold in black and white versions. In 1905 Foxy Grandpa and Buster Brown were produced, and Baby, Diana, Bridget, Uncle, Billy and Newly Wed Kid were all in production by 1907. Dolly Dimple and Tiny Tim appeared in 1909. A number of the dolls were also sold in Europe, and in 1908 the company's UK branch, in Victoria Street, London, was offering life-size dogs, cats, kittens and puppies, Punch and Judy and 'noiseless' skittles, in addition to the dolls available in the US. The company continued in production until 1910.

MRS T.K. BEECHER

Mrs Beecher of New York produced her Missionary Rag Babies between 1893 and 1910. The features were stitch-moulded and hand painted, and the dolls were given woollen hair. Both black and white baby dolls were made from old silk jersey underwear, and this gave the figures a much softer, cuddlier feel than the printed, cut-out figures offered by such companies as Arnold Print Works and Art Fabric Mills.

ALBERT BRUCKNER

The company was founded in Jersey City, New Jersey, in 1901 by Albert Bruckner, who patented a rag doll in that year. This was a pressed

B

C

B

Mrs Martha Jenks Chase was inspired by a doll by Izannah Walker that she had owned as child to make a soft, unbreakable and washable toy for her own children in the closing years of the 19th century. The Chase Stockinet Doll enjoyed unexpected success, and Mrs Chase went on to make a wide range of dolls. The Martha Chase doll illustrated here is 20in (50cm) tall and has painted cloth, rigid arms and cloth legs, which are hinged at the knee. She is unmarked, and the painted hair has been rather crudely overpainted at some stage.

C

Six of Palmer Cox's Brownies made up from sheets printed by Arnold Print Works. The figures were designed to be stuffed with bran or sawdust, and Cox's copyright, dated 1892, appeared on the sole of one foot.

CERESOTA FLOUR

The North Western Consolidated Milling Company produced a figure of a farmer's boy to advertise its flour from c.1895 until 1900. The words *Ceresota Flour* appear on the front of the printed shirt. The company registered the trademark *Farmer's Boy* in 1895.

MARTHA JENKS CHASE

Inspired by a rag doll by Izannah Walker, which she had owned as a child, Mrs Chase of Pawtucket, Rhode Island, made a soft, unbreakable, washable doll for her own children in the closing years of the 19th century. The result, the Chase Stockinet Doll, was an unexpected commercial success, and Mrs Chase, the wife of a physician, went on to make a wide variety of cloth dolls. The dolls' heads were formed by stretching stockinet over a mask and finished with pasted and painted in oils. Ears and thumbs were applied separately, and the eyes and hair (which was usually blond) were painted. Early dolls had sateen bodies, but white cotton was used later. Although these dolls tend to look rather crude, they do have a certain realistic charm, and they are keenly collected in the US, although they have few enthu-

siasts in Europe.

Before 1920 the dolls' bodies were jointed at the shoulder, hips, elbows and knees, and they were marked *M.J.C. Stockinet Doll Patent Applied For*, although in many cases the marks have worn off. Some dolls were not marked at all, and sometimes the dolls' names were stitched on their collars. Among the most famous dolls created by Mrs Chase was a series of 'Alice in Wonderland' characters, which were inspired by Tenniel's illustrations. Alice appeared in 1905, and the Duchess, the Frog Footman and Tweedledum and Tweedledee in 1921. Other dolls included Mammy Nurse and George Washington in 1905, and Bessy Brooks, Pickaninnies, Silly Sally and Tommy Snooks in 1921. She also made both adult and child-size 'hospital dolls', which were used for training nurses, and a caricature of a nurse, with *Chase Hospital Doll* across its head-dress, became her trademark.

COLUMBIAN DOLLS

Established in Oswego, New York, in 1891, this company produced hand-painted rag dolls, which were stuffed with cotton wool over a sawdust core. The dolls that were made before 1900 were stamped in ink on the torso *Columbian Doll, Emma E. Adams, Oswego, N.Y.* The costumes were particularly well made.

E.I. HORSMAN & CO.

During the 1870s Edward I. Horsman, a toy distributor based in New York City, began to import dolls from Europe. By 1900 the company was also manufacturing dolls, and from its earliest days it showed a talent for exploiting the latest trends and fads. When fabric dolls became popular, Horsman developed its range of Babyland rag dolls with painted faces, which were made from 1904, until 1907, when Horsman gave them 'life-like faces printed in colour'. International events such as Cook's and Peary's expedition to the North Pole in 1907 were recognized, as was the outbreak of World War I – Uncle Sam's Kids and British Tommy were registered in 1917.

The company employed notable artists to design its dolls, including Charles Twelvetrees, Grace Drayton, Helen Trowbridge and Laura Gardin. In 1909 Horsman obtained exclusive rights to the production of the Aetna Company's Can't Break 'Em dolls' heads, and in 1918 the two companies merged, leading to the development of a new composition material that was called Adtocolite. Horsman also worked with Fulper Pottery of Flemington, New Jersey, to produce bisque heads. After 1925 the rights to Horsman's name were acquired by Regal Doll Manufacturing Co. of New York City, which still uses the name.

RAVCA

Bernard Ravca was born in Paris in 1904 and emigrated to the USA in 1939; he has worked there with his wife ever since. Ravca's cloth art dolls first became famous in the 1920s and 1930s, when he made figures representing entertainers such as Maurice Chevalier and Mistinguette. He and his wife have produced window dolls, portraits of celebrities, royalty, sports figures and others, but they are perhaps most affectionately known for their character dolls representing old people. Ravca's dolls originally wore circular paper tags, but these were easily lost, and many dolls are now unmarked. The dolls were also widely imitated, and expert guidance should be sought if you are offered a doll purporting to be by Ravca.

SAALFIELD PUBLISHING CO.

In 1907 Saalfield, of Akron, Ohio, introduced its first set of cutout muslin doll patterns with characters inspired by the illustrations of the popular artist Kate Greenaway. In 1908 it produced Aunt Dinah, Delft Girl, Little Red Riding Hood, Papoose and Santa Claus, and in 1909 Baby Blue Eyes, Dottie Dimple and Goldenlock appeared, to be followed in 1918 by Dolly Dear. The company's greatest success, however, was in obtaining the exclusive rights to produce Shirley Temple paper dolls in the 1930s.

MODERN DOLLS

It is difficult to define the modern period for doll manufacture. Madame Alexander, Lenci and Steiff are still in production and their modern creations are much collected, particularly by the young. Such firms as Arranbee were in operation in the USA from 1922 until the 1960s. Mattel Inc.'s Barbie and Ken are a source of renewed interest for the modern doll and bring us into the age of hard plastics and vinyl. Dewees Cochran of California is a modern manufacturer of latex dolls, signed under the arm or behind the ear. The Ideal Novelty & Toy Co. of Brooklyn (1907) is another well-known American name. Under the guidance of Benjamin Michtom, whose father, Morris, popularized

A

The Ideal Novelty & Toy Co. was founded by Morris Mitchom c.1909. This composition doll was made in 1934–9 and is marked *13 Shirley Temple*, which was one of Ideal's most successful dolls of the 1930s. The doll is 13in (32cm) high and has straight limbs. The dress and wig are original.

the teddy bear, Ideal has had much success. Michtom specialized in 'purpose' dolls and linked them with advertisements for certain products. As well as product dolls, Ideal has made well-known characters such as Judy Garland, Snow White, Deanna Durbin and Pinocchio.

EFFanBEE is the trademark of another well-known American doll manufacturer, Fleischaker & Baum. The company was founded in 1910 by Bernard E. Fleischaker and Hugo Baum, and the trademark was registered in 1913; the company is more commonly known as Effanbee. During the first few years, Effanbee produced 'Unbreakable' composition dolls and by 1918 it had added stuffed-body dolls to its range. In 1922 the They

A

These four English dolls have been made since World War II. On right, with blond mohair plaits, is a cloth doll. In the centre at the back is a doll by Pedigree Soft Toys Ltd, a company whose name was first registered in 1942. It is a composition, bent-limb baby doll with sleeping eyes; the face is badly crazed. The other two dolls are 'pot head' dolls with bent limb bodies.

Walk and They Talk line was introduced, and a year later the They Walk, They Talk, They Sleep dolls appeared – although many of the dolls so marked did none of these things. Baby Grumpy was introduced in 1914, and other favourites included Lovums (1918), Skippy (c.1930), New Born Baby (1925) and the American Children series (1939). The company also made historical dolls, portrait dolls (in the 1940s) and Effanbee Limited Edition Dolls (1975). It continues to make a wide range of dolls, although the most keenly collected are those produced before World War II.

Peggy Nisbet of Somerset, England, has become a specialist innovator in the art of the costume doll with such characters as Henry VIII and his wives, Mary Poppins, Christopher Robin and Pooh Bear. More recently, she produced a limited edition of 1,000 Prince Charles and Princess Diana wedding dolls, a limited edition set of Royal Children (Princess Diana with Prince William and Prince Harry) and a royal wedding collectors' limited edition set in hard styrene of Prince Andrew and Sarah Ferguson (The Duke and Duchess of York).

Dolls

Pedigree Dolls and Toys Ltd (1938) of Canterbury, England, is another well-known English modern doll manufacturer. This was the first firm in England to make high quality composition dolls. Among its products were period miniatures (1959) and story book dolls. Perhaps it is best known today for the Sindy doll, first produced in 1962, a teenage doll, 11½in (29cm) high, with a wonderful array of accessories. Barbie and Sindy were launched at the same time, because they were the first modern fashion dolls. Sindy was the first doll to be promoted in television advertisements. The doll became fully posable. Sindy had a monopoly of the British market until 1980.

Palitoy, another big English manufacturer, brought out the popular Tiny Tears crying and wetting doll in the 1950s.

Dolls are not only playthings for the comfort, warmth and entertainment of children; they are also on-going records of our traditions and way of life.

However, the doll success story of the century is the Cabbage Patch doll, which has had record-breaking sales. The earliest examples are now collectors' items.

A new generation of doll artists is at work producing its own interpretations of our world. The American

A

First launched in 1984, the cloth Cabbage Patch Dolls became one of the best-selling products in the history of toy making. The early dolls, which had their own 'adoption' papers, are now collectors' items.

A

Doll Artists Association has high standards and guidelines in this respect, as does the British Doll Artists Association. Other creative people are making their own reproductions of old dolls from kits and moulds and this has become a fast-growing hobby, combining history, craftsmanship and a love of dolls to provide highly satisfying personal creations.

Modern dolls have been included not so much in conclusion of the doll story, but to point to a new beginning, for they are tomorrow's collectables, if not already today's. The mechanical gimmicks of the future will be light years away from those wonderful innovations loved by yesterday's children: the age of the microchip and the computer may revolutionize future doll collecting, but what materials will be used is hard to imagine. We have already trodden a long road to Palitoy's Tiny Tears or Mattel's Cheerful Tearful with its changing expressions. Many of today's children find it hard to relate to yesterday's playthings just as the children of tomorrow are unlikely to relate to the toys of today. It is left to the collector to bridge the generations so that tomorrow's children may at least have an awareness and understanding of their past through the things that earlier generations loved.

Doll-related terms

The following words and expressions are often used by doll collectors, auction houses and dealers to describe different types of doll or doll attributes or marks.

Applied ears: the expression used to describe ears that have been applied to the head after it has been moulded rather than ears that are an integral part of the head.

Bébé: the word used to describe a doll that has the proportions of a young child and a shorter, fatter body than a lady doll.

Bisque or biscuit: a ceramic material that can be poured into a mould or pressed into shape before being fired at high temperature. Bisque dolls' heads were often painted before being fired for a second time at a lower temperature. Bisque has a matt, unglazed surface.

Bonnet-head: the term used to describe a doll with a hat or bonnet moulded as an integral part of its head.

Breveté or Bt^e (French): patented.

Carton: cardboard.

China-head: the term used to describe a head of glazed porcelain, a ceramic material that was used for dolls' heads before being superseded by bisque (q.v.) in the second half of the 19th century.

A

This bisque-head, closed-mouth doll with 'googly' eyes is 7in (18cm) tall. The head is marked *A 253 M Nobbi Kid Reg US Pat Germany 11/0*. The doll was made *c.*1914 and has a composition, toddler-style body. She is wearing her original dress but a later, real hair wig.

This early Schmitt doll is 17in (43cm) high. The head is marked with the crossed keys in a shield that was the trademark of Schmitt & Fils, which produced dolls' heads and bodies between 1879 and 1890.

C

A beautiful bisque-head doll marked *K * R Simon & Halbig 80*. She has a real hair wig, moulded eyebrows and a fully articulated body. She is 31in (79cm) tall.

Composition: the name given to a number of substances (including papier mâché, q.v.) used to make dolls' bodies and heads. It was usually made of a wood pulp and an adhesive mixed with colouring agents.

Déposé (French) or **Deponiert** (German): an application for a patent has been registered; often abbreviated to Dep, and these letters are sometimes found incised in a doll's bisque shoulder-plate or head.

D.R.G.M. (**Deutsches Reichs-gebrauchsmuster**) (German): design or patent registered; these initials were used after 1909.

D.R.M.R. (**Deutsches Reichs-Muster-Rolle**) (German): German government roll of design patents.

D.R.P. (**Deutsches Reichs-Patent**) (German): German government patent.

Fixed neck: the term used to describe the head mounting when there is no joint between the head and shoulder-plate, which are made in one piece.

Ges. Gesch. (**Gesetzlich Geschutzt**) (German): registered or patented.

Papier mâché: a paper pulp, combined with a whitening agent and a suitable glue, that was used for the manufacture of dolls' heads and bodies in the early 19th century. Towards the end of the 19th century a type of papier mâché was developed that could be poured into a mould rather than having to be pressure moulded; it was both stronger and more durable than the earlier mixture.

Parian: true Parian (i.e., marble from Paros) was never used for dolls, but imitation Parian, a pure white, fine porcelain, was sometimes used for dolls' heads; the features were generally painted, although glass eyes were used.

Pat or Pat[d]: patented in US or UK.

S.F.B.J. (**Société Française de Fabrication des Bébés et Jouets**): a syndicate of French manufacturers, founded in 1899 by, among others, Bru, Fleischmann & Bloedel, Jumeau and Rabery & Delphieu, to counter the threat posed by German manufacturers. Later, companies such as Pintel & Godchaux, Genty, Girard, Remignard, Gobert and Gaultier also joined.

S.G.D.G. (**Sans Garantie du Gouvernement**) (French): without government guarantee.

Shoulder-head: the term used to describe the head mounting of a doll in which the head and shoulders are moulded as one piece.

Wax over: the term used to describe dolls that have a core of a material like papier mâché or composition (qq.v.) that is dipped into, or painted with, molten wax.

A

A musical automaton by the French manufacturer Leopold Lambert. Made *c*.1880, the figure is all original. It has a closed-mouth bisque head, which is stamped, in red, *Déposé tête Jumeau Bte, S.G.D.G. 1*. The eyes are fixed and the ears are pierced. The fore-arms are bisque. Both head and arms move to the musical movement, which is activated by a stop/start mechanism in the base. The doll is 16½in (42cm) tall.

A

Automata & Mechanical Dolls

Many toy enthusiasts like to describe the items they collect

as works of art, but it is in the area of automata that the

term is most justified. The

finest of these creations, ones

that imitated the movements

of people and animals, were individually made to the

highest standard as exhibition pieces, and they are such

rare objects that they are almost impossible to value. In the field of top-quality automata mass-production techniques had no place; each figure was meticulously decorated and costumed for a most discerning market – that of the adult rather than the child.

Representations of objects that appear to live and move have appealed to people through the centuries. The Greeks used articulated statues to answer questions and perform in miraculous ways, usually with the assistance of a small man or boy concealed in the base. The greatest advances were made by Hero of Alexandria (285–222 BC). His writings and diagrams reveal complex machines that made figures turn and move by means of hydraulic and pneumatic power. Among his automata were a figure of Hercules, which shot an arrow at a hissing dragon lying under a tree, and another of a group of singing birds that were operated by water pressure.

In medieval Europe Bernadino Baldi also created automata that worked by a hydraulic system, and there are references to mechanical animals and figures that were seen at various courts. The development of the commercial automaton began with the 16th-century clockmakers, who included central figures such as Death striking the hours or the Adoration of the Magi. Augsburg and Nuremberg were the first important centres of this mechanical art, examples of which have survived in some churches and public buildings. Small table clocks with articulated scenes from Italian comedy or classical mythology were also made in Germany. The skill of the Nuremberg craftsmen in creating flying and moving creatures was revered, and their workshops were the source of many princely gifts.

The golden age of automata was the late 19th century, when French, German and Swiss makers exported a galaxy of colourful figures and tableaux all over the world. In the early Renaissance German clockmakers created the first commercial mechanical children's toys combining music and some form of movement. As Germany developed as the toy-making centre of the world, movement was given to doll and animal figures produced cheaply for the infant market. Some of the bisque-head figures mounted on paper-covered musical boxes, very similar to those made in the 18th century, were still sold in the 1920s, as the manufacturers preferred well-tried, economical designs.

French makers concentrated on the luxury trade and delighted in complicated mechanisms and extravagant clothes and accessories. Sometimes the small fan that a fashionable lady is holding is so exquisitely painted that it could find a place in a collection of miniatures, while even the shoe-buckles and gloves are exact copies, finished with an attention to detail that is not found on clothes made for automata in any other country.

The finest automata were made in and around Paris, mainly during the latter half of the 19th century, where manufacturers such as Théroude, Decamps, Lambert and Vichy relied on the creative skills of hundreds of outworkers, who produced the costumes and accessories. Swiss musical movements were often used by the French makers, as their quality was exceptionally high, and German dolls' heads were also utilized, so that a single automaton frequently incorporates parts from all three countries.

A

EVALUATING AUTOMATA

Top quality automata have to be purchased with extreme caution or expert advice. They are a minefield for the novice. Among the many problems are replacement heads, simplified or changed mechanisms and marriages of sections from other structures. The musical movement, which can be concealed in a 'landscape' base or fitted into the body of the automaton, is sometimes found to be a modern replacement. Experienced collectors prefer to buy

B

examples in completely original condition, even if the piece is not in full
working order. They are especially
wary of pieces that have been thoroughly cleaned and re-costumed;
enthusiastic restoration can cause
irrevocable damage.

Valuing automata can be difficult. Some models that look very
impressive are in fact fairly common,
while others with less immediate
appeal have rarity value. Any old
automaton in original condition, even
if it is one of the more common types,
is well worth buying, since relatively
few models come up for sale internationally each year. Some guidance
as to current market values is provided in the estimates that are published in auction room catalogues,

although the buyer should remember that the cataloguer might not be an expert in this field and is unlikely to have risked damage to the costume by opening the figure to examine the mechanism. In general, new collectors are advised to buy from an automata specialist, who will provide a written guarantee with the piece and will be willing to supervise any restoration that might be needed in the future. Unfortunately doll dealers also sell automata, which they value more on the quality and make of the head and costume than the mechanism, in which they are often uninterested. Occasionally the figure is worth more as a doll than as an automaton – which poses yet another problem for the new collector.

Simpler clockwork toys are not a problem as anyone with a basic knowledge of them can satisfy themselves that the piece has not been tampered with. The degree of restoration and re-costuming that is acceptable to collectors varies from country to country and even from locality to locality. In France, complete originality of costume is most important, whereas in the United States a completely re-dressed item will sell well. Attitudes in Great Britain and Germany vary, and there are collectors in both countries who re-costume any figures that are not in pristine condition. However, as interest in conservation increases, fewer automata will be unnecessarily restored, but this will also demand a higher degree of expertise on the part of the owner.

Although damage puts off the leading dealers in automata, very distressed items often fetch high prices when they are purchased speculatively by non-specialists, many of whom are unaware of the very high cost of good restoration. There are specialist restorers of automata in all countries, but it is advisable to use someone who has been recommended by a satisfied client. Anyone can set up as a restorer, and some disastrous work is sometimes carried out on valuable pieces. Some restorers, more interested in the mechanical side of the figure than the costume, repair

A

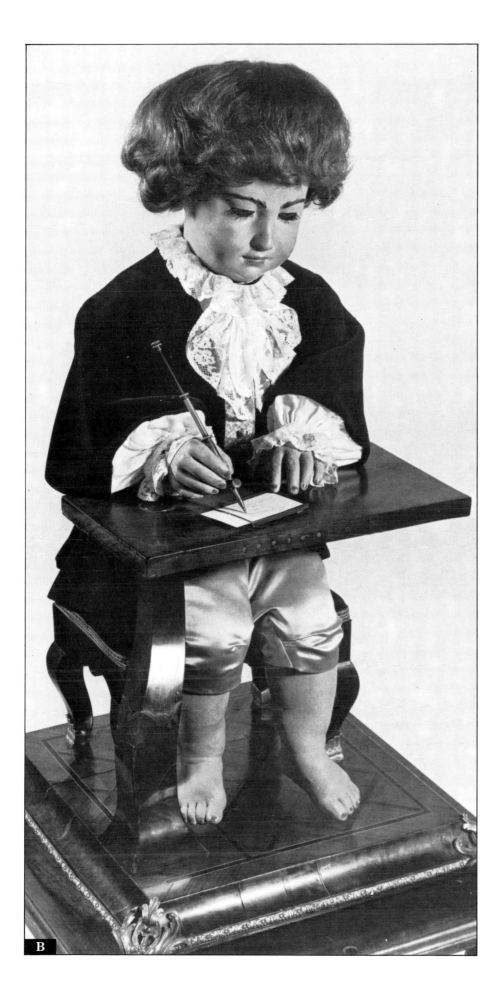

the movements at the expense of the textiles; others pretty up the clothes to such an extent that the figure looks modern. In general, it is best to ask for advice from a collectors' club, a museum or a reputable dealer. Before leaving the piece with a restorer, insist that the costume remain intact and that any replacement, as opposed to mending, of parts be undertaken only after consultation. The best restorers list the work they have undertaken on their bill, which should be retained with the figure to assist when future work has to be done.

The automata market remains very stable. Once hooked, enthusiasts rarely abandon the speciality. They also keep pieces for a long time, so few come on the market. Each year, the number of good automata sold internationally declines, forcing up prices and making these aristocrats of the toy world very attractive as long-term investments.

THE 18TH-CENTURY MASTERS

Automata manufacture had become a specialized art form by the 18th century and was already divided into two sections, one for children, the other for wealthy adults, who appreciated the complexity of the latest novelty. Tableaux such as game hunts, a blacksmith's shop or a coach and horses that moved around a cabinet give some indication of the luxury piece that could be purchased in exclusive shops. The curiosity of the

A

general public was satisfied by exhibitions, where specially constructed display pieces, such as a 6-foot (2m) figure that played the flute when air was forced through his mouth, could be viewed.

Jacques de Vaucanson (1709–82) of Grenoble was the most famous early 18th-century maker. His automata included a gilded copper duck that drank, ate, splashed about in water and then digested its food, presumably with the aid of chemicals. Other figures made by him for public display were worked by weights, cams and levers; these included a figure that could play 11 melodies on a flute. Such figures exploited some of the most advanced mechanical skills of the period and it is not surprising that Vaucanson, bored with creating novelties, should, in 1743, have sold his automata to a travelling showman and turned his attention to more serious scientific work, later becoming inspector of mechanical inventions at the Académie Royale des Sciences.

Sadly, Vaucanson's creations are all lost, but his work was carried on by a Swiss clockmaker, Pierre Jaquet-Droz (1721–90). The most famous figures that he made can still be seen performing at the waterside museum in Neuchâtel, Switzerland. Pierre, his son, Henri Louis (1752–91), and his adopted son, Jean Frédéric Leschot (1746–1827), made figures that were more realistic than anything previously attempted, and it is little wonder that they were exhibited all over Europe, together with a charming country scene that contained a number of animated characters.

Pierre Jaquet-Droz had run a very successful clockmaking business before he decided, after a nervous breakdown, to create automata. They were more lifelike than anything previously attempted. He finished a boy draughtsman and, in 1773, in collaboration with Leschot, a writer – figures that were to make his firm famous throughout Europe. The Writer, representing a boy about three years old seated at a table, is believed to have been constructed

B

One of the most famous automata of all, the Writer, made by Pierre Jaquet Droz, was first exhibited in 1774. It can inscribe any phrase of under 40 letters by means of a pre-set mechanism. The figure's eyes follow the pen as it writes.

B

The Lady Musician is one of the highly sophisticated automata made by Pierre Jaquet Droz. It was first shown to the public in 1774. Not only do the figure's fingers move as she 'plays', but her head and eyes move, and she bows slightly over the instrument, her breast rising and falling in imitation of breathing. The figure illustrated here has been given a new wig and has been re-dressed. The mechanism can be seen left.

by Pierre. The mechanism is extremely intricate because so many moving parts had to be fitted inside a child-size body. As the boy writes, with a goose-quill pen, his eyes turn to follow the words in a realistic manner. The complex mechanism allows the boy to write sentences that contain a maximum of 40 letters. The problems that collectors face in caring for the mechanisms of fine automata is highlighted by the Writer. If the temperature drops too suddenly, he is liable to make spelling mistakes and space his words unevenly.

The Little Draughtsman and the Writer were put on display at all the European courts and centres of fashion. In order to flatter Louis XV of France the Little Draughtsman drew a delicate portrait of him, copies of which can still be purchased at Neuchâtel. The Draughtsman is completely different in construction to the Writer. The paper on which he draws remains stationary. Three interchangeable sets of cams, each having 12 cams, enable the boy to make four drawings, and a system of bellows enables him to blow the dust

B

off his paper with great realism. This automaton was made over a two-year period and is now visited by every automata enthusiast, who can study the detail of the mechanism in films and diagrams.

A third figure, the Lady Musician, is so complex and functional that her mechanism is often studied by makers of robots. She is much larger than the boys and her fingers move individually so that she actually plays the instrument by means of a complicated system of rods and levers. Such complexity of movement was rarely attempted, as the cost was prohibitive, but it was the ideal that all later craftsmen attempted to imitate more economically. As the Lady Musician plays, her breast rises and falls, a relatively uncomplicated movement that is seen in a number of later, more doll-like figures. When the lady pauses in her play, she turns her head, moves her eyes, glances down modestly and then up again, bends forward and straightens up. On the completion of each melody she brings a fourth mechanism into action, which enables her to bow graciously as if acknowledging the audience's approval.

These three Neuchâtel figures represent the peak of automata manufacture and mark the beginning of the modern development of the art; other figures are always judged against them. The problems that this trio have posed to the restorers are the same as those faced by collectors, who have to make decisions about re-costuming, re-painting and replacing damaged parts. Like many lesser automata, they suffered badly in the hands of several owners, who considered them purely as amusing spectacles. Not until the early 20th century was the importance of their mechanisms fully appreciated and a painstaking programme of restoration and conservation begun.

19TH-CENTURY FRENCH MASTERS

Although collectors like to own a few examples of early automata, the majority are mainly interested in pieces made after 1860, when commercial production began in earnest. The rich European merchant classes, eager to find new and eye-catching gifts, offered the makers a ready and ever-expanding market. As Paris was the centre of international fashion, with a whole variety of beautiful luxury items produced by small, exclusive manufacturers, it was inevitable that the most

beautiful and highly refined automata should be made there.

Automata that represented beautiful children and women were difficult to produce if the heads had to be made of papier mâché or painted wood, but from 1855 French and German porcelain factories began to manufacture dolls' heads of great delicacy and elegance. The availabilty of these attractive bisque heads seems to have inspired the makers to create a procession of finely costumed ladies and beautiful, large-eyed children, and they continue to delight their owners. Court ladies fan themselves or powder their noses; children play the piano or chase a butterfly, a nurse pushes a pretty baby in a perambulator; or circus and stage char-

acters perform their antics to a musical accompaniment.

Many of the French automata contain Swiss musical movements, which were mass-produced from the 1870s. The first means of reproducing music mechanically had been the barrel organ, but the musical box was much more adaptable and was invented in 1796 as a novelty for snuff-boxes. In the early 19th century, Geneva was the international centre of the trade, although the larger sizes were usually made at Ste Croix. With dolls' heads and musical movements available, together with an army of skilled outworkers who could create ravishing costumes from scraps of tinsel, silk and lace, a galaxy of automata was ready to move on stage. As the heads have remained in pristine condition, these figures are still as lovely today as when they were first created.

In contrast to the sophistication of the faces, the bodies of automata are surprisingly crude; parts that were to be concealed by the costume were neither decorated nor well finished. As most of the figures were made to order in very limited numbers, there was no reason to use mass-production methods, such as those used for making the bodies of play dolls. Instead, the makers worked more in the manner of artists, and created simple moulds into which sheets of carton spread with glue

could be pressed. On some bodies the individual layers of carton are obvious; in others, especially those intended as children's toys, a composition substance which gave a smoother effect was used. If the legs and arms were to be revealed, a more refined composition was necessary and any joins were well sanded before flesh-coloured paint was applied. Sometimes, especially on figures of ladies, porcelain or bisque lower arms or hands gave a more delicate effect. In many instances, bisque heads were used in combination with composition hands, a mixture of materials which sometimes makes new collectors suspicious.

To sophisticated automata enthusiasts, the interest of the figure depends more on the complexity of the movement than on the beauty of the head. When the automaton is small, but contains a large number of cams and levers for several movements, the great skill of the manufacturer is especially apparent. Sometimes the musical movement is contained in the figure or hidden beneath a chair or a table, again evidence of the skill of the designer. In cheaper, more commercial, examples, the musical box is fitted in the base, which can be covered with velvet or imaginatively disguised as a rock, a tower or a moss-covered bank.

As most automata play only one or two airs, those with a larger number are especially valuable, especially if the musical box itself is of high quality. As the figures and pieces of scenery were mounted in different ways, the same doll might appear in combination with musical boxes of varying quality, so that it is necessary to become very familiar with a piece before any valuation is attempted.

The French makers of automata worked to the demands of their customers and, as their products were always expensive, they often made only 10 or 20 examples of a particular model. Little wonder, then, that some figures are extremely rare and command very high prices. All makers produced some of their simpler, more economical, figures and groups in larger, more commercial numbers. Leopold Lambert, in particular, produced some of his doll-like figures again and again, but since he used very pretty dolls' heads, usually made by Jumeau, his less rare automata sell for good prices.

ROULLET & DECAMPS

One of the most famous of all French firms to manufacture automata was Roullet & Decamps. Jean Roullet (c.1832–1907) was renowned for making performing characters and animals at his workshop at 10 rue du

A

B

Parc, Paris, where he worked from 1865. He entered into partnership with his son-in-law Ernest Decamps (1847–1909), and the company produced a wealth of exceptionally fine automata. The catalogues show automated, fur-covered cats, foxes, dogs, elephants and smoking and drinking figures, and, in 1893, they patented a walking doll and also made an elephant that sucked up water and blew it out again. A series of simpler, pull-along pieces was also made, including dolls mounted on wheeled platforms. When the toy was pulled forwards, the movement of the wheels activated some part of the doll.

Some of Roullet & Decamps finest work was produced when the company was in the hands of the founder's grandson. Gaston Decamps (1882–1972) followed in the family tradition and made automata and robot-like figures.

Some concept of the variety of automata made by Roullet & Decamps at this time is provided in the pages of a 1912 catalogue, which illustrates male and female clowns, Mexican men, Arab girls, Japanese ladies fan-

A clown with a composition head, brown glass eyes and a protruding tongue. The figure, which is mounted on a musical box, was made by Lucien Bontemps in the late 19th century. It is 26in (66cm) tall.

B

Left to right: the
Lady with a Basket of
Flowers was made by
Decamps in the late
19th century. The
musical Jester, which
has a Jumeau head,
was made c.1900 and
pumps a bellows. The
Magic Cupboard by
Vichy is one of the
most famous of
automata; it is
described on page
119. The Musical
Magician was made
by Vichy c.1885.

ning themselves and magicians who perform conjuring tricks, all, of course, costumed in rich satins trimmed with braid and sequins. The idealized life of country people has always appealed to French artists, and we find silk-dressed peasants carrying a piglet that moves its head, shepherds in court dress serenading the birds and Breton peasants wearing clogs with their satin, 18th-century-style dress. Domestic work was also idealized, and there are exquisitely costumed washerwomen and ladies ironing in charming, but improbable, costumes. In the more interesting automata the musical movements are concealed in the torso or beneath a chair, as in the Peasant with a Piglet.

Not only French bisque and papier mâché heads, but German bisque, composition and celluloid heads (some by Simon & Halbig), were used by Decamps, who, over a long period of manufacture, created knitters, a number of clowns, figures dancing on the moon and magicians that perform the cup-and-ball trick. One of the most alluring figures is the Snake Dance believed to have originally represented Loïe Fuller, who performed at the *Folies Bergère*. Many versions of this lady were made, and they are usually dated by the style of the costume. Some of the doll-like figures, which perform simpler actions, have bisque heads made by Jumeau. Among them is the charming

Flower Seller. This lady turns her head and gestures to a rose in her basket, which opens to reveal a small doll that throws a kiss.

The fantasy world of Decamps included a large number of animals: rabbits that emerge from tree trunks or cabbages, naughty dogs and cats, elephants, tigers and lions. The Puss in Boots automaton is always a favourite, as are some of the bears that are covered with rabbit fur and have moving jaws and front legs. Some of the bears play drums, others drink or smoke. As the bears are not rare, they are among the least expensive of the Decamps automata. So are some of the more toy-like figures, such as babies and animals that emerge from flowers or baskets.

After 1906, electricity was sometimes used instead of traditional clockwork mechanisms, allowing the creation of even more complex tableaux and window-display pieces. Decamps now produces a variety of figures using the most up-to-date technology. Sadly, even the luxury trade now finds such work too expensive, so that the finest modern automata have become the province of show business and the advertising world. One of the most complex figures made in recent years was created for the *Tales of Hoffmann* when it was performed at the Paris Opera. This automaton, operated by remote control, walked, sang and danced on the stage each night and then fell to pieces.

The manufacture of window-display pieces was important until the 1930s, when shopkeepers seem to have lost interest in this method of attracting custom. Alongside the complex figures made by firms such as Decamps there were many basic structures that performed only one or two actions, such as lifting an arm or nodding the head. As no great skill was required for the manufacture of such pieces, especially after the advent of electricity, negro minstrels, nodding Chinamen and dwarfs, shoemakers and cheerful Father Christmas figures were made in every country. They were rarely marked by

A

Left to right: the Magician was probably made by Decamps; her breast rises and falls as she 'breathes', and her head nods as each hand raises a cone to reveal various balls of thread; she is 34in (86cm) tall. The Jester, also by Decamps, hammers the lid of a crate, and the lid opens repeatedly to reveal a Blackamoor trying to escape. The Hunchback Pierrot by Vichy, which has a total of 11 different movements, tempts a monkey with sugar; the monkey leans over, blinks and moves its jaw. The schoolboy Dunce, another automaton by Vichy, is endowed with donkey's ears; as he turns and raises his head, his ears move and his legs kick impatiently. The musical Harpist, which may also be seen in the inset, by Vichy moves her head and eyelids as she plays. The clockwork mechanisms of this figure and of the Dunce have been replaced by electric ones.

A

C

A

The musical
Pumpkin Eater by
Gustave Vichy,
which was made
c.1870, has a
papier mâché head
and fore-arms. A
section of the
pumpkin opens to
reveal a mouse.

B

Gustave Vichy made
the Lady at her
Dressing Table
c.1880. She raises a
hand mirror in one
hand and a powder
puff in the other,
while her head turns.
The musical
movement and
mechanism are
concealed in the
dressing table.

C

This musical
automaton by
Gustave Vichy,
which was made
c.1880, has a bisque
head by Jumeau. The
figure's arms and
head move as she lifts
the lid of her basket
to reveal a bleating
goat.

the maker, but the country of origin is sometimes stamped or embossed under the base. Such figures offer an attractive collecting area for those who do not want to spend too much money and yet want to create an unusual collection that is of period interest.

VICHY

A much wider range of automata was created by Vichy, a firm that was founded c1860 by Antoine Michel, Henry and Gustave Pierre Vichy. In general, the Vichy products are much more artistic than Lambert's and the heads, usually of papier mâché, have more character, as they were especially made for the various subjects. The man in the moon was often portrayed. One version shows a small clown seated on top of a full moon that pokes out its tongue and rolls its eyes, while another has a crescent moon, whose eyes roll as a clown, seated at the base, plays a guitar.

The stage and the circus provided all the makers of automata with a variety of subjects, and Vichy was especially fascinated by the artistic potential of clowns and pierrots. One of the firm's more striking figures shows a pierrot seated at a writing table. His head turns to follow the pen as it moves across the page, but sleep is overcoming him and his eyes close and the light in the lamp dims. Awakening, he reaches to turn up the lamp and begins to write again. Another wistful pierrot, again with a papier mâché head, is a hunchback who tempts a monkey perched on his shoulder with sugar.

Vichy acrobats perform delicately on the backs of chairs or on ladders, moving their weight from the right hand to the left hand before completing their act. Sometimes a monkey performs tricks or plays a banjo as he blinks and bares his teeth. Characters from many countries were represented in papier mâché, some of the negro fruit sellers standing 30in (75cm) high. A Japanese girl with a tray, an African lady sitting on a stool and playing a lyre, and even Buffalo Bill, made c1880, all came from the busy French maker.

B

Made *c*.1876, this musical Acrobat by Gustave Vichy balances on a gently swaying ladder with both hands, nodding his head and arching his back before levitating sideways on one hand. The musical movement plays two airs.

C

The musical Gypsy by Gustave Vichy moves her head from side to side as her breast rises and falls and her arms move to play the castanets. The musical movement, which plays two airs, and the mechanism are hidden in her body.

A

The plaster head of Vichy's the Negro Smoker has glass eyes that move up and down. The figure rocks in the chair while lifting his pipe. The smoke is drawn through a hole in the middle finger, down his arm and out through the hole in his mouth. The stop/start mechanism works a musical movement that plays two airs.

Though not the most artistic of Vichy products, the Magic Cupboard is one of the pieces that every collector dreams of possessing. A naughty boy is seen sitting on a wooden sideboard.iHe turns and reaches towards an upper door, which opens. A fly then appears, but moves out of his reach. In the open cupboard he sees his goal, a pot of his grandmother's jam. He reaches for it, but it spins around to reveal his grandmother's face, her mouth opening and closing as she scolds him. He nods his head, gestures with his right hand and sticks out his tongue as the cupboard door closes. As though Vichy had not sufficiently proved its skill, a mouse then runs up the back of a cheese on the serving area. This very complex automaton is similar in style to some of the penny-in-the-slot machines that were also made by the firm, such as a pair of naughty boys who have been kept in at school. In 1905 Vichy was taken over by Triboulet, and in 1923 it became part of the Société Jouets Automates Français.

LEOPOLD LAMBERT

An automaton by Leopold Lambert is usually one of the first purchases of the new enthusiast. The firm specialized in mechanical figures of a doll-like nature with bisque heads made by the leading makers. Lambert

This automaton by Leopold Lambert has a bisque head by Jumeau. The figure turns and nods her head as she raises and lowers the strings of the toy *pulcinello*, which has a composition head.

D

Leopold Lambert made this musical Mexican Guitar Player *c.*1885. The figure has a papier mâché head, which moves from side to side and nods, and its jaw drops to reveal a row of teeth. The base on which the figure stands contains a key-wound, stop/start mechanism and musical movement, which plays two airs.

had originally worked for the respected firm of Vichy, in whose workrooms he learned many of the methods of making figures appear to smoke or blow bubbles. Most of the child-like figures he created stand on bases that contain the musical movement and they perform fairly basic actions, such as lifting the lid off a basket to show a bleating lamb or a singing bird. The simple cylinder musical movement usually plays only one air. His products are marked *L.B.* on the keys. The firm also made some very complex and rare automata, which are among the most expensive. One of the best-known figures is a smoker, which inhales and blows out smoke. The bubble blower, with a bellows in the base connected to a tube at the mouth, is much rarer and less likely to be in working order if it is bought at auction.

A

The 'crying' musical automaton by Leopold Lambert has a bisque head by Jumeau and was made *c.*1890. The wired body has bisque fore-arms, and the left hand holds a handkerchief, which the figure lifts to her face as she shakes and nods her head. The key bears the incised mark *L.B.*

B

The Smoker by Leopold Lambert stands 20in (50cm) high. The key-wound mechanism causes the figure to turn its head, smoke a pipe and tap the cane.

C

The Tea Pourer was made by Leopold Lambert *c.*1880. It has a tinted bisque head, which turns from side to side and moves up and down as the figure 'pours' the tea. A stop/start lever activates the musical movement, and the maker's mark, *L.B.*, is incised on the key in the base.

D

The Bread Seller was made by Leopold Lambert *c.*1885. The bisque head is by Jumeau. The automaton plays one air as the figure offers a loaf of bread while nodding and turning its head.

THÉROUDE

In contrast to the sophisticated automata made by Vichy for an adult market are the much more toy-like versions produced by Alexandre Nicholas Théroude, who worked from 5 rue Montmorency, Paris. Between 1845 and 1872, Théroude registered 20 patents that related to automated animals, groups of musicians and various dolls. Collectors are most familiar with the dolls that come frequently on the market. They are marked on the base. The first patent (1845) was for a life-sized rabbit that moved its feet, ears and mouth before lifting its tail and dropping chocolates on the ground. Known as Le Lapin Mal Elevé, the toy also carried a sugar carrot.

A later patent described a hen, covered with feathers, that laid gilded

E

This figure of a child, which has a composition head, was made by Alexandre Théroude c.1855. The figure moves on a clockwork-driven mechanism with a platform, on which her feet rest, and the platform bears the maker's mark.

F

F

The wheeled toddler by Théroude wears a padded cap on its papier mâché head. The two simple voice boxes say 'mama' and 'papa' and 'coucou' (part of a French children's game). The maker's mark appears on the three-wheeled metal base.

E

One of various characters produced by Théroude, this gentleman lifts his arms as he moves forwards on the three-wheeled base found on many of Théroude's automata. The head of this figure is of papier mâché. In the mid-19th century Théroude patented a number of automata, including a mechanical rabbit (1844), a chicken that 'laid' sweets as eggs (1846), a tumbler (1848), a talking doll (1852), dolls that moved on wheels (1853–4) and a monkey violin player (1862).

B

wooden eggs. Théroude's fascination with animals was also shown in a series of life-sized goats and sheep, which made his factory famous. By 1850 Théroude was described as a specialist maker of automata and toys and the inventor of a talking baby in a cradle. As he was, above all, a toy maker, many of his products were inexpensive items intended for the nursery. His dolls had papier mâché heads and were relatively simple, although some had turning heads, opening and closing eyes and arms that lifted to throw a kiss or smell a flower. Most moved on a wheeled mechanism, and some were made more complicated after 1854, when Théroude developed a device for making a doll play the game 'cuckoo', during which it lifted its apron over its eyes. This toy carries the firm's mark on the metal mechanism.

PHALIBOIS

Théroude's figures, such as monkeys playing violins or rabbits stroking their whiskers, often appeal more to toy collectors than automata specialists, who prefer the sophistic-ation of the drawing-room pieces such as those made by J. Phalibois. This firm, working from 22 rue Charlot in

A Monkey Trio, possibly made by Phalibois c.1870, has a pull-string musical movement that plays two interchangeable airs. The harpist moves both its arms while the other two figures move their right arms.

Phalibois made the Unexpected Return c.1860. This musical automaton plays two airs, the key-wound and pull-string stop/ start mechanism being contained within the base. The man's jaw, head and eyes move as he lifts the posy, and the woman's and the baby's heads lift.

C

D

base *J. Phalibois, 22 rue Charlot, Paris. F'gue Pièces Méchaniques, Fantasies à Musiques.* The clock-maker Durand & Jacob was also associated, and scenes that were created by Phalibois sometimes have keys marked *D.J.* Such associations of makers, combined with the occasional pirating of designs, often makes the attribution of unmarked automata very difficult, so that many are cautiously described as 'Phalibois type'.

Some of the groups under domes are 30in (75cm) high. They were intended as important pieces to be set in motion for visitors or to amuse children as a special treat. Scenes of a lady at a dressing table, stitching at her sewing machine or playing a piano were made with a flair for detail that is unmistakably French. One exceptionally decorative scene shows a tightrope walker carrying a flag in each hand. A negro and a Chinese musician stand on either side, the richness of their costumes reflected in the mirrored glass panels. The musical movement, incised *J. Phalibois*, plays four airs.

MANIVELLE TOYS

French manivelle-operated, or tinkle-box, toys are often so similar to those made in Germany that they can be differentiated only by their decorative detail or, sometimes, their subject matter. As relatively few French dolls' heads were exported to Germany, any examples with marked French bisque heads are attributed to France. The problem is further complicated by the fact that many French assemblers often used German dolls, which were cheaper. The collector has, therefore, usually to be satisfied with the loose term 'French type'. Among the subjects that were made in France are farm-yards, stables and twirling, dancing children. One amusing scene showed a cook working in front of an oven. When the lid of a pan is lifted, out runs a mouse.

Father Christmas was an especially popular subject, large ver-

Paris, specialized in complex mechanical groups arranged under glass shades, The quality of the automata is often reflected in their bases, the finest of which have an inlay of brass, mother-of-pearl or ivory. Some of these prestige items play as many as six airs, although the majority play only two. The musical movement is occasionally marked *J. Phalibois* or

the initials *J.P.* are incised. Such marks are sometimes difficult to find, as they can be seen only when the mechanism is revealed.

Phalibois' favourite subject was the satin-costumed monkey, who is seen painting at an easel, nursing a baby, mending shoes or performing conjuring tricks. One automaton of a monkey artist was stamped inside the

D

The Monkey Cobbler by Phalibois moves its head from side to side, nods, raises its upper lip, blinks its eyes and hammers with its right hand. The musical cylinder in the base plays two airs.

This exquisitely made figure of Punch on a Bicycle was produced by William Britain *c*.1890. Punch rides around a central weight, which contains a clockwork motor. The overall height of the toy is 8¼in (21cm).

B

The spectacular Silver Swan was made in the late 18th century by James Cox. When the mechanism, which is operated by chains and cams, is set in motion, the swan appears to catch a fish and swallow it.

A

sions of which were an important feature in window displays in December. Automated white-bearded figures ride in sleighs or simple motor cars. They are valued by their appearance rather than their place of origin, although examples containing a musical movement are more expensive. Some of the display automata are deceptively old in appearance, as papier mâché heads, have continued to be used for limited production items to the present day. Negro minstrels, clowns, Japanese ladies and tea-drinking Chinese have remained popular since the mid-19th century. Some subjects were especially made for butchers, fishmongers and shoe repairers. Gnome cobblers and old gentlemen, sometimes carrying the name of the shop or the product, often appear in the auction rooms and are popular with collectors of advertising material.

Because of the high price of good French automata, many collectors now concentrate on manivelle-type boxes or advertising figures, which are still relatively cheap.

BEYOND FRANCE

BRITAIN

One of the few 18th-century British makers whose work has survived is John Hempel, who signed his somewhat crudely made display pieces on the base. His figures were sold by Edlins Rational Repository of Amusement and Instruction of Bond Street, London, and the shop's rectangular labels are also found on the underside of scenes such as the snuff taker, spinning or the influenza sufferer. These automata, with plaster heads and a wooden body framework articulated by a series of leather hinges and wire springs, are quite primitive, but they are frequently included in collections as the first available commercial products. Somewhat similar figures combining music and figures that are ironing or spinning were made in France and they attract interest if in good condition.

The Silver Swan, exhibited at Bowes Museum, Barnard Castle in County Durham, England, gives some idea of the quality and elegance that was achieved in the 18th century. The life-sized swan preens itself and then gives the illusion of catching a fish from the surrounding water. Originally, the swan was accompanied by a canopy of mirrors, which added sparkle and glamour to the scene but

these were lost in the Victorian period. The swan was first exhibited by James Cox, a London watchmaker who ran a museum of automata that contained more than 50 exhibits. At that time, the leading clock and automata manufacturers sold their products to a limited, very wealthy, clientele, and they were already combining their skills to take advantage of the international market. After James Cox died in 1788, his son combined with Jaquet-Droz and Henri Maillardet (b.1745), and Cox's automata were dispersed across the world, from Russia to China, where they were exhibited at the courts.

Although Britain was never a producer of luxury automata, some very fine advertising and window display figures were produced, some of the rarest pieces being made by William Britain, a name more commonly associated with toy soldiers. These figures were strongly made, with lead heads, hands and legs. They are activated by clockwork. Somewhat smaller than many display automata, measuring less than 17in (42cm), the figures have the maker's label fixed under the base. One figure, representing a Scotsman, pours whisky into a glass and appears to drink. He performs for half an hour at each winding, as did a Mandarin who drank tea. Such figures were expensive in relation to the toys sold by Britain, a toy merchant, and they were mainly intended as trade pieces. The clockwork Khedive, who could smoke cigarettes or a pipe and blew out clouds of smoke, was suggested as a novelty for a Christmas party, as was the Indian Juggler, a much larger toy than the Khedive. He taps a basket in front of him and raises the lid to show a child. He replaces the lid and lifts it again to reveal a snake. Automated collecting boxes for charity were also made by the firm, any of whose products are of great interest, as so few automated figures were made in the UK.

Some interesting, but primitive, versions without musical movements were produced in the UK by William Tansley in the late 19th century. Using

commercial dolls and horses, Tansley created scenes at the races, performing minstrels and fairground dioramas with doors that open to reveal anything from marching soldiers to bellringers. Pieces by known makers always attract interest, but any fairground amusement machine with an especially well-made or amusing tableau will find a ready buyer. Such items are on the border-line between amusement machines and automata and are in general more attractive to collectors of fairground art.

GERMANY

Because German manufacturers were always more interested in the large-scale production of children's toys than in individually made luxury items, German automata, like most British and American examples, are of the most basic kind. The major-

ity perform simple actions such as lifting their arms and turning their heads, movements that are controlled by wires or cords. Costumed clockwork figures, such as those made by Ives in America, were not made by the German tin toy makers. Simple automata became a speciality of the town of Sonneberg, especially famed for its production of dolls.

Activated German toys of the 1830s relied on two methods: a squeeze box with an animal or figure fixed to the sloping surface or a simple mechanism concealed in a box with a small crank at the side, which set figures and, sometimes, music in motion. The tableaux arranged on hand-cranked boxes are particularly charming: soldiers come to attention, a pair of goats fight, a fox chases a squirrel and women take sheep to market. A few of the toys represent contemporary life too truthfully for comfort: a butcher brings a chopper

The British manufacturer William Tansley of Coventry made this automaton which represents the spectators at a race meeting with horses that move in a circle, c.1870. The height, including the metal stand, is 37in (94cm).

William Britain was one of the few UK manufacturers to make automata. The Automatic Foot Race was marketed by the company in the 1880s. The heads and limbs of the figures are made of lead, and the figures are dressed in fabric. The central column is covered with lithographed paper. The two figures race around in circles, passing and re-passing one another.

down on a bullock's neck, a man beats his donkey, and a hunter kills a hare. Some of the box-like bases were painted with bright flowers, but more frequently they were decorated with paper. Some idea of the vast range of figures sold in the early 19th century can be gained from the hand-coloured sample books of merchants such as J.S. Lindner of Sonneberg.

The most expensive versions of these early German toys have dolls with papier mâché heads, dressed in fashionable gauze or muslin frocks with high waists and low necklines and playing musical instruments. One elegant gentleman is seated at an organ; another plays a violin with a jerky, simple movement. These hand-cranked scenes were brightly col-oured and form an interesting com-mentary on the daily life of the period. Soldiers fired guns and cannon, street musicians have small monkeys as an added attraction, and monks, wood-cutters, market traders and farm workers, blacksmiths and stone-masons all perform their daily tasks in the most basic way.

Circus and fairground life has provided automata makers of all countries with a constant source of inspiration, and the workers of Sonne-berg created tightrope walkers, con-jurers, trapeze artists and clowns galore riding goats along with pigs and donkeys. Some of these early activated toys are complete scenes, with a backdrop against which ele-phants and giraffes parade with their keepers and ladies water their flower gardens or drink coffee in a sitting room. A few are nothing more than boxes with a roof, in which the figures perform in an enclosed, magical world of their own.

As the scenes and figures were made from composition, thin wood, wire, string and scraps of fabric and paper, they are extremely fragile. Few have survived in pristine condition. When they come on the market, they are bought both by toy and automata collectors, as they are among the most imaginative and well-made commercial figures ever produced. Variations on the types of figures marketed by Lindner continued to be produced throughout the 19th century. They are dated by the mat-erials used and, especially, by the costumes. Squeaking, barking, tinkling and rattling, these toys performed in the nurseries in Europe and the United States and they can now be found almost anywhere in the world. They are, obviously, most expensive in Germany, where they represent the beginning of the great toy industry that developed from the folk art of Seiffen and the southern regions.

The clowns, roundabouts, and crying babies in cradles all became larger as the century progressed and complete dolls rather than the simple constructions of wood and wire were employed. Those made c.1900 are particularly collectable, as they are very decorative. Dolls with pretty bisque heads swing garlands of flowers above their heads, dance under arches, play musical instruments or ride in a sleigh or on a roundabout. Sometimes the products of several manufacturers are combined in a single piece: the dolls' heads from Simon & Halbig or Armand Marseille, the skin-covered horses by F. Graeffer or Louis Lindner, and the musical movements provided by one of the specialist firms based at Marburg in Hesse.

Most of these tinkle-box automata, often described as manivelle-operated, are covered with marbled or patterned paper that is sometimes further decorated with flowered or embossed gold borders. Pretty children and animals were the most popular subjects such as kittens having tea at a small table, bears dancing, and dogs and elephants performing simple tricks. A simple construction could be made up in a variety of ways, by substituting bisque dolls' heads for cats or bears and changing the colour of the clothes and the patterned papers on the base. Few of the individual manufacturers of such toys are known and when a piece does carry a mark it usually relates to the seller rather than the maker. Because of the time needed to assemble, paint and finish such ephemeral items, they were produced only when peasant labour was very cheap, and their quality declined sharply after 1910, when workers became aware of the conditions in which they worked and came to demand a better standard of living.

B

C

A

This fiddler automaton with a bisque head by Jumeau was made for M.M. Heriot & Cie of Paris in the 1880s.

B

A musical acrobat clock, which was made in France c.1870. A boy acrobat in a mirrored alcove performs balancing tricks on the soles of his fellow artiste, while raising his cap. The musical movement in the ebonized base plays four airs.

C

A rare 25-key monkey duo organ, which was made in France during the late 19th century. It plays nine tunes on pipes mounted below the bellows. The winding handle is at the back, and the tune-changing slide at the side. The cello player has five movements, and the violin player has six.

D

A musical Monkey Artist, made, probably by Blaise Bontems, c.1870. Six movements activate the eyes, jaw, head and the three actions of the painting arm. The bell-striking clock by Lapy Frères has a Broco escapement.

Automata and Mechanical Dolls

SWITZERLAND

The industrial manufacture of musical boxes began in Geneva c. 1810, and larger boxes were made at Ste Croix. As the century progressed, their structure and ornamentation became increasingly complex. Superb coin-operated display automata were a speciality of Swiss makers, especially those based in Ste Croix. One of the most famous makers, Auguste Lassueur, entered into an agreement with a Swiss railway company in 1897 that allowed him to place his work in all waiting rooms. After the Swiss Federal Railways took over in 1938, these machines were electrified and many of them can still be seen in operation. Typical of Lassueur's work are groups of dancing dolls on stages backed with mirrors, though the roundabouts with dolls sitting in boats and on horses are more lively. These coin-operated automata can play as many as six airs, and they are collected by mechanical music enthusiasts as well as automata collectors.

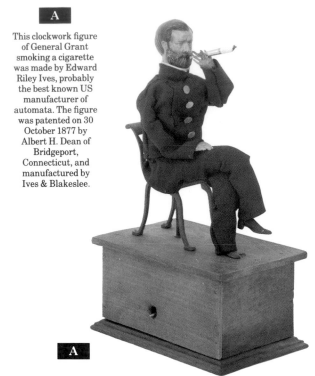

A

UNITED STATES

Colourful coin-in-the-slot automata and window-display pieces were made in the United States, although never to the standard of the exclusive luxury products of France. In the mid-19th century, wealthy Americans relied on imported luxury goods from France and Germany. Although several firms were set up in America by immigrant craftsmen, there seems to have been no serious attempt to create automata to rival the French luxury products that were sold in the most exclusive stores. Instead, American manufacturers concentrated on the simpler automata that would appeal to children and be strong enough to withstand transportation to all parts of the country without damage. One of the most imaginative mid-19th-century makers was George W. Brown, who worked at Forestville in Connecticut, a centre of the clock-making industry. Brown himself was a clockmaker by trade and was obviously interested in mechanized figures, registering sev-

B

B

The Monkey Fiddler musical clock automaton was possibly made by Blaise Bontems. The figure has a papier mâché head and glass eyes. Humming-birds perch in the branches, and the scene even features a 'waterfall'.

C

A musical Monkey Marksman dating from c.1860 and possibly made by Blaise Bontems. The monkey, which has a papier mâché head, raises its rifle and aims at the target. Its head nods and turns, and its jaw and arms move. The base contains the pull-string musical movement, which plays two airs.

C

D

Arthur E. Hotchkiss patented a design for a clockwork walking doll on 21 September 1875. Seen here are Santa Claus, General Benjamin Franklin Butler and a 'heathen Chinese', and their cast iron feet move on rollers. The figures were manufactured by Ives & Blakeslee.

E

The Autoperipatetikos was produced with a variety of different heads and costumes. This doll has a porcelain head, and the skirt has been lifted to reveal the cardboard cone that conceals the mechanism, which was patented by Enoch Rice Morrison on 15 July 1862.

eral patents for walking dolls.

Edward R. Ives, who also worked in Connecticut, is a much more important figure to collectors of automata. Although intended mainly for children, some of his figures are so beautifully made and dressed in such fine fabric that they hold their own against more sophisticated European products. Ives originally made toys that were activated by hot air, but by the 1880s a range of charming metal toys, such as a costumed lady driving a hippodrome chariot, was being made. The window-display figures, typical of the strong toys that Ives created, could run for long periods without re-winding.

Ives increased his range of automated toys after taking over a small New York maker, Robert J. Clay, who specialized in figures such as fur-covered bears, negro preachers and crawling babies. Ives also used the talent of Jerome Secor, who made singing birds in cages and metal headed dolls performing such actions as playing the piano. Most famous of all the Ives' products are the stiff figures that 'walk' on wheels concealed under their large feet. Father Christmas, figures of various nationalities, Uncle Tom and General Benjamin Franklin Butler all marched out of the Ives factories costumed in fabric

outfits. They were highly popular toys and examples frequently appear in the specialist salerooms.

WALKING AND TALKING DOLLS

While automata manufacturers like Jaquet-Droz were especially concerned with complex hand movements and manufacturers like Vichy were attempting to coordinate as many individual movements as possible into one piece, commercial toy manufacturers were more interested in the apparently mundane task of attempting to make a figure appear to walk by placing one foot in front of the other. Doll-like toys that moved forwards by means of wheels concealed under a

E

skirt had been made since the Renaissance, but the Swiss automata maker Charles Abram Bruguier (1788–1862) is believed to have been the first to make a doll, introduced in 1821, with a more realistic walking movement.

A common American toy is the Autoperipatetikos, a doll that appeared to walk without support. It was patented on 15 July 1862 by Enoch Rice Morrison. The dolls move forwards by a key-wound clockwork mechanism that operates the feet independently, so that the figure takes actual 'steps' forwards on rollers concealed under metal boots. Large numbers of these toys were produced, all with the characteristically thick body that was necessary to conceal the mechanism. The commonest figure of the type is a lady in a crinoline dress, a toy whose value depends on the type of head used and the quality of the costume. Parian, wax, papier mâché and porcelain shoulder-heads were used by the manufacturers, although the rather rarer, if less appealing, examples of portrait figures representing such characters as Napoleon III were made of composition with moulded beards.

Another American walking doll was the one patented in 1868 by William F. Goodwin of New York. However, this cannot truly be described as a 'walking' doll as it pushes a pram, against which it leans as it moves forwards.

The innovative French doll maker, Jules Nicholas Steiner founded a company, sometimes called Société Steiner, in 1855 to specialize in making mechanical bébé dolls that walked and talked, Steiner was a clockmaker by trade, and many of this company's dolls have complex mechanisms, including voice boxes that produced the sounds 'mama and papa'. In 1890 Steiner introduced a doll with a moving head, arms and legs, and it was patented as Bébe Premier Pas (or First Step Baby). The doll has a bisque head, while the body, which contains the mechanism, is partly carton, partly composition. The Bébé Premier Pas head has an open mouth with two rows of sharp, rather

pointed teeth, and some collectors find this an unattractive feature, which means that such dolls are often underpriced.

Various mechanisms have been used to imitate the human voice in dolls and automata. In 1824 Johannes Jean Maelzel (b.1783) was granted a patent for his talking doll, which had won an award in the Exhibition of French Industry in 1823. The sound was produced by a bellows action activated by arm movements, which blew air across a reed. The resulting 'papa' sound could be modified to become 'mama'.

Théroude took out a patent in 1852 for a talking doll that uttered

the sounds 'mama', and 'papa' and 'coucou', and there is some evidence that a talented doll maker working in London in the 1850s also made talking dolls; sadly, however, his name has not survived, Christoph Motschmann of Sonneberg, Germany, seems to have been the first manufacturer to have patented a talking doll mechanism that could be mass-produced fairly inexpensively for insertion into a doll's body. A stamp bearing the words *Patent 29 April 1857 Ch, Motschmann Sonneberg* has been found on dolls manufactured between 1857 and 1859. There is, however, no evidence that Motschmann actually made the dolls in which the mechan-

A

Ondine, the swimming doll, has a clockwork mechanism that was perfected by Charles Bertran of Paris. The doll was made by E. Martin, a manufacturer of automata, using a Simon & Halbig head, which is marked *Halbig S & H*

2½. Ondine does the breaststroke, her cork body keeping her buoyant and a metal casing protecting the mechanism. The limbs are wooden and the hands metal. Ondine is wearing an original outfit, probably made by Au Nain Bleu of Paris.

B

B

This Autoperipatetikos has a key-wound mechanism. The braided hair-style is rare, and the doll has leather arms and metal feet. The dress is original to the doll, and the carton base reads: *Patented July 15, 1862, also in Europe 20 Dec 1862.*

C

A Steiner Bébé Premier Pas or 'kicking' Steiner, which was made in 1875-80. The cardboard body contains a key-wound mechanism, which activates the leg movements. There is also a voice box, which says 'mama' and 'papa'.

isms appeared; rather it seems that the patent applied only to the apparatus that worked the eyes and voice box by two strings that emerged at the doll's hip.

If the easily reconizable Autoperipatetikos was the first mass-produced doll to move forwards with individual steps, another American inventor must take the credit for designing the first talking figure to be manufactured in large numbers. Thomas Alva Edison (1847–1931) of Orange, New Jersey, is better known as the inventor of the phonograph and incandescent lamp, but in 1879 he made the first talking doll, a rather crude assembly of tin and wood, which enjoyed mixed success. Ten years later, however, he produced a more attractive version, which had wooden limbs and a metal torso containing a phonograph and playing mechanism. The head was a Simon & Halbig bisque head, bearing the company's mould number *719* or *917*. The doll was wound from the back and recited a number of nursery rhymes and short sentences. Complete models are now rarely found; they can be identified by an impressed mark on the mechanism, *Edison Phonograph Toy/Manufacturing Co./New York* together with the patent date. The most frequently found phonograph doll – although frequent is hardly the appropriate word as they are very rare – is the Jumeau Bébé Phonographe, which was made in 1893–8.

The quest for sound led also to the quest for lifelike movements, and in 1876 in Paris, E. Martin produced Ondine, the swimming doll. The bisque socket head was by Simon & Halbig, but the body was of cork, so that it would float. The clockwork mechanism was housed in the body. The arms and jointed legs are of painted wood, and the cup-shaped hands were made of metal. Ondine could swim on her front as well as her back, but out of water the strange angles of her legs and arms give her a rather frog like look.

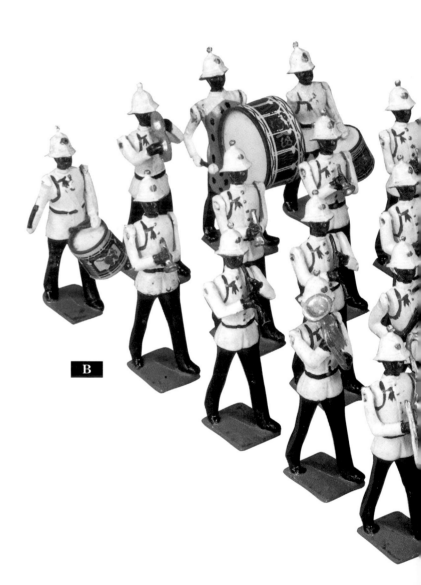

Made in the
Erzgebirge region of
Germany *c.*1870,
these wooden toy
soldiers are from a
boxed set of infantry
that includes an
officer and a
drummer.

B

Britains set 2186, the
Band of the Bahamas
Police, is a famous
and rare set, made
after World War II.
The complete set
achieves high prices
in the sale room.

3

Upright young men in gorgeous uniforms, well-fed and

groomed horses, fairy-tale forts and immaculate army

vehicles — all present a

Toy Soldiers

picture of military life that

was very far from the reality

of war. When every boy played with toy soldiers, life in the

army must have represented excitement and the romance

of dressing up in splendid eye-catching uniforms for deeds of valour. In Germany, where military service was compulsory in the 19th century, the uniforms were especially striking and must have offered a young man some compensation for a period spent away from career and home.

Throughout their history, model soldiers have appealed to adults as well as children, and expensive versions in precious metals and precise detail have been made alongside cheap, mass-produced examples. As so many figures have survived in good condition, soldiers form one of the most active collecting areas, with their own specialist groups: those who collect antique figures in near-perfect condition for display and those who use the models for their war-games and accept examples in different materials, adaptations and re-paints.

As the value of soldiers in original condition has increased, collectors treat their acquisitions with great

A

respect and there has been a marked decrease in the amount of repairing and re-modelling work done to them. The importance of original packaging is also respected, as the additional value of a boxed set is generally recognized. It was once quite common for respected collectors to remove complete sets for their war-games and forget where they had put the boxes. Sad tales of auction room staff desperately trying to marry boxes and figures without success abound, especially in executors' sales.

Toy soldiers were commercially made from a number of materials, including wood and composition, but those made of metal are the most avidly collected. Anyone beginning to collect model soldiers is advised to consult price guides and lists of auction realizations as well as specialist magazines; the proliferation of

adapted and repainted figures can gull the uninitiated into making expensive mistakes. Some auction rooms hold sales devoted to soldiers and the catalogues carry estimates of the prices that are anticipated, estimates that help new collectors to avoid the more common pitfalls.

So many toy soldiers have been produced and are still being produced by manufacturers in Europe and the US that it is impossible to do more than touch briefly on some of the better known names that collectors will come across in the sale room. Many smaller manufacturers are not included here, even though their work is interesting and attractive, nor are those from countries like Italy, Spain and Denmark, all of which have produced notable pieces.

B

A

A rare boxed set of the Royal Fusiliers, which may have become Britains set 7, although this particular box is not numbered. The set was first made c.1895, and such sets are seldom found with the original packaging intact.

B

Britains set 148, the Royal Lancaster Regiment, in foreign-service dress. The complete set, first issued in 1907, included a mounted officer, a foot officer, a colour bearer, a trumpeter, three men at the trail, three men at the slope, two gunners and a gun.

C

One of the earliest methods of mass-producing soldiers was by turning them on lathes. This group, which was made in the Erzgebirge region of Germany c.1880, shows how even simple added detail could give variety.

WOODEN SOLDIERS

Carved wooden soldiers have a special appeal to collectors. Hand-carved wooden toys were produced in large numbers only in countries where there was a cheap supply of peasant labour. There are, consequently, few examples from the UK and USA, although in New England villages where the German influence was strong, craftsmen brought their traditional wood-carving skills to their new homes; the output was, nevertheless, slight.

Germany, in particular Saxony, is the homeland of the wooden toy. By 1864 there were, in Saxony alone, 697 manufacturers of wooden toys, and Saxony is still an important wood-carving area. Toy soldiers were produced together with other toys, and the peasants would carry the week's work to merchants, who paid, usually by weight, for the articles that they then distributed throughout Europe. Nuremberg was one of the major trade centres; it lay on one of the main routes of the Holy Roman Empire, which enabled merchants to avoid the heavy customs duties imposed by the multitude of small states. From the 17th century Nuremberg was supplied with toys made in Thuringia, the Groden valley, Berchtesgaden and Oberammergau, and these were taken across Europe by pedlars and merchants.

By the 18th century the darker, natural stains that had been used for toy soldiers had given way to bright, attractive colours, and in the 19th century trading depots were set up to carry the toys by wagon, train and river. The oval, chipwood boxes that contained the soldiers became as common in the nurseries of the UK and US as in Germany, and German-made toys were so cheap that competition was almost impossible.

Toy soldiers made in various parts of Germany were assembled at just a few collection points, and it is not usually possible to identify accurately the exact place of manufacture. The customers' requirements were paramount, and regional differences were soon obscured as figures were produced to set designs offered in catalogues.

One of the most important of the Oberammergau merchants was

A

Very fine painted detail was added to flats. This set of mid-19th-century German cavalry was modelled with the greatest skill.

B

Carved soldiers of this type are typical of the wooden soldiers produced in many areas of Germany in the 19th century. The detail added to what are, on the whole, crudely carved figures gives them enormous charm and vitality.

Georg Lang, who had begun to develop his organization about 1750. So that the toys he offered should satisfy customers in other countries, Lang closed down overseas agencies manned by Germans and relied instead on local merchants. By 1821 Lang's business employed more than a hundred carvers, most of whom were members of the same family and who were bound by strict guild rules to ensure that they worked only in certain materials and passed down to ensure that they worked only in certain materials and passed down their skills only to members of their own families.

Some of the finest wooden soldiers were made in the Berchtesgaden region of Germany. A school of design was founded there in 1840 to encourage the development of the

industry at a time when 120 turners, 60 carvers and 120 box-makers were working in the area. Skilled carvers could produce more than 300 soldiers a day, and these were passed to members of another guild for painting. The most basic figures were lathe-turned with stick-like arms and a sword or a gun that was glued in position. The base was sometimes part of the figure; more often, however, it was a separate, green-painted disc of wood.

Any boxed sets of soldiers made in Oberammergau or Berchtesgaden are now collectable, especially in Germany and Switzerland, where they command high prices. Large scenic pieces, representing complete battles, are extremely rare and attracted considerable interest even when first made. In 1816 Alois Lechner, a

carpenter in Oberammergau, constructed a scene representing the capture of several fortresses, triumphal marches and battles in a table-top setting that included many hundreds of figures, which were set in motion by a lever. The articulated scene included detachments of marching infantry and soldiers on horseback.

In the southern Tyrol, the centre of the toy industry was St Ulrich, which produced military bands and regiments in various state uniforms. By the end of the 19th century some three out of every five of the town's inhabitants were involved in the wooden toy industry. Trading depots were established for work that was collected from the Groden valley, and even in 1905 peasants could not sell their work directly to visitors but

C French toy makers tended to specialize in cleverly designed, beautifully constructed items made from cheap basic materials. Paper soldiers were the most economical to produce of all, and they quickly became familiar to children in nurseries in both Europe and the US. This reprint obviously cannot reproduce the fragile quality of old paper.

had to sell to the merchants, of whom the best known were Insam, J.B. Purger and Prinoth. Their warehouses were packed with horses, wagons and soldiers, often painted in improbable but bright colours.

The wood carvers of St Ulrich were among the more fortunate toy makers, for they were better paid than those in some of the less-fashionable areas of Germany. The cheapest toys came from the Erzgebirge (Ore Mountains), where Seiffen was the major centre. Although there was a long tradition of wood carving in the area, the peasants were so poor that they could not even afford to buy their own lathes, which were leased to them at a charge that was based on their output. Whole families were forced to work for 14 or 15 hours a day, but despite the conditions, the soldiers produced in the region are bright and light-hearted in effect, movement being suggested by a few simple shapes and a dash of colour. Some of the best figures are those that are mounted on rockers or have a wire spring attaching the horse to its rectangular base.

Boxed scenes of battles, ships with sailors, horse-drawn gun carriages and military bands, all painted in somewhat gaudy colours, typify Seiffen work, which was exported by agents in Grunhainichen, Olbenhau and Waldkirchen. Agents overseas used catalogues and sample boxes to obtain orders for the toys, some of which could be made to a higher standard by special arrangement. Simple turned soldiers are still made in small factories in Erzgebirge, and although wooden toy making in other regions is now limited, factories in Seiffen continue to supply children with amusing and well-made playthings.

PAPER SOLDIERS

Paper and card figures are among the most ephemeral of toy soldiers. They are believed to have originated from the sheets of printed uniforms and battle scenes first produced in Germany, but Strasbourg in France is often regarded as the birthplace of the paper soldier. Inspired by the interest shown by the citizens of Strasbourg in the troops of the visiting Louis XV in 1744, the printer Seyfried quickly produced some sheets, which he sold around the streets. Although prints of military uniforms had been available since the previous century, it is thought that Seyfried was the first to produce sheets especially designed to be cut out. Seyfried's sheets, which included a series showing the mounted troops of the Regiment Orleans Cavalerie, sold remarkably well, and other printers in Strasburg soon took up the idea.

One of the leading manufacturers of printed paper sheets of soldiers was H.R.G. Silbermann (1800–76). In 1845 Silbermann developed a way of oil printing in colour, and soon soldiers were decorated with gold and silver detail. On the whole, however, the basic sheets were simple and cheap. Silbermann's business was taken over by Gustave Fischbach and Fritz Kieffer, who remained in production from 1872 until 1914. Their sheets of soldiers bore the name of the company and *L'Imprimerie Alsacienne*.

Most famous of all the French printers of paper soldiers is the firm established at Epinal in the Vosges by Nicholas Pellerin (1703–73). Under the leadership of Nicholas' son, Jean Charles (1756–1836), the firm used lead plates made from old woodcuts and began to print thousands of sheets of various kinds, including soldiers. Some of the sheets were designed to be assembled as three-dimensional models, and guns could

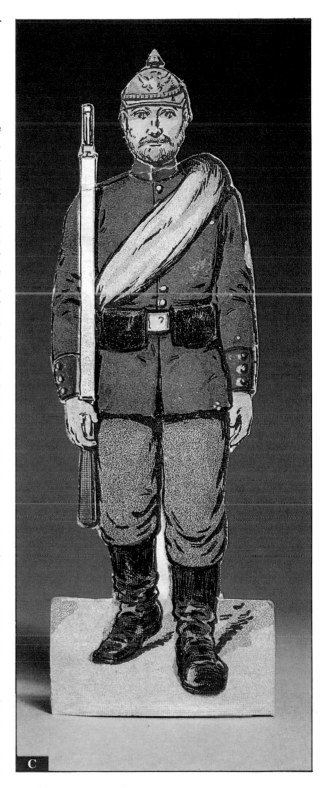

be made to move by attaching wheels, made of paper and backed with card. Although some of the sheets were coloured, others were left plain.

Pellerin soldiers were the cheapest available in the early 19th century. They were sold by pedlars who went to Epinal to collect their stocks several times each year, and

A selection of paper soldiers. The enduring popularity of these most ephemeral of soldiers has inspired modern reprints of old sheets.

A

sheet upon sheet of different armies, printed on thin paper, were produced to meet the demand. Some of the firm's best work was produced during the Napoleonic Wars, and it was quick to capitalize on new conflicts and to include representatives of troops of all kinds, sometimes printing several dozen sheets of different regiments of the same army.

Other companies followed Pellerin's example. C.H. Pinot, for instance, produced sheets of soldiers, and Nancy in northeast France became a centre of paper soldier production in the 19th century. Sheets of single figures and of groups are sometimes found with the imprint *Imagerie de Nancy*. Similar sheets were also produced in the UK, and the London-based firm of Michael Henry Nathan & Co. is known to have printed a set of the Black Watch. All of the French paper sheets were intended for the mass-market, and they continued to be issued until this century, although it is difficult to date accurately many of these sheets as the styles were unchanged for decades. There are, too, many modern reprints of such sheets, some of which are 'aged' so that they will resemble the older editions. It is hard, however, to imitate the fragility of really old paper.

It would be wrong to believe that paper soldiers were enjoyed only by the poor. King Ferdinand of Naples had a procession of 2,000 paper figures representing lords and ladies of the Bourbon court, the uniforms of the Kingdom of Naples and detachments of the Italian army, and these may be seen in the San Martino Museum in Naples. Other collections of paper soldiers are in the Musée de l'Armée in Paris and in the Army Museum in Naples.

A

TIN SOLDIERS – FLATS

It was not until the 1730s that the toy soldier as we know it today – that is, an article intended primarily as a child's plaything and, to some extent, mass-produced – first appeared. Inititally made of tin or pewter and cast in engraved slate moulds, these figures were the flat, two-dimensional pieces, known as *Zinnfiguren* or, simply, flats. Flats were first produced by the tinsmiths of Nuremberg. As early as 1578 Nuremberg was, according to the records of the guild of pewterers, a

centre for the manufacture of toys, which were produced as a sideline to the main occupations, those of producing pewter-ware and jewellery. The metal was readily available from the many mines in the area, and pedlars and merchants quickly carried the toys across Europe along the trade routes that had existed since the Middle Ages. Flats were economical to produce, easy to distribute as they were light and not bulky and, on the whole, resistant to damage during transportation and display. A wide range of subjects, not just military ones, was covered by the flats, and the individual pieces were often designed to very high artistic standards.

The engraver of the original mould, on which the success or other-

wise of the flat depended, worked painstakingly from the published prints and books illustrating the uniforms worn at the time. Working in stone, wood or, more often, slate, the engraver was required to depict as accurately as possible the details of buttons, fringes and feathers. The two halves of the mould had to fit together perfectly, and deep pouring channels were gouged so that, when the two halves were fixed together, a tin alloy could be poured into the pre-heated mould. The composition of each pewterer's alloy was a carefully guarded secret, but usually tin and lead were combined with a small amount of bismuth or antimony so that the soldier could be bent without snapping. Each time the mould was used, it had to be dusted with a

powder so that the alloy would run
smoothly. Poor quality soldiers can
be recognized by a thin but untidy
line of metal that shows where the
two halves of the mould were joined.
Usually, this 'flashing' was cut away
before the figures were painted.

A skilled worker could produce
hundreds of soldiers in a day from
moulds that were, when treated carefully and not subjected to rapid
changes of temperature, almost
indestructible. The durability of the
moulds has made it difficult for collectors to identify any one manufacturer's work, for they were frequently
passed on to other makers or bought
up when a factory closed.

The flats, often only a milli-
metre or two thick, were at first cast
in a variety of sizes, but many makers

later standardized to the Nuremberg scale of 30mm (1⅛in), which was introduced by Heinrichsen in 1848. They were sold, both painted and unpainted, by weight, 1kg (2.2lb) representing approximately 330 soldiers. The cheapest were those left completely unpainted, while others were only partly decorated. Some boxes were packed with the same type of foot soldier; others contained complete military encampments, a historical battle scene or a military band. In general, today's collectors prefer the group settings, which make effective and attractive displays.

The production of flats flourished throughout the 19th century. Although Germany is regarded as the home of *Zinnfiguren*, there was some production in other countries, notably Spain, Italy and France, but output was limited and some firms operated for only short periods. Records of the pewter toy workers in the UK in the 19th century mention a small production of pewter toy soldiers but they were presumably so fragile that none has survived.

Neither the engravers nor the painters marked their work, and the merchants who assembled the completed flats at central depots packed the soldiers into boxes labelled with their own names. Some of the engravers worked for several makers, and the copying of successful designs was commonplace. Most flats, therefore, are bought for their individual qualities, not because they are the work of a known manufacturer. Some of the names of individual manufacturers can be found in the reports of the national and international exhibitions, but even though specialists sometimes claim to be able to recognize the work of particular makers, this is really possible only when a soldier is marked or is identical with one that can be positively attributed. Although superseded as toys by hollow-cast soldiers, the interest of adult collectors has stimulated the continuing production of both new flats and reissues from old moulds.

A

A

Britains set 75, the Scots Guards, was made between 1897 and 1966. The set shown here, with its box lid describing the regiment's battle honours, was made *c.*1900. The figures – an officer, piper and six men at the slope – have movable arms; after *c.*1911 the set was made with marching figures.

LEAD SOLDIERS

Although lead was used in the tin alloy from which flats were produced, a far higher proportion was incorporated in the alloy from which semi-flats (or semi-rounds) were made. These were developed by German manufacturers who wanted to introduce more realism into their work by making the bodies of both men and horses slightly rounded while the legs were still fixed in a straight line on the base. Lead was also used in the manufacture of the other two main kinds of toy soldier – solid and hollow-cast figures – that now form the most popular areas for collectors.

SEMI-FLATS

Semi-flat figures, like flats, originated in Germany, and they became popular in the second half of the 19th century. As the name suggests, they were thicker than flats and could have more detail worked on them. Bulkier and with a higher lead content than the flats, they were a sort of halfway house between the flat and the fully round figures that were to follow. Some attractive and well-modelled pieces were produced, but, on the whole, semi-flats are less

desirable than other types of toy soldier.

Like flats, semi-flats – *halb massif* – have always been more popular in Germany than elsewhere. Allgeyer and Schweizer were two of the earliest craftsmen to produce these figures, and Kober of Vienna enjoys a well-earned reputation for the attractive figures it still produces from old moulds.

Some collectors of flats and solids tend rather to look down on semi-flats, and in the 1900s the German company Gebrüder Schneider sold semi-flat moulds for home-casting. In consequence, some poorly made pieces have appeared on the market. Schneider's moulds were very popular in the US, where the moulds themselves are collected.

SOLIDS

The French have never been very interested in either flats or semi-flats, and while the Germans were producing *Zinnfiguren*, a French metal worker named Lucotte began to make fully modelled, rounded figures, which were known as 'Lucotte's little men'. Also cast from alloys of tin, lead and antimony, but sold ready painted, Lucotte's figures were cheap enough to be available to a wide section of the public, and his firm did very well. Lucotte is said to have begun producing solids at the time of the French Revolution (1789). Later, Cuberly, Blondel and Gerbeau produced boxes of fully rounded figures, marked C.B.G., and they and Lucotte eventually combined with Mignot, another Frenchman, to become C.B.G. Mignot.

In the mid-19th century German companies, possibly as a reaction to the success of the French fully modelled figures, began to turn out *ronde-bosse* figures too, one of the best-known manufacturers being Heyde of Dresden.

By this time, French and German manufacturers had established the production of toy soldiers as a viable commercial undertaking, and they offered a remarkably wide and varied range of figures, which were exported throughout the world, making the toy soldier a familiar figure in nurseries everywhere by the closing decades of the 19th century.

HOLLOW CAST

So far, cast figures, in one or other of the lead alloys, had been produced as solid items. Flats were, of course, nothing more than thin sheets of metal, but the *ronde-bosse* or solid figures used an appreciable amount of metal in each casting, which added not only to the production costs but also to the costs of transportation.

In 1893 an English toy maker, William Britain, who already had an established business making mechanical toys, saw the advantages inherent in hollow-cast, fully modelled figures, and he began to market the first examples in competition with German flats and French solids. So successful were these figures that the name

Britains has, for many people, become synonymous with toy soldiers. Beginning with British Army subjects, the firm introduced more and more representations of foreign forces into its range, until by 1900 over one hundred different sets were available. New designs continued to appear, showing improvements in standards of modelling and finishes. Soon outstripping its European rivals, Britains became the largest manufacturer of toy soldiers in the world.

Hollow-cast figures are produced manually. A molten alloy of tin, lead and antimony is poured into a hinged metal (usually brass) mould, which often incorporates handles with protective gloves. The metal is swirled around the mould and poured out again very quickly, leaving a skin of cooling metal on the surface of the interior of the mould cavity. When the two halves of the mould are separated, the fully modelled figure is revealed. Hollow-casting always leaves a characteristic aperture at the point where the surplus metal flows back

A

Britains made regiments from all parts of the British Empire. These figures are from set 66, the 1st Bombay Lancers, which included four troopers with lances and one officer and dates from the 1900s. Set 66 was made from *c.*1896 until 1966

A

B

Britains also made soldiers that reflected the involvement of British forces in various parts of the world. These two sets first appeared during the Boer War (1899–1902). The box for set 105, the Imperial Yeomanry, which contained five troopers with fixed arms, mounted on trotting horses, is dated 1 June 1900. The set was made from 1900 until 1941. Set 38, the South African Mounted Infantry, had originally been entitled Dr Jameson and the African Mounted Infantry, but Dr Jameson's popularity plummeted after his surrender to the Boers, and the set was thereafter known always as the South African Mounted Infantry, although the contents remained the same – four mounted figures with rifles and one mounted figure (representing Dr Jameson) with a pistol. The set was made from 1896 (when it presumably celebrated Dr Jameson's success in the Matabele Wars of 1893) until 1941.

C

This fine example of a modern model soldier was made by Frederick Ping (1930–77). Ping had begun to make soldiers in the 1930s, and he is widely admired among the collectors of model soldiers for the accuracy and individuality of his figures. This model of Henry, Duke of Lancaster, in full armour, is approximately 4in (10cm) high.

out of the mould, but this is usually obliterated during painting.

Between 1900 and 1955 hollow casting was the most widely used method of producing toy soldiers in the world. Although the designs and finishes of Britains figures were undoubtedly the finest, the company had many imitators and competitors whose work is of interest to collectors. The increase in the cost of metal after World War II, combined with the development of plastic, led to a decline in hollow-cast production, and in 1967 even Britains turned to the production of plastic figures. There are still, however, many thousands of hollow-cast figures produced by Britains and other makers in the first half of this century to enable new collectors to build up interesting and unusual displays at reasonable prices.

NEW TOY SOLDIERS

Although the large-scale production of toy soldiers is now dominated by plastic, some manufacturers have taken account of the interest of adult collectors in toy soldiers, and several companies now produce accurate models aimed at the adult market. These figures, made as solids in tin and lead alloys, became successful in the mid-1970s, and although there is no large-scale collectors' market in these figures, as there is for genuine toy soldiers, they have a wide and appreciative following. There are several notable manufacturers in both Europe and the USA, and Britain itself has introduced a range of diecast metal figures, aimed both at collectors and at the souvenir market.

COMPOSITION

Composition substances have been made a variety of ingredients since the earliest times. The word 'composition' has, however, been used to describe a wide range of materials, including papier mâché and carton (a thin cast of compressed paper). Toy makers in Sonneberg used brotteig, a sort of bread dough, to mould dolls' bodies and heads, and it was in Sonneberg, in the first half of the 19th century, that composition (that is, a brotteig-like substance containing rye-flour, plaster, sand and glue) was used in the mass-production of toy soldiers.

Although composition is more difficult to mould than metal, and the smaller figures are, therefore, less detailed, the charm and attractive finish of the early Sonneberg soldiers bring them many admirers. Like good carved wooden soldiers, such figures appeal to both antique collectors and toy soldier collectors, and they are in such short supply that they are also of interest to museums and folk art.

Some of the finest examples of composition armies dating from the first half of the 19th century may be seen in German museums, A few of these are made of such dense material that they resemble earthenware and are much stronger even than the composition used after 1900. To give greater realism, Sonneberg-made mounted soldiers sometimes had springs fixed under the horse's hoofs or under the girth strap to create an illusion of movement, while the bases were occasionally made to resemble stone or grass.

By the end of the 19th century composition was used mainly for the mass-production of cheap figures. In general, it had been superseded by papier mâché for the manufacture of dolls' bodies and heads and by lead for the manufacture of toy soldiers. Sets of rather child-like toy soldiers were made in France, and these are sometimes found in boxed military games or used as targets for shooting practice. Unless the game is specially attractive, these sets hold little attraction for the collectors of toy soldiers, although they are of interest to general toy enthusiasts, who are not concerned with the poor detail.

Composition figures suddenly enjoyed a new lease of life in the early years of the 20th century when a more durable mixture was evolved.

A

Grand Admiral Raeder and General von Blomberg made by Hausser in the late 1930s. These Elastolin figures are on the oval bases used by Hausser.

Sawdust, casein, kaolin and dextrin were mixed with bone glue to make a strong but relatively inexpensive modelling material. The breakthrough was made by Emil Pfeiffer of Vienna in 1895. Pfeiffer owned a company, which traded under the name Tipple-Topple, that made zoo and farm animals, Christmas cribs, railway figures and some cleverly modelled cowboy and Indian scenes. The advertisements claimed that Tipple-Topple specialized in wood and 'papier mâché' animals, but the line drawings of the wares suggest that the animals, cowboys and Indians and the farm buildings the company produced have been mistaken for the Elastolin products of Hausser, the waste sawdust from Pfeiffer's wooden toys going into tpe composition used for the 'papier mâché' pieces.

The figures were made by pressing the pulpy mixture by hand into a two-piece brass mould. More complicated figures or ones with especially thin legs were strengthened by a wire armature, which was inserted at this stage. The two halves of the mould were then pushed together, the stickiness of the composition making additional glue unnecessary. The figures were then 'cooked' in a low-temperature kiln. When they were ready, the edges and joins were neatened, and, as the glue size in the composition acted as an undercoat, paint could be applied directly to the surface.

Max and Otto Hausser had been making similar figures for some time, possibly as early as 1904, although the company, Hausser, was not registered until 1912. The company used for its composition figures the tradename Elastolin, a name that was not officially registered until 1926 but that may have been used for some years before then. In 1925 Pfeiffer's company was sold to Hausser, which moved to Neustadt near Coburg. As late as 1924 Tipple-Topple and Elastolin pieces were being advertised separately, but the figures are so similar that it is possible to distinguish between the two only if they are marked.

During the 1930s Hausser raised the production of military figures to an art, and the company is particularly noted for the 'portrait' pieces of Nazi leaders. Hausser was not alone in using composition however; Lineol and Leyla in Germany and Durso in Belgium also produced well-modelled toy soldiers until the competition posed by plastic injection moulding proved to be too strong.

B

These comparatively large figures – they are 100mm tall – were made by an unknown French manufacturer c.1914. Beautifully detailed and accurately painted, they are unusual in being made of plaster, and they have clearly been played with little for they are in excellent condition.

A

Just a small part of the wide range, said to total more than 3,000 items, of soldiers, cowboys and Indians, Arabs and tradesmen that continues to be made by C.B.G. Mignot.

FRANCE

When a collector finds an unusually well-fashioned figure or a spectacular painted cardboard scene, created with no apparent thought for commercial production, the most likely origin is French.

LUCOTTE

For most collectors of toy soldiers the names Lucotte and Mignot are all important. Lucotte is generally regarded as having been the first maker of solid lead soldiers in

Paris, although the early history of the firm is uncertain; however, it is thought to have been operating at the time of the Revolution in 1789. Lucotte's mark, the letters *L* and *C* separated by the Imperial bee, is found on some superb figures, mostly representations of the French Army of the Revolutionary and First Empire periods. The early figures, which were 52mm (2in) high, must have been expensive toys: each section was separately cast, the parts of the horse and rider then being soldered together. An alloy of lead, tin and antimony was used, which was cheaper than the predominantly tin alloy that was used in Germany.

Writing in 1811, Goethe described French toy soldiers that were round and solid, quite unlike the flats

he was accustomed to seeing at home, and it is clear that by the mid-19th century the fame of Lucotte's 'little men' had spread throughout Europe. Figures that could be lifted off their horses and that were fully three-dimensional pieces must have been irresistible to children, which makes it difficult to understand why Lucotte seems to have disappeared in the early 19th century. A group of French makers, Cuperly, Blondel and Gerbeau, appears to have taken over Lucotte but this firm, C.B.G., was itself acquired by another manufacturer, Mignot, in 1825. C.B.G. Mignot is still operating and can claim the longest unbroken existence of any toy soldier manufacturer, as it traces its origins to Lucotte's operations at the time of the Revolution.

C.B.G. MIGNOT

Until a few years ago Mignot operated from the same premises in the rue Charlot that it had occupied since its foundation. At the time of writing, the business is run from an address in the Latin Quarter of Paris, 14 workers smelting, soldering and painting the soldiers in the traditional manner that means that no two figures are identical. During its long history the company has built up a stock of nearly 3,000 moulds for solid and semi-flat figures, as well as some 800 moulds for the manufacture of traditional flats. Although Mignot is better known for its 54mm solid figures, it also produced an attractive range of 40mm (1½in) semi-flats, including French-Algerian troops and, in 1914, a series of Allied forces including Belgian, Russian and British infantry.

In its own account of its history, C.B.G. Mignot claims that the Lucotte moulds were acquired as recently as 1930. Many collectors, however, believe that Mignot made soldiers from these moulds before that date. On the whole, Lucotte figures are better modelled than those by Mignot – the arms were cast separately and located on lugs before soldering, while the arms of Mignot figures were bent into position and the weapons soldered on. Lucotte's cavalry horses have longer tails than those by Mignot, and they have separate reins. Examples of marked Lucotte figures are extremely rare, and although experienced collectors may be able to distinguish between Lucotte and Mignot pieces, novice collectors should always seek the advice of long-established and reputable dealers.

In the 20th century Mignot became more energetic in its export policy, and soldiers in the company's distinctive bright red boxes with the C.B.G. labels are as likely to be found in the US as in France. Most of the figures are made to the standard 54mm scale, but some other, rarer sizes have been produced. The presentation of the figures is particularly

French in style, and some are packaged in tiered boxes with trees, buildings and other accessories. Unlike Britains cavalry horses, which were made to balance on their slender legs, Mignot horses are fixed to bases, which does make them easier to display.

GERMANY

Until World War I Germany supplied the children of the world with toys of all kinds, including metal flats, most of which still represented the traditional colours of the regiments that had participated in the Napoleonic Wars, Despite the success of Georg Heyde in exporting solid toy soldiers to Britain and the US, German children seemed to prefer the flat figures and, to a lesser extent, the semi-flat soldiers, and their production continues in Germany to this day.

ALLGEYER

Johann Christian Allgeyer, who was based in Fürth, near to Nuremberg, was established as a manufacturer of flat figures by 1800. His son, Johann Friedrich (1821–76), began to use the family name on the bases of figures that represented Greek and Roman battle scenes, medieval figures

B

and soldiers from the Napoleonic Wars. At the Great Exhibition in London in 1851 the Allgeyers showed semi-flat figures, well before any other manufacturers had adopted the style. Allgeyer's figures were packed in marked boxes, which helps collectors in dating and attributing the many unmarked pieces that are found.

AMMON

Some of the most desirable of all toy soldiers are the large, individual figures such as the knights on horseback made by Ammon of Nuremberg. Johann Wolfgang Ammon, a master

B

These Mignot figures are modern reissues, dating from c.1960, made using moulds that were originally produced c.1900. The soldiers, which are 54mm tall, represent a horse-drawn gun and supply cart of the Union Army during the American Civil War.

A

This group of knights, made by Ammon of Nuremberg c.1840, is part of a tournament setting. The figures are decorated in gold and red, and both the visors and arms of the figures are articulated.

pewterer, is believed to have made a number of flats at the end of the 18th century, basing his designs on the soldiers of the Napoleonic Wars. Johann was succeeded by his son Christoph (who became a master pewterer in 1836) and later, by his grandson Christian, who continued to run the firm until 1921. The marks on some of their fine-quality soldiers include *C.A., C. Ammon* and *C. Ammon in Nurnberg*. These figures, with their beautiful decoration, were made as part of a large tournament, and they are unusual in that both the arms and the visors are articulated. They may be seen in the National Museum in Nuremberg together with various standing figures, such as heralds and drummers. The original setting must have been full of colour and movement, as it included musicians, court ladies and a posturing

king, and it was made c.1840, when the production of flats was at its peak.

Like most other German toy soldier manufacturers, Ammon started to produce semi-flats in the 1860s, manufacturing tournaments, Austrian lancers and Turkish soldiers in quantity. Among the many engravers working for Ammon at this time was the ambitious Ernst Heinrichsen (1806–88), who founded his own factory in 1839.

BERGMANN

The company A.J., C.T. and Charles Bergmann was based in Strasbourg between 1800 and 1904, and manufactured flats. It was the most important employer in the town at the time.

DU BOIS

A company was established in Hanover in 1830 by J.E. du Bois, who had been an engraver for Wegmann (q.v.). The main output was of flats, but a few, now very rare, solids were also made. The founder was succeeded by his son, Ernst, and the company continued to manufacture toy soldiers until the end of the 19th century. The figures produced included troops modelled on the Hanoverian Arm, Napoleonic troops and both infantry and cavalry men from the Roman era. Some of the pieces, all of which are of excellent quality, were marked *J.E. du Bois*, but most were unsigned.

DENECKE

This company, which was based in Brunswick, produced flats in the early 19th century. Part of the business was sold by the founder's widow to Wegmann (q.v.) in 1820, while the remainder was taken over by Wollrathe Denecke in 1842 and later sold, in 1870, to L. Link. The company's output included soldiers from the Napoleonic wars and Brunswick militia, and some of the figures were to the Nuremberg scale of 30mm. Figures made by Wollrath are marked *W.D.* The workshop eventually passed to Bernhard Borning, and it may now be seen in the Stadtisches Museum, Brunswick.

DORFLER

Hans Dorfler was manufacturing toy soldiers in Fürth between c.1890 and 1945. The company made semi-flats and solids, basing many of its figures on the armies of World War I. It also produced some large figures based on the pre-World War I German Army, which included cavalry men that could be detached from the horses.

HAFFNER

Johann Haffner founded the company in Fürth in 1838. He was

B

A military parade of
flats, made by the
Berlin manufacturer
G. Sohlke during the
first quarter of the
19th century.

succeeded by his son, and it was later known as United Toy Factories and based in Nuremberg, where it had taken over the company owned by Christian Schweigger. Haffner produced the usual range of figures based on the armies of the Franco-German War and also some French dragoons, but was unusual in manufcturing flats, semi-flats and solids. The company was eventually taken over by Albrecht Stadtler, an engraver for Heinrichsen (q.v.)

HASELBACH

This large company was manufacturing toy soldiers in Berlin between c.1848 and 1900, and it is said to have been used between 5,000 and 6,000 different moulds. The figures were made to a scale of 40mm – sometimes known as the

Berlin scale – and they represented the armies of the Thirty Years' War and the Crusades. There was also an unusual series of sailors. The figures were sold in boxes with a large *H* on the lids.

HAUSSER

Composition came into its own in the early years of the 20th century when Hausser started to produce figures under its tradename Elastolin. The date of the first Elastolin soldier is not known, but catalogues produced in the 1920s have survived, and it is clear that by 1924 the company was offering a range of 65mm (2½in) and 105mm (4in) figures. One boxed set contained ten men, two officers, a colour bearer and a striped sentry box (made of cardboard). The advertisement claimed that Elastolin

soldiers were available 'in all positions and of all nations', but in fact, most of the company's figures were based on the German Army and were adapted for special orders. By 1924 Hausser was producing English and Danish guards at the march, as well as troops from the Indian, Greek, Austrian and French armies. The company's range of Highlanders was especially popular in the UK, and they are the most often found Elastolin figures there.

Hausser's takeover of Pfeiffer's Tipple-Topple company in 1925 proved to be extremely important as Pfeiffer had used not only composition for figures but also tinplate for vehicles. Today, the most keenly collected of all Hausser's products are the ones that combine the two materials – portrait figures seated in finely made tinplate cars. Among the most desirable of all are Nazi figures in appropriate vehicles.

There is a tradition among collectors of Elastolin figures that Hausser had to show all its personality models to the government before they could be put into production, and some of them are certainly idealized. Porcelain heads were used on a number of the figures, since the bisque gave a more flattering, natural appearance to the face, and these figures are now extremely expensive. Figures of Hitler himself were, of course, produced, but Hausser's output included many prominent personalities – Benito Mussolini, for instance – and members of the Nazi party in their uniforms – Hermann Goering and Rudolf Hess, for example.

HEINRICHSEN

At first Heinrichsen produced flats in a variety of sizes. He was a skilled engraver and a good businessman, and his work quickly attracted international interest – Tsar Nicholas I, for instance, ordered a set of mounted Russian guards. Other figures included Prussian guards, Napoleon I and the Old Guard, the 1856 expedition to China and scenes from the Crimean War. The firm's rapid expansion was aided by the growth of railway communications and the increasing wealth of the middle- and artisan classes, who were now, for the first

A

B

time, able to buy toys for their children. Probably as some form of promotional aid, Heinrichsen wrote a book, *Kriegsspiel (War-games)*, which was aimed at children. He also sold some of his sets of soldiers with paper guidelines for setting out effective battles.

At this time, toy soldiers tended to be made in a variety of sizes, and although most were between 50 and 60mm (2–2⅜in), some were smaller and some were considerably larger. This variation in size made it difficult for children to set out convincing battle scenes – battles from the Napoleonic Wars must have been difficult to stage with flimsy tin flats ranged against solid wooden figures. In 1848 Heinrichsen standardized his soldiers to a height of 30mm (1⅛), and this scale, known as the Nuremberg or Heinrichsen scale, was adopted by many of his fellow manufacturers.

The establishment of the Nuremberg scale helped boost not only Heinrichsen's own business but also that of his rivals, who imitated his engravings and offered almost identical sets. Ernst's son Wilhelm took over the company in 1869 and continued to produce contemporary and historic pieces; scenes from the Trojan War, the Crusades and the Napoleonic Wars were exported all over the world in characteristic grey or brown cardboard boxes.

Ernst Wilhelm Heinrichsen, another member of the family and a skilled engraver, took charge of the company in 1908 and introduced even more designs, some created by Ludwig Frank (1870–1957), one of the greatest soldier artists.

Heinrichsen's work is marked *E.H., E. Heinrichsen* or *W. Heinrichsen*. Although many of the figures are stiff and somewhat reminiscent of old toy-theatre prints, they have great appeal for collectors, who like the artistry and are not concerned with realism. All the flats are fragile and the colour is easily chipped, but fortunately a large number has survived, and, apart from the larger sets, which command high prices, they are still available relatively cheaply.

A

These fine quality Belgian infantry men, which are 70mm tall, were made by Haffner c.1910. Johann Haffner founded the company that bears his name in Fürth in 1838, but, as the box here indicates, it was taken over and moved to Nuremberg.

B

These small figures – they are 30mm tall – are known to collectors as 'tinies'. They were made in Germany by an unknown manufacturer in the 1890s, and they are typical of the toy soldiers that were used by Victorian children for their war-games.

C

A splendid group of the Indian Camel Corps made by Heyde c.1900. The presence of the original box adds greatly to the value and desirability of the group.

C

HEYDE

Toy soldier production in Germany tended to be dominated by flats and, to a lesser extent, by semi-flats. Few solid figures were produced. In the early 1870s, however, probably encouraged by the success enjoyed by Lucotte and Mignot, Georg Heyde of Dresden began to produce solid lead figures.

The company was known to have been in operation by 1872, although there is a tradition that it had been producing figures as early as the 1830s. In the 1870s, Heyde introduced a range of attractive solid figures, and the company quickly became one of the most prolific producers of toy soldiers, exporting huge quantities all over the world.

Heyde's figures are found in a wide range of scales, although 43mm (1¾in) and 52mm (2in) were the most frequently used. The smaller figures sometimes look rather dumpy and badly proportioned, and occasionally Heyde used flat tin guns with coloured flashes of fire with his solid figures, because of this design technique that makes some of the pieces look older than they actually are; this should not mislead the amateur collector.

Among the company's vast range were soldiers from many countries and many periods. North American Indians were made alongside Roman legionaries, and one of the most eye-catching sets is the 1910 Durbar, which includes colourful rajas and splendid elephants. One of Heyde's sets, the Triumph of Germanicus, which contains some 200 figures, is a tour de force of toy soldier manufacturing.

Collectors who are more interested in military models than in toy soldiers sometimes find that Heyde figures lack realism because of their poor proportions and because so many sizes were made. The figures are also fragile, and thin guns and swords are often bent completely out of shape due to the delicate nature of the materials used. But these faults are, in fact, part of the charm of these

pieces. Unlike other manufacturers, Heyde offered children soldiers going about their everyday chores in interesting and individual poses; the company also provided complete scenes, including trees and piles of rocks, so that imaginative displays could be mounted – tiger shooting in India; soldiers striking camp; soldiers feeding horses, map reading or launching observation balloons; and massed

groups of soldiers in great ceremonial parades. Such diversity was very popular with children.

By 1900 Heyde was the chief supplier of toy soldiers to the US. The company also enjoyed great success in the UK, but it never succeeded in overcoming the popularity of flats and semi-flats in Germany itself. Its output continued unabated until World War II, when the factory and its records were lost.

Heyde produced such a vast range of toy soldiers that is tempting to attribute almost any unmarked solid figure to the company. It should, however, be borne in mind that other companies, in Spain and Denmark, as well as in Germany, were producing interesting and attractive solids at the same time. If there is any doubt about a manufacturer, always seek the advice of a reputable dealer.

HILPERT

Every collector of flats dreams of finding a figure marked by a member of the Hilpert family, although these are now so rare that a chance discovery is unlikely. Johann Gottfried Hilpert (1732–1801), the son of a tinsmith, was born in Coburg and in 1750 moved to Nuremberg where he established the manufac-

ture of tin soldiers as an industry in its own right.

Although early figures by Hilpert were made in large quantities, few are now available for collectors as so many are in museums; they are marked on the bases with *H. Hilpert* or *J.G. Hilpert*. Several generations of the Hilpert family were associated with the firm, which produced not only strikingly modelled soldiers but also animals, circus figures and scenes. One of the most famous soldiers is the 15cm (6in) equestrian portrait of Frederick II, which was produced in 1777 in two versions, the first marked *H.* the second *J.H.* Frederick II's successes in the Seven Years War (1756–63) had increased interest in all things military, and Hilpert was quick to expand his Nuremberg workshop and develop mass-production techniques for the

B

cheaper soldiers, which were exported throughout Europe in chip-wood boxes. Potsdam guards, and French, Russian and Turkish soldiers were engraved with artistic assurance, and some of the finer figures seem more in the nature of ornaments than playthings. The model of the Prince de Ligne issued in 1778, is widely considered to be an especially fine example of toy soldier manufacture.

LINEOL

Hausser was not the only company to create contemporary portraits. Its great rival was Lineol, which produced models standing on square or rectangular bases, unlike Hausser's round or oval bases. The composition used seems to be almost identical to Elastolin. Lineol's trademark was three marching geese with their heads in the air, and the company's toy soldiers are marked *Lineol/Germany* under the bases. Hausser seems to have produced more figures than Lincol, but Lineol's representations of leading Nazi figures are generally considered to be superior to its competitor's products. Lineol also made a number of rare non-German characters, including the Duke of Windsor.

Like Hausser, Lineol produced a range of toy soldiers, many to the 70mm (2¾in) scale, but larger (100mm, 4in) and smaller (40 and 60mm, 1½ and 2⅛in) versions were also made. The company disappeared during World War II, but it has recently resumed production using the old moulds.

The other main German manufacturers of composition figures were Leyla and Durolin, which was taken over by Hausser in 1936.

RIECHE

Founded in Hanover in 1806, Gebrüder Rieche made flats based on a wide range of subjects, including the Indian Mutiny, the battle of Waterloo and the Conquest of Mexico. It also produced some portrait figures, such as the Duke of Wellington, which were engraved by Franz Rieche and designed by Richard Knotel. The company ceased operations in 1936.

SCHWEIZER

Adam Schweizer, a tin founder, established a company in Diessen-Amersee in 1796. By 1821 it was

making flats, which were sold by the pound and were probably unpainted. The figures included representations of infantry men, Bavarian dragoons and German sailors, and they were much in the style of the early cheap tin toys. The company is still in existence and produces a range of flats and semi-flats in various sizes of both military and civilian subjects.

SOHLKE

At the Great Exhibition in London in 1851 G. Sohlke, a toy manufacturer from Berlin, was awarded a medal for his display of lead soldiers and figures representing a military review held at Windsor during a visit of the Empress of Russia to England. Sohlke, whose figures were described as 'pewter toys', was one of a number of Prussian manufacturers specializing in the casting of intricately designed outline figures that were painted in such minute detail that their beauty can be fully appreciated only with the aid of a magnifying glass.

Sohlke originally specialized in the production of flats. His display at the 1855 Paris Exposition, a representation of the Battle of Alma in 'tin soldiers', was described as: 'a

A

Boxed sets of toy soldiers always attract interest, but this Britains set 2112, the Band of the US Marine Corps, a magnificent 25-piece group, is especially desirable as it has never been removed from its box.

B

Britains set 79, the Royal Naval Landing Party, contains a petty officer and eight running men with a limber and gun. It was first issued in 1897 and continued to appear in Britains' catalogue until 1963.

C

Before World War I Britains made models of many foreign armies. Set 175, the Austro-Hungarian Lancers, contained an officer, trumpeter and three troopers. It was based on Britains own set of Scots Greys, and many of the overseas armies tended to be less detailed than the models of the British Army.

complicated work, full of movement and interest. The attitudes of the people are of such naturalness as one rarely finds in this type of toy.' Such prestige pieces were not typical of the firm's work. In the 1860s Sohlke introduced the slightly round semi-flats, and most of the later output was of only average quality. The firm went out of business in 1872.

WEGMANN

Carl Wegmann, who was based in Brunswick, made flats from c.1820 to 1825, when he was succeeded by his son, Theodor. The company used moulds made by Denecke, and the figures were marked *C.W.* on the bases. The pieces were based on troops from the Napoleonic wars, Prussian infantry and figures from the Franco-German war. The company was later acquired by Bernhard Borning.

WEYGANG

A maker of flats, who worked from c.1820 until his death in 1872, Carl Weygang was based in Göttingen. He was succeeded by his son, Victor, who worked until 1919. The figures were representations of Hanoverian infantry and civilian characters, and they were signed *C.W.G.*, *C.W.* or *W.* occasionally the full surname was used. The moulds are now in the Göttingen Museum.

BRITAINS

It was in Great Britain that the most realistic soldiers, meeting the demand from children and war games enthusiasts, emerged. British production of toys had never compared with that of Germany and France, but by the end of the 19th century some makers were making efforts to capture a larger part of the market. William Britain (1828–1906) was typical of this more progressive breed of businessman and made a variety of toys and window-display pieces that almost qualify as automata. His eldest son, who was interested in the various methods of creating model soldiers, devised a hollow-cast process that revolutionized production.

The first Britains soldiers appeared on the market in 1893, and the success of the venture was assured once Gamages, the London store that supplied toys by mail-order all over the world, marketed them as 'English-made'. This was a useful selling ploy in the days of Empire and became increasingly so as anti-German feeling developed just before World War I.

B

Hollow-cast figures, being standard-sized, were ideal for war games: the men were always 54mm high with complementary horses and equipment. Accuracy of uniform was especially important, a feature that the colourful German soldiers had often lacked. Britains soldiers were ideal for the nursery, cast from alloy and therefore relatively light. The first to be marketed were Life Guards with an officer and four troopers, quickly followed by subjects like the Boer Cavalry, the 5th Dragoon Guards and the Royal Fusiliers.

The characteristic bright red, almost lacquer-like boxes that Britains used have excited recipients ever since they first appeared under Christmas trees and it is soldiers in the original packaging that are most coveted by collectors. The first special display boxes were sold from 1894 and were made up from four existing sets, which made them expensive. A reporter in *Athletic Sports, Games and Toys* (October, 1895) commented that the firm had already placed on the market more than 20 sets of soldiers from the regiments of the British Army and that the Royal Horse Artillery, the Regimental Band of the Line and the Full Band of the Coldstream Guards were to be added to the list.

Britain's advertising literature claimed that the soldiers were produced entirely by British labour and that only innocuous paints and spirit varnish was used in their decoration. Some of the large presentation cases were very expensive and contained two inside trays for the display of as many as 275 pieces of cavalry and infantry. Alongside the basic soldier

C

A

Britains set 39a, the Royal Horse Artillery in service dress, is an unusual variant on the more normal full-dress version. This set was exactly the same as its full-dress counterpart, although painted in khaki and with heads with peaked caps, as were the Royal Field Artillery, the Army Medical Corps Ambulance and the Army Service Corps Wagon. The set illustrated was made c.1920, and such sets always attract strong interest among collectors.

B

This painted wooden army barracks is particularly well equipped and contains hollow-cast soldiers marked *Johillco* and *John Hill & Co.*

sets there were pieces such as the horse-drawn ambulance of the Royal Medical Corps. In addition to soldiers, there were railway scenes with passengers and luggage and sets of football teams like Sheffield Wednesday and Aston Villa. There was even a model of the Football Association cup in silver or gilt.

Foreign armies, such as the Japanese infantry, the Austro-Hungarian lancers and the United States infantry, were sold in attractive boxed sets. Red Indians, the German Army, Arab horsemen, the Second Bombay Native Infantry and the Gurkha Rifles all appeared in the early years of production. The paper box labels that described the contents were individually designed for the same sets. Titles such as Dr Jameson and the African Mounted Infantry, the Turkish Infantry and Africa's Savage Warriors, Zulus all evoke the past and are collected by military as well as toy enthusiasts.

Britains attention to accuracy was always paramount. In 1900 one customer complained that the rifle

regiment was modelled with rifles at the slope instead of 'at the trail' and this was corrected in subsequent issues. After World War II, an American colonel wrote to say that the lance heads of US Marine Forces were silver, not gold, and this was at once corrected. Since the company has continued to produce toys for such a long period, there is an abundance of material for the collector's market and the price range is very wide. Worn or slightly damaged individual figures can still be purchased for next to nothing, while an 1893 set of the Royal Scots Greys, with plug shoulders and contained in the original box, could set you back some £3,000 ($5,000). Condition is extremely important, as the more sophisticated collectors require sets that are near-perfect in well-preserved boxes. Prices at the top end of the soldier market can be somewhat unpredictable. Occasionally a figure or a set will hit the headlines, yet a year later similar examples will sell for much less. This is usually because several sets appear on the market in the wake

of the publicity, and it quickly becomes evident that the toy is not so rare as was originally believed.

UNITED KINGDOM

The pre-eminence of Britains in the field of toy soldier production should not be allowed to obscure the achievements of the many other companies that were quick to adopt hollow-casting techniques and follow Britains lead in producing attractive and, now, highly collectable figures. Manufacturers produced a wide range of soldiers, and there were sets and single figures designed to appeal to every pocket. Most UK manufacturers exported toy soldiers throughout the world, especially to the English-speaking countries.

C.D. ABEL & CO.

One of the many firms in north London, C.D. Abel & Co., which was in production from *c.*1898 to 1914, made some 40mm hollow-cast figures as well as a range of 54mm and slightly smaller (50mm) soldiers. There was an extensive series of regiments of the British Army in drill positions

ing a B.M.C. series with over 200 sets. These included Life Guards in 1908, Foot Guards, which were 50mm tall, in 1905 and some fine Dragoon Guards in 1906. The company continued to produce good quality, well-made figures, including some excellent cowboys and Indians, but it went out of business in the 1930s, during the Depression.

pool, Lancashire. In 1950 Cherilea took over the Fylde Manufacturing Co. and may also have taken over the moulds of Monarch, when that company ran into difficulties in the early 1960s. Later production, until 1977, was of rather over-sized plastic figures, which, while not particularly accurately uniformed, were in dramatic poses.

and some early 20th-century infantry. The figures are unmarked, but many have an inset brass socket so that they could be used in a parade-drill game patented by Abel in 1902. Some of the earlier figures were adapted and re-issued with re-moulded bases to accommodate the brass socket and locating blocks.

B.M.C./SOLDARMA

William Pickford founded the Britannia Model Co. in 1919, producing a range of large-scale models. John Hill & Co. had already registered Britannia Brand as a trademark and promptly sued Pickford, who, by 1920 was using the name Soldarma. In 1922, however, Pickford was market-

CHARBENS

Another north London company founded by ex-employees of Britains, Charbens, which began operating in 1926, produced rather poor quality, hollow-cast figures as well as some more attractive civilian vehicles. Production continued until 1968, although after World War II the company used plastic, adapting old hollow-cast moulds to injection moulding techniques.

CHERILEA

In 1948 Wilfred Cherrington (a freelance master figure designer) and John Lee (an ex-sales manager of John Hill & Co.) started to produce simple hollow-cast figures in Black-

CRESCENT

In 1922 Henry G. Eagles and Arthur A. Schneider founded the Crescent Toy Company in their north London workshop. They seem to have bought most of the moulds they used from other companies, and their soldiers have no coherent style. The company's hollow-cast soldiers and cowboys sold for 1d each and appear to have been aimed at the lower end of the market. It included a large number of British regiments in its range, and in 1948, to accompany its excellent series of die-cast artillery pieces, it introduced detachable riders. During World War II the company almost ceased trading, but in 1949 it moved to Cwmcarn in Wales and continued production until 1978.

J.W. Roden, the technical director, introduced new tooling and production methods for the die-cast toys and designed machines for plastic soldiers, although these were not as successful as the hollow-cast metal figures had been.

ERECTO TOY CO. LTD

Arthur Fry founded the Erecto Toy Co. with his brother and R. Hollyer in 1915 to produce hollow-cast 48mm and 54mm figures. The company made many World War I figures in lively and original poses. Marketed as Fry's Fighting Soldiers, the box labels claimed that they were 'manufactured in London by British labour and British capital'. Despite the innovative figures, the company went out of business in the 1920s.

JOHN HILL & CO.

Founded in Islington, north London, c.1900 by the Wood brothers, this company is perhaps the best known UK manufacturer of hollow-cast toy soldiers after Britains, John Wood, an ex-employee of Britains, established the company as a direct competitor with Britains, producing single figures in great quantities. to sell to UK and US retailers. Boxed sets are, therefore, rare. Hill produced some 42mm (1½in) figures as well as the standard 54mm figures, which were marked Johillco, the name by which the company is often known. Although of variable quality, the best Hill figures, especially those of the British Army, compare favourably with Britains. After World War II the company moved to Burnley in Lancashire, where it experimented with plastic figures, marked *Hilco*, which are rare. The factory closed in 1960.

REKA LTD

'Types of the British Army, Correct models. Well finished, London made . . . Special value boxes 1d. Cav-

alry and infantry, gilt and painted.' So ran an advertisement in 1908 for Reka's toy soldiers. The company had been founded in Islington, north London, by a toy wholesaler, CW Baker, who offered not only soldiers but a variety of metal figures and games. Some Reka figures are of high quality, and a few are dated. Most could be bought separately, and they therefore had great success in poorer areas. The boxed sets contained six infantrymen, all with movable arms, with the name of the regiment printed on the inside of the box lid. In the 1930s Baker sold his moulds to Crescent.

JAMES S RENVOIZE & SONS

Renvoize was a successful wholesaler of German-made solids (probably by Heyde and Heinrich) who countered Britain's success with hollow-cast figures by, it is thought, getting his existing suppliers to produce hollow-cast figures based on Britain's designs. This piracy led Britains to copyright and date its figures in 1900. Between 1899 and the outbreak of World War I, Renvoize offered a wide range of well-made and nicely presented figures that differed little from Britains in appearance but were cheaper. Renvoize did not resume the importation of lead toys after 1918.

TIMPO

Toy Importers Co. – Timpo – which produced toy soldiers between 1943 and 1979, was one of the most successful manufacturers of hollow-cast figures to become established after World War II. In addition to the standard scale figures, it produced some 60mm figures in a wide range of subjects, ranging from Romans to US combat troops and including King Arthur and his Knights. From the mid-1950s it used plastic in a new range of subjects. Timpo pieces have *England* on the backs of the figures.

A

UNITED STATES

'J ust arrived' was the popular advertising slogan of toy sellers in the 18th and 19th centuries, when almost all the well-made pieces on offer were imported from Europe. So many soldiers were shipped across the Atlantic that today collectors are offered equally good selections of toy soldiers in New York as in Paris or London. On the whole it was not until the early years of the 20th century that US toy soldiers appeared in quantity as cast iron had been the preferred material.

AMERICAN SOLDIER COMPANY

Founded by CW Beiser in Glendale, New York, about 1900, the American Soldier Company made hollow-cast figures so similar to Britains that they are almost copies. Britains own set 149, issued in 1907 and comprising a mounted officer, a foot officer, a colour bearer, a trumpeter, three men at the trail, three men at the slope, two gunners and a gun, was, was available as a 'Military Display and Game'. The game consisted of a card with hinged metal clips into which the bases of the soldiers could be slotted. When the figures had been 'shot down', they could be flipped back into position. Perhaps because of the variety of 'weapons' used, this game is extremely rare. Beiser, who had invented the game, also offered it with other types of soldiers, including some figures in the uniform of the Spanish-American War of 1898, and these may have been made by Barclay.

BARCLAY

Among the most eagerly collected of all US-made soldiers are the pieces, known as dime-store figures, that were sold in the 'five and dime stores' throughout the 1930s. These soldiers, at 3¼in (83mm), are rather larger than European soldiers, but they were hollow-cast, and they represent an immediately identifiable type of toy soldier.

Barclay, a company that specialized in dime-store figures, was established in New Jersey by Leon Donze in the 1920s, and it produced 54mm and 60mm figures, some of which had movable arms. The dime-store figures were, however, the ones that caught the public's imagination. Although, their chunkiness and round – or 'pod' – feet make them appear somewhat clumsy, the wide assortment of US Army and Navy troops in a variety of active and realistic poses brought them a wide and appreciative following.

COMET METAL PRODUCTS

This New York company, which was founded about 1918 by Abraham Slonim, produced a series of 55mm (2⅛in) solid lead figures, which are not considered especially appealing, as well as some flats and semi-flats. During World War II it was an important maker of recognition models for the armed services. In 1938 it produced the Brigadier range, which is distinguished by thick bases, but it is perhaps best known for its co-operation in a scheme to get European industry on its feet after World War II, when, in association with Curt Wennberg, the Swedish Naval Attaché in the US, who helped to attract toy soldier designer Holger Eriksson, it founded a company called Authenticast in Eire. After the failure of Authenticast in 1950, Comet continued to produce soldiers in New York and Wennberg moved to South Africa, where he founded Swedish African Engineers.

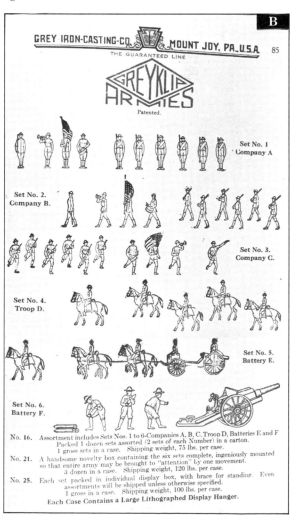

GREY IRON CASTING COMPANY

Founded in Mount Joy, Pennsylvania, at the turn of the century, the Grey Iron Casting Company was unusual in its use of cast iron to make toy soldiers. The company's 1915 catalogue shows soldiers, marketed under the tradename Greyklip Armies, in contemporary US service dress. One group, packed in a novelty box that contained the six Greyklip sets, was arranged in such a way that the entire army could be brought to attention by one movement. In the 1930s the company brought out a range entitled Uncle Sam's Defenders, which incorporated 40mm (1½in) figures of US World War I servicemen. An earlier range, also in 40mm scale, had been in nickel-plate, but the company returned to cast iron in 1933 with a range of figures in the dime-store scale of 3¼in (83mm). The figures have some curiosity value because of the late use of cast iron, but on the whole they are of limited appeal and sell comparatively cheaply.

MANOIL

Barclay's main competitor in the production of dime-store figures

was Manoil, which was founded in the early 1930s. Manoil figures are normally marked *Manoil* and they tend to be posed in rather more individualistic ways than Barclay figures. Both companies also produced vehicles and accessories, although these tend to be too small to look realistic with the soldiers.

Dime-store figures are rarely offered for sale outside the US, where they can command very high prices.

MARX

No discussion of US toy soldiers would be complete without a reference to Louis Marx, whose range of sets of unpainted plastic soldiers, sold with tinplate and plastic accessories, was not only hugely successful in the US but also sold so well in the UK that it largely replaced the hand-painted plastic figures that had dominated the market in the 1950s. Founded in New York in the 1920s, Marx became the largest toy manufacturer in the world, buying out many other toy makers.

A

B

C

Scale

The height of toy soldiers is usually given in millimetres and measured from the top of the head (without any head gear) to the soles of the feet (that is, excluding the base).

Toy soldiers were originally produced in a bewildering variety of sizes, although the early German manufacturers of flats tended to concentrate on figures that were between 50 and 60mm (2–2⅛in) high. Even after 1848, when Heinrichsen standardized his toy soldiers to a scale of 30mm (1⅛in), and although many German manufacturers followed his example, there was still a vast range of sizes on offer.

Building up a coherent collection and being able to mount satisfying displays clearly demand that most of the figures conform to a fairly standard scale. Scale can be expressed as a fraction – for example, a man who is 6 feet tall represented in a scale of 1 : 32 would be 72/32 or 2⅛in – or 54mm – high.

This size, known as standard size, which corresponded to gauge 1 toy railways, was used by Britains for most of its figures, and it was also quickly adopted by Britains' main competitors.

A

B

C

CHAPTER

4

Figures and tableaux that were made from a mixture of

materials, such as papier mâché, wood and metal, were

labour intensive to produce

Tin Toys *and made commercial sense*

only if they were

manufactured for the luxury market. As work forces,

especially in Germany, became more organized and

demanded better pay and working conditions, traditional

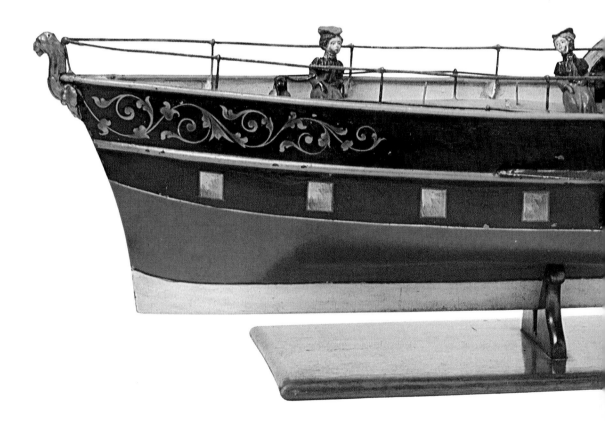

A

This elegant late 19th-century clockwork paddle-steamer, *La Sirène,* may have been made by Maltête & Parent, a company founded in Paris in the 19th century by C.H. Maltête and G. Parent. It manufactured a wide range of mechanical toys, including sculling boats, submarines and floor-running railways as well as some novelty toys, such as fish and lizards.

toys, largely made by domestic out-workers, were gradually replaced by factory products. By the mid-19th century, children were also becoming more selective, and the old folk-style coach and horses carved from wood no longer satisfied a child who was interested in the fine detail of contemporary transport, detail that could be reproduced only in a material strong enough to be cut in fine outline, embossed and twisted to create a realistic sleigh, brougham or boat.

Many of the small toy-making firms, especially in France, worked in mean backrooms, converting scrap metal into quaint, cleverly made pieces. Toys of this type, including a large number of kitchen pieces, are rarely marked, but they were made in quantity in Britain and the United States, as well as the more established centres of Paris and Nuremberg-

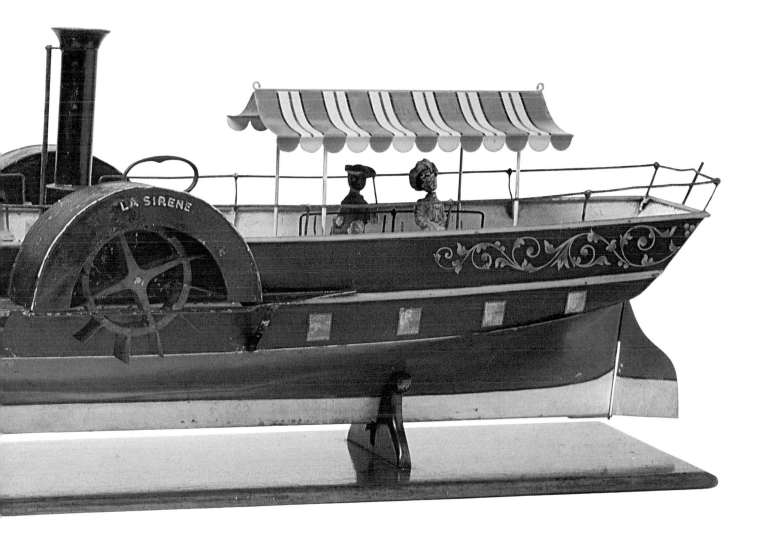

Fürth. Many tin toys continued to be made in small single-family workshops until World War I. Such work was never marked; it has to be valued purely on appearance and quality of workmanship.

The majority of metal toy-making firms had factories that were divided into sheet-metal rooms, tool rooms, moulding and pressing areas, and painting rooms. The most skilled, and the most highly paid, craftsmen were those who lined the detail on coaches and motor vehicles. By 1900 the large German firms had steam and electrical workshops, packing rooms and stores, as well as studios where the toys and their packages were designed.

The commercial production of metal toys began in Germany in the 18th century, but the great advance came after 1850, thanks to continual improvements in machinery and communications. Mass-production was not possible until factories were powered by steam and, later, electricity; nor was it possible to deliver up-to-date models to the retailers until the railway system was well established. The more complex toys, because of the expensive tooling of their parts, were not suitable for making in family workshops. They were the province of the large factories, which were proud to mark their work. The Germans were particularly skilled in merchandising and were quick to see the importance of adapting exported toys: Nuremberg-made buses and delivery vehicles carry British or American advertisements, and ships bear names that were familiar in London nurseries.

Despite improvements in decorating techniques, which made metal toys more colourful, the majority, especially in the United States, were still hand painted in 1900, although the surface was sometimes further decorated with stencils, transfers or sprayed effects. This continued use of what were really outdated techniques gives many toys a deceptive antique appearance. All the manufacturers cloaked their methods of printing on tin in great secrecy, and it is still impossible to know exactly how some effects were achieved. Printing in colours by a lithographic process had been in use since the mid-19th century, but it was not in general use on tinplate toys until 1900. The old lithographic process, involving the use of colour on a stone, was not suitable for printing on metal, but rapid improvements in specialized techniques after 1875, especially in the field of roller printing, made the process viable. It became much cheaper after 1900, when metal lithoplates were used instead of stones, and even more economical in the 1920s, when photo-lithography began to be used.

A

A spirit-fired, live-steam road roller made by Bing. The single cylinder drives a fly-wheel to maintain momentum. This hand-painted toy is based on a German prototype of a kind seldom seen in other countries, and it is typical of the fine and interesting toys made by Bing before World War I.

A

B

Märklin used a wealth of detail in the pressing and hand painting of this four-seater open touring motor. Four separate paint colours were used as well as the gold coach lining. The lamp at the front is nickel plated, and the tyres are white rubber. Altogether it is a most striking – and desirable – toy.

C

This model of a Mercedes tourer was made by Carette c.1907. It is unusual to find examples complete with sidelights, which are rather reminiscent of carriage lamps, and with headlights.

C

B

Sämmtliche Wägen mit Blechpferden, Kopf und Füsse bewegend.

HORSE-DRAWN TRANSPORT

The earliest highly collectable toys represent the various types of horse-drawn transport. Some of these pieces are surprisingly large and have perfectly constructed detail in leather, brass and fabric, which brings them close in spirit to automata. Calèches, mail coaches, broughams and hackney carriages were made in Germany and France, some of the finest measuring 24in (60cm) in length. These were expen-

sive toys, and the detail was finely executed, as the aim was to create a realistic model. The horses are sometimes made of wood or skin over wood, papier mâché composition or even zinc; the trappings and harness are often beautifully made miniatures. Some of the paintwork is also highly detailed, with enamelled and lacquered panels, those on coaches sometimes embellished with a coat of arms or a monogram. The superb quality of these horse-drawn toys can also be seen in the makers' attention to specific effects, such as embossed springs or satin-upholstered interiors.

Occasionally carriages are found with their original drivers and passengers, whose costumes provide one of the best methods of dating

the toys. Some of the most elegant date from the early 18th century period and are, obviously, fairly rare. Curiously, despite their high quality and early date, toys of this type sell for less than the motor cars made by firms such as Märklin after 1900.

Carriages, as well as furniture for dolls' houses, were produced by one of the oldest-established German toy makers, Ludwig Lutz of Ellwangen. This firm, founded about 1846, specialized in toys of high quality but somewhat fragile construction; they appear never to have been marked. Some of the finest early horse-drawn toys are often attributed to Rock & Graner, founded in Biberach an der Riss in 1813. This Württemberg firm produced toys at a small factory and used a variety of metals, including

A

Fine models of vehicles of all kinds have always been favourites with children and parents alike. This page from the catalogue of a Nuremberg toy seller dates from 1877 and shows just a few of the immense range of toys available at the time. Despite the advent of rail travel, horse-drawn coaches remained popular.

B

The fine detailing on this tinplate phaeton (four-wheeled carriage) makes it extremely attractive. Although it is unmarked, it was made in Germany *c.*1870, probably by Lutz, one of Germany's longest established toy makers. Founded *c.*1846, Lutz was taken over by Märklin in 1891.

copper and sheet zinc. At the Great Exhibition in London in 1815 the firm was awarded a prize medal. At this time the factory was producing papier mâché as well as tin toys, and its fame rested on its tinplate fountains and other water toys. The company made steam carriages as well as clockwork, steam ships and dolls' house furniture. Railways later became its most important product.

Exceptionally good German carriages are now frequently attributed to Rock & Graner, but they could equally well have been made by any of the small factories producing quality toys. The most lavishly finished carriages were made in France in the last quarter of the 19th century, with folding leather hoods, silver-plated lamps and satin upholstery. They are

A

This tinplate one-horse sleigh was made in Germany in the 1870s, and its style is reminiscent of toys by Lutz. The mechanism causes the carved wooden horse to dip up and down realistically as it moves forward. The figures are of plaster, and the two passengers are covered by a 'fur' rug.

B

This extremely fine carriage, drawn by two horses, still has its driver and two passengers. Made during the late 19th century, it was probably manufactured by Märklin.

rarely marked, but sometimes carry the label of the shop where they were sold. Any tinplate toys of this type, especially those in the larger sizes, are now rare and expensive. They were time-consuming to produce and were never made in large numbers. But the ability to make a detailed carriage proved the skill of a young apprentice, and these pieces, treasured in German families, occasionally appear in exhibitions.

As horse-drawn transport was common in town and country until the late 1930s, toy makers continued to produce fire-engines, milk-floats, mail-coaches, trams and street-cleaning carts. Some are curiously archaic in style, such as those made by the French firm of Charles Rossignol between 1920 and 1930. Rossignol was founded in 1868 in Paris, and the company made carpet (floor) trains, clockwork cars, Paris buses and fire engines, but, in spite of the number of motor vehicles on the roads, Rossignol, in company with many German and US firms, continued to make painted tinplate cabs, water carts and farm and military pieces. Some of the horse-drawn transport was sold complete with a tinplate or wooden stable, fire station or store, though few have survived complete.

Donkeys, reindeer, goats and dogs are all found pulling decorative road vehicles, as well as fairground and circus items. It is sometimes possible to attribute unmarked pieces by reference to catalogues, but in general these toys are valued mainly by their age and visual appeal. Those made after 1920 tend to be very simple: the horses are often two sections tabbed together and lithographed. Even so, many of them have a primitive charm and they are now becoming collectable. More recently, Japanese-made horses have appeared, indicating the continual appeal of this old-fashioned form of transport.

B

A good example of a pre-1914 closed landaulet, with the chauffeur sitting in the open. The steering wheel is turned to make the car run in a circle. This particular toy, although unattributed to a specific maker, is similar to a 13in (32cm) long taxi made by Carette shortly before World War I; this toy had a rear folding leather hood and two opening doors.

CARS

When motor cars first appeared on the roads, toy manufacturers were slow to accept their potential. Models were rarely seen in the shops before 1905. Motor vehicles are now, however, the most heavily collected area of tin plate, and pre-World War I pieces by known makers arouse international interest. By 1910 the makers were fully aware of the sales value of an up-to-the-minute toy, and coupés, tourers, racing cars and double phaetons were put into production, the best of them having well-finished

interiors, especially made miniature lamps and, occasionally, luggage and travelling rugs. The finest models, such as those made by the German firm Märklin, are of heavy construction and often contain passengers. Because of the painted finish, it was possible to imitate the coach-lining of actual cars, making the models especially elegant. Originality of paint work is very important in this area of metal-toy collecting, as the soft patina of age is impossible to reproduce.

The first toy cars, such as those made in France in the 1890s by H. Vichy, with velvet and silk seats, are accurate copies of the horseless carriages. They are so rare that possession remains a dream for most collectors. Other makers produced motors with either civilian or military occup-

ants in the years before World War I, but judging from the small numbers illustrated in contemporary catalogues, they remained a relatively insignificant line among the traditional horse-drawn items.

After the war simplified methods of production meant that cars became much cheaper to produce, and as they became available to a wider social group, children wanted copies of the newest models they saw in the street. Manufacturers were pleased to satisfy this demand with an ever-increasing assortment of toy cars in all sizes and prices. The majority of collectors now concentrate on the period between the wars, examples of which are available at all antique toy shows and fairs. Although the detail and individual craftsmanship that characterized the early models disappeared, the later versions provide a fascinating miniature document of the evolution of the car. Fortunately, the majority of the pieces carry a maker's mark.

GEBRÜDER MÄRKLIN

The most revered German maker is Märklin, a firm that is still in operation and still producing fine quality toys. Many of its early toys are more light-hearted than those of Carette and have painted detail that seems to have been added purely for the love of decoration. The company was established in Göppingen in 1859 by Theodor Märklin (1817–66) and originally concentrated on metal toys for dolls' rooms and kitchens. The early years, when the business was largely run by Carolyn, Theodor's widow, were difficult. In 1888 a new company, Gebrüder Märklin, was established, and in 1891 business improved when the company took over the fine quality products of Ludwig Lutz. New capital was injected in 1892, and the firm changed its name to Gebrüder Märklin & Co., a name that was retained until 1907. The company expanded rapidly, new premises were taken on and another old toy-making firm, Rock & Graner, was absorbed in 1904. Because of financial problems another partner was taken on in 1907, and the name again changed to Gebrüder Märklin & Cie, a name used until the 1920s.

After the take-over of Lutz the range of Märklin toys increased dramatically and there was tremendous concentration on transport vehicles. These were made in heavy tinplate and in the somewhat severe classic German style. Unlike Carette, Märklin did not produce a great variety of cars, so that any examples coming on the market are very desirable. By painting vehicles in different colours and adding special detail, the same model could assume a new identity: a passenger car, for instance, can become a taxi. Most Märklin toys of the great era, between 1895 and

A

B

1914, were hand-made in heavy metal, and some have extravagant detail, such as leather luggage straps and removable spare tyres.

GEORGES CARETTE

All collectors have a preference for some particular maker's work. Some like Bing and Märklin for their strength and solidity, others prefer the whimsy of Lehmann or the more romantic approach of Günthermann, whose drivers and passengers display charming detail such as minute glasses or gloves. But the work of Georges Carette is universally popular, as his toys were not only well made but were designed with true elegance and flair.

Carette, who was French by birth, the son of a Parisian photographer, founded his toy-making firm, Georges Carette & Cie, in Nuremberg in 1886 when he was only 24 years old. He had learned the trade by serving an apprenticeship in the large Bing factory, and he remained especially interested in the marketing and business side of his factory. He was always keen to produce a striking toy at a competitive price and his motor cars, though not as extravagant as those of Günthermann, are beautifully decorated in attractive colours. His firm expanded rapidly and by 1900 had depots all over Europe and employed some 400 people.

In 1911 Carette headed his range of cars with a superb motor landaulette with reversing gears and a brake. This motor, complete with a painted papier mâché chauffeur, could be adjusted for straight or circular running and was beautifully finished with nickelled head lamps and rubber-tyred wheels. The company sold boxes of assorted figures, so that a convincingly crowded effect could be achieved. These figures were especially useful for the motor buses, for which special conductors and drivers were made. One of the buses carried English advertisements and was marketed as a London bus. It remains one of the most popular Carette toys.

Delivery vans, water lorries and mail vans were produced by Carette as well as tinplate garages, which could have a workbench and vice fitted. Almost all worked by either a

A

Steam as a means of powering full-sized cars had almost completely died out by 1914, making this live-steam toy by Doll & Cie of Nuremberg especially interesting. J. Sondheim and Peter Doll founded the company in 1898 to specialize in the production of stationary steam engines and accessories, and this car was made c.1924. The boiler and mechanism are beneath the bonnet, and the car features cast metal wheels with white rubber tyres. It is 19in (48cm) long.

B

This unusual motorcycle delivery vehicle is unmarked, but it has the appearance of an Italian toy. Probably made during the late 1930s, it has bright nickel plating, and the clockwork motor, which is housed in the engine section, has a belt drive to the rear wheels.

C

Although unmarked, this handsome toy is obviously of high quality. The body pressings are detailed and suggest the deep buttoning of the upholstery. The enamel was applied by hand and is still in excellent condition.

A

clockwork spring motor or a flywheel. Carette's fire station, sold with three vehicles, had a working water jet and hose as well as removable figures.

During World War I Carette was forced to return to his native France, although the company continued to trade until 1917, when its stock and tools were dispersed, some of the cars later appearing with the Karl Bub trademark. Bub, another Nuremberg firm, was founded in 1851 and reached its peak of production in the 1920s, when large numbers of saloon cars and tourers of fairly light construction were made. In 1935, to celebrate the centenary of the Nuremberg-Fürth railway, an amusingly atavistic train with printed period occupants was made.

GEBRÜDER BING

After Märklin, the leading German manufacturer of tin toys was Bing, which was established in Nuremberg in 1863–5. By 1928, in fact, Bing had become Germany's leading toy maker, with annual sales of about 27 million Deutschmarks. The company was founded by Ignaz and Adolf Bing, and its prolific output included boats, cars and trains. Unfortunately, the trade depression that .

followed the Wall Street Crash in 1929 proved to be a disaster for the company and eventually led to its being taken over by its rival toy manufacturer, Karl Bub.

The brothers Ignaz and Adolf Bing began producing tinplate kitchenware and toys in the 1860s in Nuremberg, but little is known about the firm's early products, because real expansion began only in the 1890s, when the firm became a limited company. The brothers were excellent businessmen, and their products were on sale across the world, from Sudan to Alaska. They also saw the importance of displaying their latest toys at international exhibitions, and any medals won at such exhibitions could be used in advertising. Their finest toys were sold in specially designed presentation boxes, with a landscape forming a realistic background. Others were sold in strong wooden boxes (sometimes marked with the name of the retailer, such as Gamages) and they owe their survival after years of neglect in attics and basements to this rigid packaging.

In its heyday, Bing produced some wonderful toy cars. The tinplate had a solidity not found in all Nuremberg-made toys, and some of the cars had such refinements as glass wind-

B

screens and operating hand-brakes. After World War I Bing's products became less interesting and showed a marked decline in standards. Nevertheless, the lithographed, tinplate, clockwork-driven toys are still desirable and attract interest at auction

Bing's trademark varied over the years, but it usually incorporated the letters *G.B.N.* (for Gebrüder Bing Nuremberg) and, between 1917 and 1932, *B.W.* (for Bing Werke).

JOHANN DISTLER

Another Nuremberg company, Distler was founded in 1900 and made a wide range of penny toys, cars and trains. It was eventually taken over by Trix. In the 1920s Distler produced toys for the British and US markets, including a fire-engine with a bell that sounds as the vehicle runs along

B

Made by Bing in the early 1920s, this lithographed limousine features a chauffeur. It was fitted with electric headlights to add to the realism and has two opening doors and adjustable steering.

C

This fine steam-powered model of a fire-engine was made by Bing c.1905. The spirit-fired copper boiler has a water level gauge. This piece is typical of the detail and ingenuity of the best of Bing's work, which combined fantasy with mechanical precision and inventiveness.

C

(it was powered by clockwork) and a ladder. Distler used several marks: the letters *J.D.* on a thistle (*Distler* is German for thistle); *J.D.N.* on a globe; and, after World War II, *Distler*.

JOUETS DE PARIS

Some of the best-quality French tin toys were made by Jouets de Paris, a firm that in the 1920s and 1930s produced models of all the famous cars of the period. Its Hispano Suiza was an impressive 20½in (52cm) long and was fitted with lights; and the Delage racing car was claimed to be 'the prettiest racing car ever'. Most of the firm's products are clearly marked, and they are well worth collecting. The quality, even of toys from the late period, is always good. The company is believed to have originated in Paris in 1899 as the Société Industrielle de Ferblant-erie, the name being changed to Jouets de Paris and to Jouets en Paris (J.E.P.) in 1932. The finest toys were undoubtedly made in the 1930s. The Rolls Royce is a superb model and is both strongly and accurately made.

CITROËN

J.E.P.'s greatest French competitor in the area of model cars was Citroën, which, in the early 1920s decided to use copies of its automobiles as promotional items. Both pick-up trucks and cars were made by Citroën, with the aim of encouraging children to know the maker's name from their earliest years. Attractive posters showing infants with the toy cars helped boost sales – some 15,000 in 1923, the first year of production. In 1928 'miniature toys' that were diecast appeared on the market and were an immediate success. The tinplate delivery vans, taxis coupés and flat-bed lorries were quite accurate copies and could be purchased from car showrooms or shops. They were frequently issued at the same time as a new full-sized automobile, so that children could encourage papa to acquire the latest model.

The B2 taxi, with canework panels to the passenger section, is one of the most collectable pieces, although the B2 Torpedo, being the first to be made in 1923, is also popular. Virtually all the models carry the

Citroën trademark and are easily identifiable. The good products were made for a relatively short period, as fewer were marketed in the late 1930s, although a small range was made after the war by another company.

CHARLES ROSSIGNOL

Another great French maker of tinplate toys was Charles Rossignol, who began production *c*.1888 in Paris. Like Citroën products, the firm's models were always marked and the boxes also carried the company's monogram. Production ceased as recently as 1962, leaving collectors a very wide range of models and styles from which to choose. The earliest products are believed to have been floor trains, but motor cars, horse-drawn vehicles, field ambulances, steam boats and well-made penny toys were also produced. Friction-driven milk carts, with drivers and a group of churns, are among the most decorative pieces, although the clockwork taxi-cabs, limousines and coupés, with bright lithography, are more generally popular with collectors and attract the highest prices. Some Rossignol toys, such as the steam fire-pumps were lacquered, not lithographed, but all are clearly marked with a monogram. In several instances, indeed, the monogram is an integral part of the surface decoration.

KARL BUB

Founded in 1851, the company had offices at Tetzelgasse in Nuremberg. It made lacquered tinplate toys, some with clockwork mechanisms, and began to make toy cars in the 1920s. It made pieces in common with Carette and continued to sell them after Carette's collapse in 1917. The motor cars are well detailed, and often have finely lithographed metal wheels. Bub took over Bing in 1933 and survived until 1964.

A

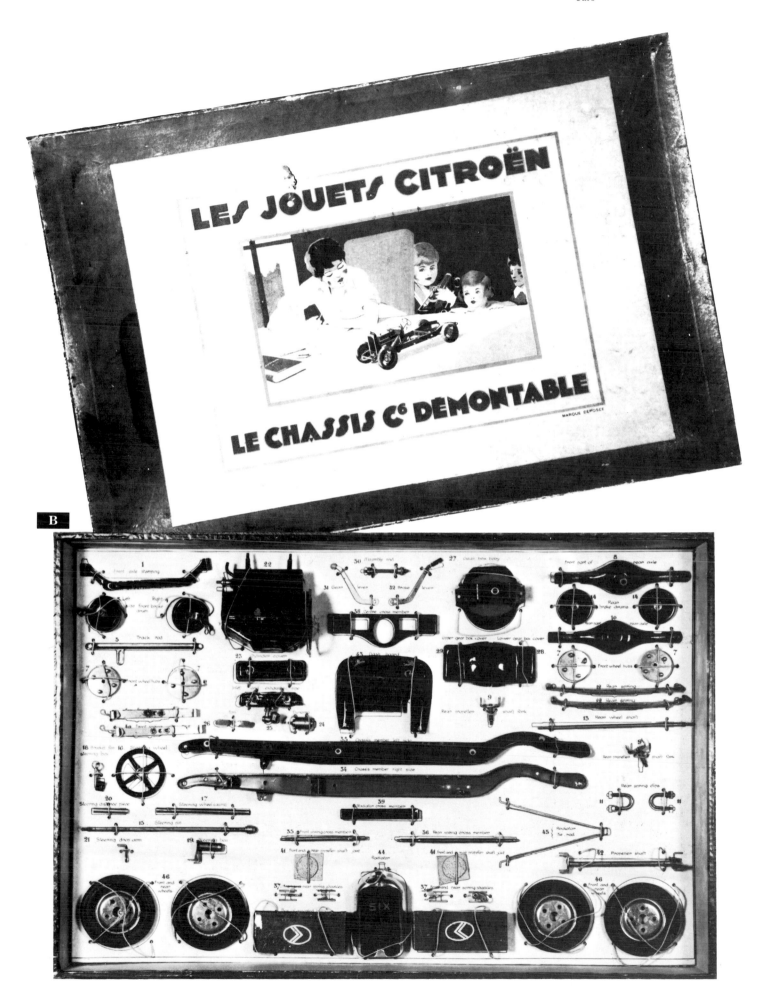

DOLL & CIE

Founded in 1898 by J. Sandheim and a tinsmith, Peter Doll, the company originally made stationary steam engines and accessories. Max Bein joined the company in January 1911, and after this time clockwork toys were also made. During the 1920s and 1930s many steam engines were produced. Doll was taken over by Fleischmann in the late 1930s, although the Doll name continued to be used until after World War II. The company is especially remembered for its brightly decorated toys with their lavish use of cut and pierced decoration.

GEBRÜDER FLEISCHMANN

Little is known of the early products of this company, which was founded in Nuremberg in 1887, but it later specialized in magnetic floating toys and tinplate ships. In 1928 Fleischmann took over the firm of Staudt, and from then other types of toys were made. During the 1930s Fleischmann tended to concentrate on boats, many of which resemble those made by Carette. The company took over Doll after World War II, and it is still in production.

GÜNTHERMANN

S. Günthermann founded the company that bears his name in 1877 in Nuremberg, and by 1901 it employed some 250 people. Günthermann, who is sometimes regarded as the pioneer of the tinplate clockwork manufacturers in Nuremberg, died in 1890, and his widow married the company's manager, Adolf Weigel, whose initials were included in the trademark until his death in 1919. After this, the mark reverted to *S.G.* The company made the typical range of Nuremberg toys, including horse-drawn vehicles, fire engines, a well-known series of Gordon Bennett racing cars and airplanes. The company was taken over by Siemens in 1965, but the production of good tinplate toys has continued.

ISSMAYER

Johann Emanuel Issmayer had made pressed metal toys in Nuremberg in the 1830s, and his son, Johann Andreas, had worked in his father's business, both as a traveller and in the factory. In 1861 Johann Andreas founded his own business at 20 Peterstrasses, Nuremberg, to make toy kitchenware and magnetic, floating toys. He is thought to have been the first Nuremberg toy maker to produce working tinplate figures. Comparatively few of the company's clockwork toys are known, as the main production was of trains, but it made amusing tins in the form of toys in the early 20th century and charmingly decorated clockwork pieces in the late 19th century. Issmayer died in 1922, and the company was taken over by his son-in-law. It appears to have ceased production in the early 1930s.

A

A lithographed London bus, 12½in (32cm) long, manufactured by Georges Carette of Nuremberg. It is of exceptionally fine quality and still has its original plaster driver, conductor and full complement of passengers. It was made *c*.1910.

A

B

Compared with the open tourer illustrated below, this lithographed limousine by Distler was aimed at the cheaper end of the market. It was made *c.*1925. At the same time Distler made a more up-market version of the same toy, with an adjustable windscreen and electric lights operated by a battery underneath the car.

C

This lithographed open tourer by Distler was made in the 1920s, a time when the construction of all tinplate toys had become much flimsier than in the pre-war years. It is approximately 12in (31cm) long and has a rear luggage rack, adjustable windscreen, rack and pinion steering and opening rear doors.

C

A

A

Märklin continued to make excellent large-scale models of warships well into the 1920s. This example is powered by electricity and has three propellers as well as a hoist for lowering a seaplane into the water.

B

The instruction leaflet shows steam coming from the funnel of the fishing boat, but the toy was actually powered by a fly-wheel mechanism, as can be seen from the handle at the stern. The manufacturer was Uebelacker, a company that was founded in Nuremberg c.1860 by Leonhard Uebelacker. This boat was made in the late 1880s.

BOATS

Every toy collector dreams of owning one of the boats made by a firm such as Märklin before World War I. Some of these fine toys measure more than 40in (100cm) and were powered by clockwork, electricity or steam. As the boats were intended to be floated, few have survived in good condition. Some of the clockwork versions could run for over a quarter of an hour, while the steam-powered *Maure-tania* could travel for an hour. No wonder so many were lost as they ploughed their way into the centre

A

of lakes and ponds! Even if the boat returned to the nursery, it was often put away wet and allowed to rust. Inevitably, such toys are extremely rare and the survival of examples complete with their sailors, lifeboats and fabric flags is almost miraculous.

By 1891 Märklin was producing a range of boats alongside its elegant horse-drawn carriages and military vehicles. Some of these early models continued in production for many years, such as the steam yachts and paddle steamers; but it is the large battleships and torpedo boats, powered by steam or clockwork, that have become the stars for collectors. The passenger steamers and naval craft offered by the firm after the war were not so lavishly equipped as the early products, and detail, such

as sailors that could be fixed in position, disappeared. The ocean liner *Columbus,* some 40in (100cm) long, with a powerful motor, could run for 12 minutes and was fitted with forward and reverse movement. All the boats had adjustable steering gear and were sold with stands for display in the nursery. Some of the larger sizes were very expensive and were owned by the richest children; production was limited. Despite the war-weariness of the European public, torpedo boats, battleships and gunboats remained popular toys. Submarines, which dived automatically at intervals, ranged in size from 9 to 30in (23 to 75cm); it is the small sizes that are now commonly found.

Carette boats are much rarer than those produced by Märklin. They

A problem with live-steam powered boats was that, inevitably, as the toy was played with the paintwork was scorched, as on this model of *Aviso Greif*, which was made by Schoenner *c.*1900. Despite the damage to the paintwork, the detailed decoration on the bow, which is typical of the period, is still visible.

A

were very well made, with a japanned
finish, and the larger sizes, such as
ocean-going steamships, were supplied with an anchor and chain as
well as lifeboats. In order to make
German-designed vessels acceptable
in Great Britain and the United States,
they were given non-German names.
Large pleasure steamers, coasting
cruisers with quick-firing guns,
searchlight and look-out stations and
torpedo boats with signalling apparatus were available by 1911. In lighter
vein there were pleasure yachts and
a splendid despatch boat, the *Sleip-
ner*, which was advertised as a scale
model of the ship in attendance on
the German emperor.

The other great German toy
maker, Gebrüder Bing, also made
high-quality boats and submarines,

B

C

The relative size of
the sailor sitting in
the bow indicates the
small scale of this
liner, which was
made, probably by
Carette, *c.*1900. It
was powered by
clockwork.

although they do not rival the finest
Märklin pieces. The early Bing boats,
dating from 1895 to 1910, are the
best, with painted detail and lavish
ornament added for the enjoyment
of the buyer. As Bing, unlike Carette,
marked its work, the firm is especially
popular with collectors. Some Bing
toys, such as the smaller submarines,
are not very expensive, as they have
survived in some quantity; but larger
boats, if in good condition, can command extremely high prices.

Both Bing and Märklin made
some boats that were 36in (1m) long
and by 1912 Bing was producing auto-
matically-firing gunboats, torpedo
boats and destroyers powered by
steam or the more expensive clockwork. Bing toys made after 1917 lack
the allure of the early work, as they
were more economically made to
compete with the products of other
toy makers in the difficult years of
the Depression. But since the early
pieces are now very expensive, the
cars, steam accessories and boats
made in the later period are becoming more popular.

D

This toy German
submarine, made by
Bing of Nuremberg,
is in fine condition,
even retaining its
national and German
Navy flags. The
clockwork motor,
which makes the
vessel dive and
surface repeatedly, is
wound through the
screw fitting in the
conning tower. Bing's
mark, *G.B.N.* (for
Gebrüder Bing,
Nuremberg), may be
seen on the label on
the box.

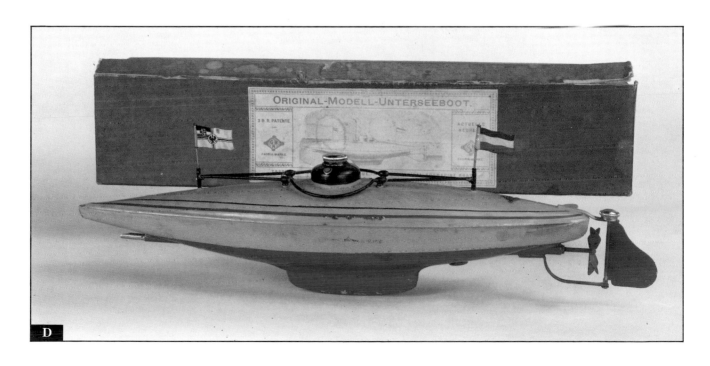

A

AIRSHIPS AND AEROPLANES

Before 1914 relatively few aeroplanes were made as toys, perhaps because the manufacturers felt that they were too remote from the daily lives of most boys. Pre-1914 models are rare and desirable, even if their condition is not superb. As Carette ceased trading in 1917, before any toy maker created planes in great numbers, its work is especially valuable.

During its short years of production, Carette concentrated as much on airships such as Zeppelins as on planes. Its Parseval airship, in the larger sizes, had two propellers that helped the craft describe wide circles. Carette's 1911 catalogue showed only two aeroplanes: Wright-type biplanes and the Blériot monoplane, a curiously fragile construction.

The exploits of daring pilots during World War I attracted the imagination of boys all over the world and toy manufacturers encouraged their interest with an assortment of aeroplanes modelled, not only on the latest designs of the 1920s, but on the fighter planes of the war years. Aeroplanes, like ships, had a hard time in the nursery and they are rarely found in good condition. They are, even so, popular with collectors.

After the famous solo crossing of the Atlantic by Charles Lindbergh in 1927, interest in model planes increased, and by 1930 there were planes that had parachutes, planes with tinplate hangers and planes which circled over ships or aerodromes. The German firms Günthermann, Lehmann, Distler and Tipp all made quite accurate models of civil and military aircraft as well as seaplanes. Some of these toys were made of very thin tinplate; it looked effective when it was freshly lithographed, but it soon dented and rusted. The penny toy versions, so small that they were usually played with indoors, have often lasted better.

A

Tinplate toys of all kinds have become collectable and therefore expensive in recent years, and enthusiasts should beware pitfalls such as this clever reproduction of a World War I Focke-Wulf tri-plane. This tinplate model has all the appearance of age, but it is, in fact, of recent manufacture.

B

Deceptively antique in appearance as well as being a fairly accurate representation of the World War I twin-engined bi-plane, this toy is, in fact, of recent manufacture.

C

Airships captured the public's imagination in the early years of the 20th century, and many toy manufacturers produced representations of this novel means of flight, including Märklin and Tipp. The model shown here was made by Lehmann between 1920 and 1930, and that company's mark may be seen on the side: *EPL – II 652 Marke Lehmann* [with the Lehmann metal-press mark] *Made in Germany*. When the airship is suspended from a string, the celluloid propeller pushes it around in circles. All Lehmann toys are collectable, and this is an especially desirable example of the company's output.

B

C

A

An unmarked figure
representing Charlie
Chaplin. Made
c.1930, it is dressed in
felt clothes and
shuffles along,
twirling its cane.

B

Made c.1909 by
Fernand Martin, this
toy is known as La
Conquête du Nord. It
was inspired by
Robert Peary's
expedition to the
North Pole.

C

Made in the
immediate post-war
period, this brightly
lithographed novelty
toy of a porter
steering a luggage
trolley pursues an
erratic course when it
is wound up. It is
marked: *Made in the
US Zone of Germany*.

B

A

NOVELTY TOYS

All the tinplate toys were, in a sense,
novelty toys, but there is a large
group of toys made specifically
to amuse. While toy cars, buses
and even aircraft are expected
to be enjoyed seriously, novelty
toys are designed to entertain,
and many of the toys made by the
larger factories retain a lightness of
touch that provides a contrast with
the more serious work of Bing or
Carette. French manufacturers in
particular made some delightfully
whimsical items, which charm collectors today as much as they amused
their original owners.

FERNAND MARTIN

This typically French approach
is seen particularly in the products
of Fernand Martin, who founded his
Paris factory in 1878. Like Lehmann,
the most whimsical of the German
makers, Martin created amusing figures that reflect scenes in the streets,
in shops or the circus; but instead of
covering the surface with bright lithography, he aimed at realism and even
costumed some figures in fabric.

Martin was also especially
interested in the advertising and sales
potential of attractive boxes and
these carry the names of the toy and

the maker, as well as the dates of the medals he was awarded at international exhibitons.

Though the construction of Martin toys – a combination of wire, steel, copper, lead and fabric – seems complex and time-consuming, the firm was profitable, partly because the same models were made year after year with different finishes or detail to suit foreign markets. One toy, the Sheriff, seems to have been specially made in 1892 for the Chicago World Fair, presumably because of the success Martin had achieved with previous toys such as a jazz band and a wheelchair that were made for French exhibitions. Drunkards, street violinists, waiters, boxers, policemen, fruit-sellers, concièrges and laundry-women, all caricaturing Parisian daily life, poured out of the Martin factory. Some of these toys now appeal more to automata enthusiasts than tin-toy collectors, but they also offer a large collecting field in their own right.

Martin was fascinated by the history of toys and he gave the Conservatoire des Arts et Métiers in Paris a large collection of the toys he had made over a 30-year period – the only 19th-century toy maker to have foreseen the historical importance of his work.

LEHMANN

Ernst Paul Lehmann established a toy-making firm in Brandenburg in 1881. Lehmann approached the problem of creating models of contemporary transport in a light-hearted way and concentrated, not on accuracy and good quality, but on surface decoration and novelty. As the toys made by this company were so much cheaper than those made by Bing or Carette, they were owned by children of all income levels. Many models have survived in number, depressing their price. For Lehmann designing a simple car was not enough: it had to be occupied by a naughty boy who drove it erratically. As Lehmann toys are marked both with the name of the firm and with the design patent details, they are

immediately recognizable. Sometimes the company name was added to a toy even though it detracted from the overall effect – as on an airship or a bus, where the patent mark is carried on the bonnet.

Buses, trucks, animals and vans, all decorated in bright, eye-catching colours, poured out of the Lehmann factory after 1900. Many of these charming creations resemble auto-

C

mata in being so cleverly designed, presumably so that adults would find them irresistible and carry them home as gifts for children. A stubborn mule, with a comical clown attempting to control a bucking donkey that pulls a circus cart, is the most famous of the firm's products.

By the 1920s Lehmann was producing more than 80 different models, most of them carrying a name such as Halloh, a boy riding a motor bike, Mandarin, with two bearers carrying a sedan chair, Tut-tut, a car, and the much rarer Baker and Sweep, with a sweep attacking the baker.

Many of these toys remained on the market for long periods, and their patents were re-applied for. As this information is printed on the tinplate, most Lehmann toys are fairly easy to date. In 1921 the firm had some 800 workers and was at its peak of production; by then Johann Richter had become a partner, a man who had studied working methods in other countries and was full of new ideas.

After World War II, the Lehmann factory was sequestered by the Soviet Union, but Richter re-established the toy-making firm near Nuremberg and it is still in production.

Because of their somewhat flimsy construction, Lehmann toys are somewhat ignored by top collectors, who prefer the weight and solemnity of Carette or Märklin transport vehicles. Yet arranged as a group, especially if they are with their colourful original boxes, Lehmann toys are visually arresting, full of humour and incident. Some of the designs introduced before 1900 are extremely

A

Although unmarked, this tinplate money box (bank) is clearly German and was made in the 1950s. When the lever at the side is pulled, the woodsman hits the coin with his axe so that it falls into the base.

B

This novelty toy, a sand scoop, was made by Bing c.1925. As the small black handle is turned, a belt drives the large wheel, causing the arm to scoop sand from the bottom tray and drop it on the slope on the left, which returns it to the tray.

progressive, so simple that they might have been made in the 1920s. Gustav the Miller, who climbs a pole and sets the sails of his mill in action, was first sold in 1897, yet must have looked completely up-to-date to boys in the 1930s. Some of the firm's products were such good sellers that they were produced for a long period of time. They are relatively common and fetch low prices. Others such as the amphibious car, patented in 1905, are much rarer and make excellent investments.

Despite their apparent fragility of construction, some Lehmann toys performed extremely well, with motors that could run for an hour. The mechanical airship show, composed of dirigibles and aeroplanes circling a tower, was a continuous spectacle, as was the County Fair Tower, with cars running under arches while airships circle above, a toy that was introduced in 1914.

A

These two Lehmann toys are seen with their original boxes, which makes them even more desirable. The box on the right bears the legend *Baker and Sweep, or Good Fighting Darkness*, and Lehmann's trademark is clearly visible on the body of the tricycle illustrated on the box. This amusing novelty toy is typical of Lehmann's products. The baker rides his tricycle while at the same time attempting to beat off the sweep who is attacking him from behind. The 'cake' on the cart is actually a bell, which rings as the toy moves along. Made in the 1900s, the toy is 4½in (12cm) high. On the left is the New Century Cycle, which is 5in (13cm) long. This was made in two versions, the one shown here and one commemorating Amundsen's polar exploration. As the vehicle moves along, the umbrella turns around and the driver's right hand moves up and down. This toy was made in 1905–14.

GEBRÜDER EINFALT

The German toy industry produced a vast range of novelty toys; one has only to glance through the catalogues of exporters and toy dealers like Moses Kohnstam to appreciate the enormous variety that his firm handled. The pages of his catalogue show jousting knights, comical clowns organ-grinders, acrobats, pecking hens, billiard players, carousels, loop-the-loop aeroplanes, switch-backs, figures on see-saws – the list is almost endless.

After Lehmann, one of the most important manufacturers of novelty toys was Gebrüder Einfalt, which produced a fascinating range of track toys in the years immediately following World War II. These toys, which were always colourfully presented, are extremely appealing. There are tiny clockwork vehicles whizzing along tinplate tracks, while simple, but effective, control systems allowed the vehicles to manoeuvre along the tracks, stopping if necessary to avoid collision where tracks or roads crossed. Sometimes the vehicles vanished into mountain tunnels, reappearing mysteriously at a higher level, only to free-wheel downhill. Some of Einfalt's layouts even incorporated moving miniature figures, activated by hidden levers moved by passing vehicles. Other toys had small aircraft circling around central pillars, descending as they spiralled down.

Einfalt was founded in Nuremberg in 1922 by Georg and Johann Einfalt, and its trademark was originally *G.E.N.* and, after 1935, *Technofix*.

ARNOLD

In 1906 Karl Arnold founded a company in Nuremberg. It pioneered the sparking flint toy, producing a large range of novelty toys both before and after World War II. Its trademarks were *Arnold* and, on trains in the 1960s, *Rapido*. One of Arnold's most spectacular toys was the motorcyclist Mac. As the clockwork-powered bike travelled along, Mac would brake to a stop and realisically dismount and stand by the side of the machine. He would then throw his leg back over the saddle, sit down and drive off.

A

PENNY TOYS FOR THE MASS MARKET

Penny toys is the popular term for a variety of brightly coloured figures, animals and transport vehicles that were made in France and Germany until the 1930s. The most collectable are those that were made before World War I; their colouring is much richer and they have more embossed detail. Some have moving parts – a football that is kicked between two players, hens that peck at their food or a clown who beats a donkey. Many of them were produced over a long period and have to be dated by their colour and the general quality of their construction. Relatively few are marked, as they were made by dozens of small firms who sold their products through the big Nuremberg wholeslers, such as Moses Kohnstam, who traded as Moko.

In the 1928–30 Moko catalogue are found horse-drawn carriages and Edwardian rowing boats, alongside up-to-the-minute cars, sewing machines and motor bikes. Some of the penny toys, such as the trains, were made in several pieces and were originally sold boxed. Those made by the French firm Rossignol were marketed in this way, although the majority of makers seem to have sold the pieces loose and by the gross to street hawkers and sweet-shops.

A light-hearted, amusing approach was necessary for any firm producing penny toys. French toy makers, in particular, seemed to have the ability to make a model, perhaps from scrap materials, eye-catching and magical. While the raw materials used for the French penny toys might be of the cheapest kind, the decoration and finish is always delicate and charming. As they were made in small workshops in the back streets of Paris, the toys are rarely marked.

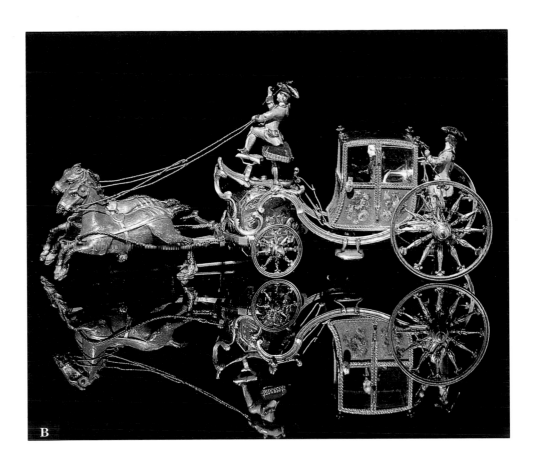

kitchens and the seaside. William Britain, in the 1880s, had produced some inventive metal toys such as an equestrienne, and they are highly collectable, but the best period for the collector is after 1930, when firms such as Wells, Hornby, Chad Valley and Mettoy were in full production. Few British makers before 1914 marked their work, as it was sold very cheaply directly to the retailers. James Norris of Birmingham was one of the leading makers of toy scales and dolls' kitchenware, while The Fancy Toy Company in the same city specialized in tin gardening tools and sand moulds for turrets and battlements.

The finest tinplate kitchenware had been made in Germany by firms such as Märklin, which created a series of spirit- and gas-fired kitchen ranges that were beautifully finished as functional items. British output was unexciting by comparison, and it was not until the 1930s that well-finished, cleverly designed pieces appeared in quantity. The quality of British printing on tinplate was good, as is evidenced by the very attractive

BRITISH MANUFAC- TURERS

Some clockwork toys were made in Great Britain as early as the 18th century, but the industry never attained the strength that might have been expected, mainly because of the high cost of labour.

As a result of the cessation of imports from Germany during World War I, the tin toy industry was forced into life. Previously, tin and metal toys had been produced in Birmingham and Wolverhampton, but these were mainly for dolls' houses, model

A

The Express Transport van by Wells was made *c*.1947. It is made of tabbed-and-slotted tinplate, and has printed, perforated-disc wheels, the rear two driven by a clockwork motor, wound by the key near the back wheels.

B

This unmarked model of an English Green Line bus represented the ultimate in luxury travel in the 1930s. The simple clockwork mechanism is wound by the key near the back wheels.

biscuit tins and containers that were made before 1910, but these skills were not at first directed towards toy transport. Some of the best model cars were made by Brimtoy, which used Nelson's column as the company trademark. This firm later amalgamated with Wells to become Wells Brimtoy, which was the main British producer of lithographed toys until the late 1950s.

Though many of the road vehicles made in the 1920s and 1930s seem light and poorly made in comparison with the classic French and German products of the turn of the century, they now have a following of their own. Mettoy, Tri-ang, Sutcliffe, Crescent Toys and Chad Valley all made models of contemporary road vehicles that were finished in bright colours. The Tri-ang toys are of a much plainer construction, without the lithography that made the Chad Valley pieces so lively, and they were usually stove-enamelled.

C

C
Although it is called Snoopy, this bloodhound seems to be of an earlier date than the US comic strip character of the same name. It is marked *Made in Britain* and wags its tail as it pursues its quarry.

A

A

The best makers of tin toys in the years immediately after World War II were the Japanese, and it is impossible to identify the makers of many of the excellent pieces that appear on the market. This black Cadillac and the Buick are both large toys, and they accurately reflect the rather garish appearance of many 1950s US automobiles.

B

Walt Disney characters were favourites with movie-going children – and adults – from the first cartoon. The brightly lithographed Goofy the Gardener, which was made in the UK by Marx in the 1950s, 'walks' along, pushing his wheelbarrow.

AMERICAN MANUFACTURERS

Early American metal toy makers, like their British counterparts, concentrated on kitchenware and very simple toys; most of the rest were still imported from Europe. The native industry developed rapidly after 1840, although the main emphasis was on cast iron. The Americans were comparatively late in making use of lithography, and many of the pieces made around the turn of the century were painted and stencilled in a deceptively atavistic manner. The toy industry boomed after 1900, although there were still fewer than 100

manufacturers. After World War I US production again increased and toy design became much more inventive. Manufacturers such as Louis Marx were eager to represent popular characters of the period such as Charlie MacCarthy, the ventriloquist's dummy, Donald Duck and Mickey Mouse, and every advance in transport and aeornautics was reflected in an accurate model.

The production of cast iron toys, a peculiarly American activity, reached its peak in the 1880s. Money-boxes, bell toys, horse-drawn transport, sleighs, animals and caricatures of politicians were all created in cast iron, which could be poured into very complex moulds. In some early toys, tin and cast iron were used together, and some of the finest bell toys, such as elephants which pivot to strike bells, were made of cast iron. The first 100 years of American independence

celebrated in 1876 fostered a spate of centennial toys, many incorporating the Centennial Bell.

Because of the current interest in primitive art, American toys have become increasingly popular internationally and prices for some of the early pieces, such as those that appear in the George Brown Sketchbook of 1870, are now classed among the greats. George W. Brown & Co. was founded in 1856 in Connecticut. It was amalgamated with J. & E. Stevens in 1869 to form the Stevens & Brown Manufacturing Company. Brown made a number of boats, some of which appeared in a wheeled version as carpet toys. Delivery vehicles, circus cages, horses in hoops, birds that balance between large wheels, pull-along trains and very elegant wire-work hose-reel fire carriages were made by this prolific and versatile maker. Brown's toys are identified

A

Trotters have always been popular toys with American children. This hand-painted, tinplate toy, which is powered by a simple clockwork motor, is designed to run in circles.

by a label that was fixed to the boxes or by reference to the Sketchbook.

The cleverly designed, but decidedly lightweight, lithographed tinplate toys made by Louis Marx in the 20th century are a complete contrast to the heavy, primitive creations of George Brown, but they are equally typical of their period. Marx, who was born in 1894, originally worked for Ferdinand Strauss, one of the major American clockwork toy makers. After a rapid rise from office-boy to millionaire before the age of 30, Marx took over several factories and acquired the rights to some of the Strauss lines. He aimed to create toys for the new mass-market, which demanded novelty at low prices. One of the most memorable of his creations is the Mouse Orchestra, with four mice around a piano. By buying out most of his competitors in the 1930s, Marx became the largest toy-making firm in the world.

A similar approach to the mass market is apparent in the light, brightly coloured tin toys made in Japan. At first, Japanese products were mainly imitative, but after 1945 Japanese designers began to create more imaginative work. Well-tried clockwork mechanisms were cast aside in favour of battery-operated electric motors which were much more in tune with space-age rockets and moon landing craft. Some of the Japanese aeroplanes are superb, complex models of contemporary advances. In addition, a wide range of cheap novelty pieces flooded the shelves of chain stores, offering children a choice of anything from a ladybird to a helicopter. Among the more expensive toys are extremely complex robots. They are among the most inventive of all modern tinplate toys and are attracting progressively higher prices as they develop a wide following.

At present, the most passionate collectors of robots are Japanese, but the appeal of robots is becoming more international and they are beginning to appear in toy auctions and specialist exhibitions. Despite this growing interest in the international market it is still possible, in the UK at least, to pick up bargains from car-boot sales.

B

This fantastic racing car was made in the US by Marx in the 1930s. The gaudy lithography adds to the splendour.

C

Among the most attractive and specifically American tin toys are the hoop toys of the kind seen here. This elaborate clockwork-powered balancing figure was made by Althof Bergman between 1870 and 1880. It is 9¾in (25cm) in diameter. Althof Bergman was founded in New York in 1856 as a partnership between the brothers Charles, Louis and Frederick Bergman, who originally imported toys but quickly turned to manufacturing their own.

C

D

One of the toys produced by Morton E. Converse between 1910 and 1920, this colourful horse-drawn 'menagerie' wagon is made of lithographed tinplate. Converse was established in 1878, and the company continued in production until the early 1930s.

D

A

This simple clockwork engine was made by Hess *c.*1895. It was designed to run on track that has raised inner edges. The same locomotive was available with different name transfers on the engine for the different markets Hess sold it in. The example illustrated here seems to have been wrongly packaged, for the box bears a label with the word *Philadelphia* on it, while the locomotive itself was clearly destined for the UK.

A

CHAPTER

5

Railways as a form of transport captured the imagination

of the public powerfully and immediately. At first people

were frightened by dire

Toy Trains

warnings of the severe

damage that the human

frame would suffer when subjected to speeds in excess of

30mph (48kph). But quite quickly the romance of the train

overcame fright, and the continuing love affair with railway engines began.

Inevitably, in the golden days of the tin toy manufacturers before World War I, many superb trains were produced in the great factories of Nuremberg and Göppingen, but although these form the centrepiece of any serious collection of toy railways, they were by no means the first to be made.

The opening of the Stockport to Darlington railway in 1825 led to the great rush of building across the world, and the major events were celebrated by many of the traditional toy makers. Among the earliest is a representation of the first train on the Nuremberg to Fürth line, made as a flat figure, in the manner of the early lead soldiers. It shows an engine pulling a tender and two stage-coach-type carriages, with a guard sitting on the roof of the last. Dating from 1835, it is in the tradition of the pleasure gardens and zoos that appeared

A

A lead flat, made in four sections, representing the first train to run between Nuremberg and Fürth in 1835. Note the guard sitting on the roof of the last carriage, as in the horse-drawn coaches of the time.

B

This primitive early train set is made of painted wood and was sold with a wooden truck. It was made in Germany c.1845 and is 3¼in (8cm) high.

from the early 18th century period onwards, and was more a decorative than a practical toy.

The makers of wooden toys also sold representations of trains, some complete with wooden rails, and while these are crude, they give some idea of the style of engines and rolling stock of the period. More realistic were the early scale models, mainly produced by the makers of scientific instruments, which often served as selling aids or as prototypes before production in full scale. These are so rare and fine that they are out of the reach of the ordinary collector.

When caring for railway items, as dry an environment as possible is needed to prevent the onset of rust, which can be caused by excessive humidity. Cleaning must never be done with an abrasive substance, however mild, but with a soft, oily cloth. Moving parts sometimes benefit from the application of a light machine oil, but care must be taken to wipe off any surplus. Even if a piece is worn, it is never wise for anyone other than an expert to attempt restoration, for unless the right components and paints are used, the value of the piece is lost.

Railways have always been an important part of a boy's childhood, and they fascinate some men throughout their lives. The trains made for boys in the early part of this century, like their full-scale prototypes, have now earned an honourable retirement – providing enjoyment by the artistry of their workmanship rather than the excitement of their operation.

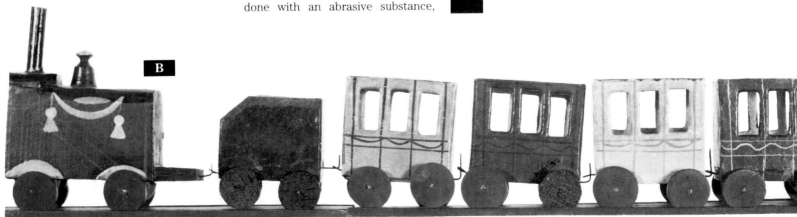

B

The Paris-based company of Charles Rossignol specialized in making flimsy but attractive toys. The finish on this 0-6-0 floor train was originally bright and shining, but it has aged. Rossignol's mark, *C.R.*, may be seen on the side of the locomotive.

CLOCKWORK AND STEAM

It was not until the second half of the 19th century that the production of toy railways began in earnest, with trains that ran either by clockwork or live steam. Oddly, many of these were retrospective in design, representing prototypes that had been obsolete for up to 30 years, perhaps pandering to fathers with fond memories of their own childhood.

The simplest of the clockwork locomotives held a motor in a central box, and the train was drawn in a circle by means of a long arm of wire. Known as the Rotary Railway Express, this is one of the first tinplate toy train sets. Small in size, it was only 1⅞in (44mm) high and the engine, tender and two carriages a total of 12in (30cm) long. Similar small tinplate trains, not intended to run on tracks, were made, particularly in France, which was at the time more successful than Germany in the production of metal toys. Most of them were without any form of motive power, and were simple push or pull toys, which are often known as carpet or floor trains.

The earliest toy engines were mainly steam-powered floor runners – not designed to run on tracks – and, because of their propensity for leaking water from their valve gear, they were known as Birmingham dribblers or piddlers. Most had the front, non-driving wheels set at an angle, so that the engine would always run in a circle. These little engines, fired by methylated spirit burners, must have been an immense fire risk, as they were prone to turn over!

The British and the French were among the most prominent makers of this type of engine and firms such as Stevens's Model Dockyard of London and the Clyde Model Dockyard of Glasgow were particularly well known in the field. Neither appears to have been a very large concern, and while their advertisements proudly proclaim the products as 'our own make', there is strong evidence that most of the smaller manufacturers bought in parts, or indeed complete models, from each other. One of the sources of such supply was the Paris-based firm of Radiguet & Massiot, whose products may easily be identified in the catalogue produced by the Clyde Model Dockyard.

Most of the early companies would supply either the completed engine, ready to fire, or a kit of parts for home assembly. While, as always, the more expensive the model, the greater the degree of realism and the better the finish, it should not be thought that these toys were in any sense true scale models; they were merely reasonable representations of the prototypes. Nor was there, in the early days, any attempt to stand-ardize gauges – manufacturers simply used what seemed reasonable for the size of the toy.

Engines are classified by the number of wheels, both in full-size locomotives and in toys and models. The first number indicates how many leading wheels there are, the second the number of driving wheels and the third the number of trailing wheels. Thus a 2-4-0 engine has two leading, four driving and no trailing wheels. Very rarely on toys an additional set of driving wheels is encountered, and the configuration is then written, for example, 0-6-6-0. Most of the late-Victorian engines in Europe were in fact of the 2-2-0 type, the leading wheels being strikingly small. These trains have been given the nickname 'stork legs', although the origins of the expression are not known – it may have come from America.

Not all of the early models were crude. Newton & Co., of London, turned out excellent examples, made almost entirely of unpainted brass, with ebony being used for the buffer beams. Newton was primarily a manufacturer of scientific instruments, producing models only to special order, and its work is much finer than that normally found in the products of the model dockyards.

Another British instrument maker who produced exceptionally fine models was H.J. Wood, father of the conductor, Sir Henry Wood. The quality of his work varied greatly, presumably in accordance with the

A

amount of money that his clients wished to spend, but his best models do qualify as true scale models, not simply toys.

It was only at the end of the 19th century that the revolution in model railway occurred that was to make them truly accessible to a wide public. At the Spring Fair in Leipzig in 1891, Märklin showed for the first time trains running on a standard system of gauges, from 1 to 4.

The size of the railway system, whether in full scale or miniature, is expressed in terms of the width of the tracks, which in Germany was measured, until 1930, from the centre of the railheads; since that date, by international agreement, it has been measured from the inside edge of the

rails, a difference in model railway terms of around ⅛in (3mm). Confusion is added by the fact that, for a long time, there was no agreement among manufacturers as to which gauge corresponded to a given number: thus Bing's gauge 4 is the same size as Märklin's gauge 3. When smaller sizes were later introduced, the gauge below 1 logically was called 0, and even later the half gauge 00 or H0. Further miniaturization destroyed the earlier numerical pattern, and the smallest size now available is N.

The trains of the late 19th century, even those made by the major manufacturers, are almost surprisingly crude, with the clockwork versions being little more than primitive sketches of the prototypes. The

wheels look large and clumsy and the rolling stock is simply stamped from the tinplate and hand-painted; indeed the charm of these pieces lies in their very crudeness. They were, of course, intended chiefly for the lower middle classes, who had neither the space to house nor the money to buy the larger scale steam-fired locomotives, which might cost as much as a poorer manual worker earned in a year.

Among the best, and most sought after, of the late 19th-century German toy trains are those manufactured by Jean Schoenner, whose factory in Nuremberg opened in 1875. Schoenner's output remained fairly small, but he produced some of the most impressive engines in a mixture of pressed tinplate and brass. Perhaps the most remarkable was a large 5⅖in (137mm) gauge model, the *Luitpold*, which was shown at the Paris Exhibition of 1900. The Bavarian State Railways 4-4-0 locomotive, which stands 15⅓in (39cm) high and is 38½in (98cm) long, is sufficiently large for a wealth of detail, and the work is finer than that found in the work of any other maker of the period. While this was obviously a special exhibition piece, Schoenner's more commercial examples, which were often sold in Great Britain through the Bassett-Lowke company, were also often extremely fine, and there are still some that, although known through catalogue drawings, have not yet appeared on the market.

Bassett-Lowke also retailed the products of other makers from Germany, particularly Georges Carette, the Nuremberg-based Frenchman. Carette was perhaps the first of the toy makers to produce locomotives that were reasonably true to their prototypes. One of the earliest was the Lady of the Lake, an unusual gauge 1 2-2-2 London & North-Western Railway locomotive with a very large driving wheel. It appeared in the catalogues at the turn of the century. Because of the accuracy of the models and relatively short life of the company, Carette's pieces always command high prices.

The wealth of Great Britain led

Early toy trains were
often simple and
rather crude,
especially when they
were made for the
cheaper end of the
market. This
locomotive, tender
and carriage, in
approximately gauge
00, was made *c.*1910
by Gebrüder Bing of
Nuremberg.

most of the major German toy makers
to concentrate their marketing efforts
on that country, although the United
States, both as a selling area and a
source of prototypes, was not ignored.
American designs held an appeal on
both sides of the Atlantic. The Bassett-Lowke catalogue of 1904, for
example, shows a Carette model of
the Vauclain Compound engine which
ran on the New York Central railway
and was, at the time, one of the most
famous American locomotives. In
common with most other models of
the period, it was available with either
clockwork or steam power. Its appeal
to the British was that it was totally
unlike the engines with which they
were familiar, having such exotic
accessories as cowcatchers.

Probably the most famous collaboration between Nuremberg and
Great Britain was that between Bing
and Bassett-Lowke. Stefan Bing met
the English businessman, Wenman J.
Bassett-Lowke, at the 1900 Paris
Exhibition, and shortly afterwards
Bing engines and rolling stock were
introduced into Bassett-Lowke's catalogue. One of the earliest, and most
famous, results of this collaboration
was the London & North-Western

Railway's 4-4-0 locomotive, the *Black
Prince*. Bing's work was invariably
heavier and less detailed than that of
his main competitors, but the output
of the factory was so great that
examples of the firm's products are
more easily available than any other
German manufacturer, except perhaps Märklin.

By the turn of the century, and
in the years preceding World War I,
Märklin produced a large quantity of
excellent models, based on prototypes
from all over the world, which
achieved wide international sales.
Märklin did not compete with the
best of the work of Jean Schoenner
or Georges Carette, but the company
pursued a consistent policy of excel-
lence and realism that led it to dominate the world market and its early
work commands substantial prices.
Throughout this early period, Märklin's major emphasis, in common with
most other European manufacturers,
was on gauge 1 or larger; gauge 0 did
not really gain a hold until the inter-
war years.

Railways could provide horrify-
ing copy for the newspapers when
accidents occurred, and there were
several spectacular crashes at the

A

B

This naïve 2-2-0 locomotive and tender were made by Bing *c.*1895. It is gauge 1.

B

A

A

The illustration on the box promises far more than the rather ordinary lithographed set by Hess, made *c.*1900, contained therein delivered.

B

Among the most sought after toy trains are Bassett-Lowke's *Black Prince* (at the rear), which was made for Bassett-Lowke by Bing, and Hornby's *Flying Scotsman*. The Hornby train was made betwen *c.*1928 and 1940 in all the major liveries, and it is, therefore, one of the easier Hornby locomotives to acquire, although it will be expensive.

B

C

Hornby's Dublo – i.e., gauge 00 – system immediately recognized contemporary developments in railway transport. This British Railways diesel locomotive is made partly of plastic and dates from the late 1950s.

beginning of the century. Children who enjoyed engineering such catastrophes for themselves were assisted by Märklin, which brought out a complete train that disintegrated on impact. Springs threw the sides and roofs off carriages, and only mangled corpses were lacking for total realism.

Many smaller German firms produced interesting and, in some cases novel, trains. Karl Bub of Nuremberg, in addition to making many fairly unexceptional (but nevertheless collectable) trains, produced the *Whatsamatter*. After running a short distance, the train stops and the driver's head appears through a trap in the cab, as if to inspect an obstruction. Satisfied, he re-enters, and the train runs on to the next delay.

Small, crude trains were also produced by Hess, mainly in very small scale and either flywheel- or clockwork-powered, or indeed unpowered. These were brightly lithographed, as opposed to the hand-painting that was common on the better toys, and they were floor runners. Cheap and amusing, they were more in the nature of stocking fillers than serious models.

Ernst Planck of Nuremberg, a firm that specialized in scientific toys such as projectors, magic lanterns and stationary engines, made a number of trains. Rather crude, both in scale and finish, they are characterized by coarse wide wheels with deep flanges. Interesting because of their rarity, they are prevented by their crudeness from attaining the high prices that more common, but better made, models of other makers reach.

In Britain, the early years were dominated by Bassett-Lowke, which imported most of its stock but did have a manufacturing facility, which supplied mainly larger gauge, well-engineered models. The firm's output increased after World War I, when, even though Carette had ceased production in 1917, Bassett-Lowke mysteriously obtained many of that firm's dies and was thus able to continue to make models previously supplied from Germany. Similarly, after the Bing family lost control of its company and fled from Nazi Germany, Bassett-Lowke assisted Bing in the setting up of the English Trix company, which produced smaller gauge railways.

After World War I, many people

felt that it was unpatriotic to buy German toys. A gap opened in the market, and to fill it, Hornby, which had previously made only the Meccano construction kits, began to produce train sets. The early products were gauge 0, and some excellent models appeared. Hornby quickly achieved a position of market dominance in the United Kingdom, so that its name became almost synonymous with toy and model railways. Hornby also made an early entry into the European market, establishing its French manufacturing facility before the outbreak of World War II. Its range was wide, from simple, cheap, clockwork-powered tank engines to sophisticated and reasonably accurate representations of mainline express locomotives, such as the London, Midland & Scottish Railway's *Princess Elizabeth*, powered by electricity, which was made from 1937 to 1939.

Lionel made these two gauge 0 electric locomotives in the 1930s. On the left is a pressed steel and diecast set based on the famous *City of Portland* of the Union Pacific Railroad. This three-car diesel unit, which was made *c.*1934, is one of Lionel's most convincing trains and accurately represents its prototype. On the right is a super-detail scale model of the *Hudson*, a 4-6-4 locomotive of the New York Central Railway. This train dates from *c.*1937, and it is one of the most important pieces by Lionel and is keenly collected. Both trains are seen emerging from another Lionel item, the Hell Gate bridge, which was made in the late 1920s.

THE AGE OF ELECTRICITY

Although electric power was used as early as 1880 by Ernst Planck, which exhibited the system at the 1882 Bavarian Trades Exhibition, no examples from this early date have so far been found. Among the earliest commercial producers of electric toy trains was the American firm of Voltamp, which was marketing them from about 1890. In Europe they did not become available until some 10 years later, when all the major manufacturers were almost forced to offer electricity as an alternative to clockwork and steam. Because of the difficulty in producing a satisfactory transformer to convert high-voltage alternating current to low-voltage direct, as well as stringent government regulations, the method did not become generally accepted in Britain until the 1920s.

The smaller houses built after World War I forced the makers of toy railways to re-assess the market. Bassett-Lowke was again in the lead, persuading Bing to produce the first Table Top Railway, which was half the size of 0 gauge and known as either H0 or 00. This eventually became almost the standard, and few manufacturers now produce models above this size.

In the United States, the market was served at an early date by native manufacturers, who worked mainly in gauge 1 or larger. One of the first was Eugene Beggs of New Jersey, who in 1875 obtained a patent for a model engine made of cast iron. To compensate for this increased weight, his rolling stock had cardboard bodies, covered with lithographed paper. These colourful, but fragile, toys are now avidly collected but are in very short supply. The firm did not have a long life, ceasing production in 1906.

Tinplate toys were made in Forestville, Connecticut, a centre of the clockmaking industry, and the first American tinplate engines were made there by George W. Brown who,

American Flyer was
the only US toy train
manufacturer to
produce a European-
type train. This
clockwork Great
Northern Railway
tank locomotive was
made in gauge 0 in
the early 1920s and
marketed as British
Flyer. Unfortunately,
British toy train
buyers were
unimpressed with the
cast iron construction
and the lithographed
coaches and by the
inclusion of a tender
with a tank engine,
and British Flyer had
a short life.

B

C

This group of gauge 0
locomotives and
accessories was made
by Märklin in the
1930s. At the rear is
the two-car diesel
unit, the *Flying
Hamburger*, which
was produced from
the early 1930s until
World War II. It was
available in gauge 1
as well as gauge 0
and in both electric
and clockwork
versions. In the
centre is Märklin's
famous *Der Adler*,
which was produced
in 1935 to
commemorate the
centenary of the
opening of the first
commercial steam
railway in Germany
between Nuremberg
and Fürth. The toy
train was complete
with driver and
passengers, and only
a limited number was
made: it is a rare and
desirable item. In
the front is an
electrically powered
version of the
Southern Region
Merchant Taylors.

C

in common with European manufacturers, produced many toys other than railways. By the 1870s there was a fairly large-scale production, and although some models were clockwork-powered, the majority were simple push-alongs, and almost all were floor runners.

The most famous name in American model railway history is that of Edward R. Ives, who established his business in Plymouth, Connecticut, in 1868, moving two years later to Bridgeport. The company slogan, 'Ives Toys make Happy Boys', featured prominently in its advertisements. For a period the company held in the United States the market dominance that Hornby had in Great Britain, but Ives was an early victim of the Depression, running into financial difficulties, which led to bankruptcy in 1928. Ives produced a wide variety of trains, from

A

The gauge 0 electric locomotive was made by Ives; the carriages are by Ives and Lionel and date from c.1932. On the right is a cast iron train by Ives, dating from c.1916, which was made in the company's 3200 series; it, too, is powered by electricity.

early tinplate and cast iron floor runners to steam-powered cast iron. In 1910 the company produced the first gauge 0 electric system in the United States.

Although the name of Ives continued for a time after the bankruptcy, by 1933 the company had been absorbed by Lionel, which had been founded in New York in 1906 and had pursued its own distinctive style, even to the extent of using a non-standard size. Slightly larger than normal gauge 2 at 2$\frac{1}{10}$ (54mm), it was promoted as the American Standard Gauge. An advantage to the company was that only its rolling stock and accessories could run on the system, ensuring brand loyalty once the first purchase had been made. Larger than most of its competitors, a Lionel train of the 1930s, with streamlined bodywork and silver paint, is a stylish evocation of the

great US railway era.

The third giant of the US scene was American Flyer, which also started operations at the beginning of the century. Its major emphasis was on gauge 0, and the range of its products is wide, almost entirely based on United States prototypes, although there was a short-lived attempt during the 1920s to break into the English market with a clockwork-powered, cast iron engine. For its domestic market, the company mainly produced electric-powered trains and its products are rarely found in Europe.

A

B

A gauge 1 coach from the *Kaiser* train, Germany's royal train, which was made by Bing *c.*1902. The clerestory roof opens to reveal tables and chairs.

B

C

C

A Hornby Dublo Royal Mail van. When the car passed a switch by the side of the track the door opened to collect a sack of mail.

ROLLING STOCK AND ACCESSORIES

Inevitably collectors place most emphasis on the locomotives, but much of the attraction of a railway setting is in the rolling stock: here, the variety is greater than in the engines themselves. From the very beginning manufacturers have provided all the necessary accessories to complete the trains – passenger carriages, goods wagons, guard vans and even mobile cranes. There are,

too, some wonderfully decorated stations complete with newspaper kiosks and lights.

The earliest commercially made rolling stock items were mainly passenger coaches, and, like the engines, they were relatively crude, simply stamped from tinplate and hand painted in the appropriate livery, with the windows left as empty spaces. As the sets became more sophisticated, so did the carriages. By the early years of the 20th century, a bewildering array, with good detail, could be found. They were still rather untrue to the originals, but were better than the mere sketches that had been provided at first. Particularly interesting are the coaches based on continental prototypes, such as the

Swiss gallery carriage, which has an observation platform running the length of the carriage, the guard rails ornamented with Gothic tracery and heavy mouldings to the pillars supporting the roof. Produced by Märklin from 1909 to 1920, it has opening doors leading to the compartments. Passengers could be purchased separately to complete the scene.

The search for increasing realism led to the introduction of coaches with opening doors, windows glazed with mica and seats in the compartments. So that the passengers might sit neatly when the train was in motion, Märklin and Bing soldered pins on to the seats, and the composition figures had corresponding holes into which the pins fitted. Carette

Unusual items of rolling stock are always keenly collected. This gauge 1 Rüdesheim wine tanker was made by Märklin c.1910.

passengers, however, had the pin fitted to them, which slotted into a hole in the seat – a ready means of identifying some unmarked figures or coaches.

With the introduction of lithography, the presentation of the same basic body in different guises became easier, and dining cars, sleeping cars and Pullman carriages became more commonly available. Many of the manufacturers supplied department stores under contract with sets which were sometimes marked only with the store's name. Märklin, for example, was a regular supplier to Gamages of London, and the make of these models is mainly identified by reference to known and marked models sold through other sources. The finest detail was on the larger gauge models; with the introduction of the smaller 00, the surface became more important than the interior.

It would be almost impossible for a collector to obtain a complete set of all the goods wagons made by one manufacture, for the range of service vehicles was even greater than that of passenger coaches. As each advance was made, it was recognized by the toy makers. Thus, when the British used armoured trains in the Boer War, Märklin reproduced them in miniature. With the advent of the motor car, the distribution of fuel became important and was mainly undertaken by rail: tanker wagons, decorated with company logos, such as those of Shell or Anglo-American Oil, were quickly introduced into the catalogues. Coal trucks and timber wagons, complete with twigs for tree trunks, became a commonplace in the toy cupboard, especially as goods vehicles were cheaper than passenger carriages. More easily found, they are now consequently less expensive in the collector's market.

Unusual and rare items obviously command the highest prices. In Britain, the Colman's Mustard truck, painted in the distinctive bright yellow and decorated with the royal coat of arms, is at a premium because of its scarcity, especially the gauge 1 version produced by Carette. Märklin recognized the beginning of the trend towards containerization as early as 1910 and produced flat-bed wagons on which the containers were loaded. These are also rare items which are consequently expensive to purchase.

No layout was complete without the appropriate station buildings, and in this area the toy makers excelled themselves. Little effort was made to recognize styles of architecture other than that found in Germany, but the buildings are impressive examples of the tin workers' skill. Frequently the brickwork and tiles were impressed in the metal; and with windows, shutters, ticket collector's gates, waiting rooms and ticket offices, they remain charming examples of the Bavarian's ability to create exciting and attractive toys. The platform scenes were completed with passengers, railway staff, newspaper stands, benches and even cafés. Working oil lamps could be used to light the scene, while there were signals, level crossing gates and tunnels to provide excitement and realism to the layout. All of these items command respectable prices, especially those made before World War I, for they provide the necessary background to the trains themselves.

With all this realism available to the collector, it is surprising that the track itself is of little or no value. This is partly because it is in abundant supply, but chiefly because the engines are now far too valuable to be used: steaming an early engine risks damage to the paintwork. Restoration always decreases the value. Steam engines are especially susceptible to damage, as the heat of the boiler scorches the paint, while neglecting to drain the boiler results in corrosion. Even clockwork engines are seldom operated, to prevent possible damage to the spring. If they are wound up, care should be taken not to wind the motor fully, in order to prevent excessive pressure, which can cause the metal to snap.

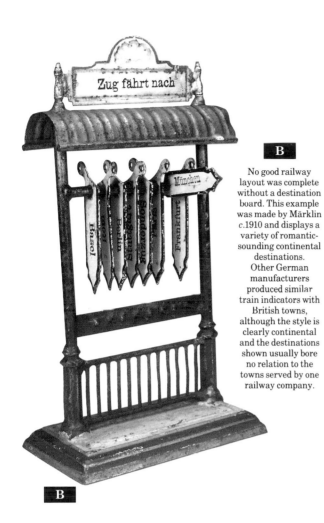

B

No good railway layout was complete without a destination board. This example was made by Märklin c.1910 and displays a variety of romantic-sounding continental destinations. Other German manufacturers produced similar train indicators with British towns, although the style is clearly continental and the destinations shown usually bore no relation to the towns served by one railway company.

B

C

A gauge 1 Compagnie Internationale des Wagon-lits sleeping car by Bing. The coach is hand painted, except for the gold lettering, which is transfer printed. Bing's mark, *G.B.* (for Gebrüder Bing), may be seen at centre front.

D

All the major manufacturers made carriages and rolling stock compatible with the liveries of the countries in which their products were marketed. This gauge 1 luggage car, made c.1925 by Bing, is in the livery of the New York Central Railway, and it includes a section for the guard with a desk and a chair, as well as a kitchen with a dresser and stove.

D

CHAPTER

6

The imitiation of transport in toy form reached its widest

market with the introduction of the diecasting process,

similar in concept to the

Diecast Toys

method used by William

Britain for the hollow-casting

of soldiers. The earliest models were not, in fact,

recognizable as particular types or makes of vehicle, but

were merely generalized represent-ations of cars or aeroplanes. Made of a soft lead alloy, they were quite well detailed, with delicate wheels. They appeared almost simultaneously in both France and the United States in *c*.1910, being made by S.R. and Toot-sietoy respectively. Small in size, they were about 2in (5cm) long, a scale that increased to a standard 3in (7.5cm) about five years later. In 1915 the first model based on an actual prototype was made. The Model T Ford, probably the most famous car of its period, was then in its heyday, and a toy version was marketed sim-ultaneously by both S.R. and Tootsie-toy in the new, larger size.

Although the majority of people associate diecasting methods almost exclusively with models of road trans-port, from the very beginning other toys, such as guns, and aeroplanes,

A

A boxed set of Tootsietoy diecast toys, made in the US. Although the mould joints are crudely made and can be clearly seen and although only generic types were made, a boxed set such as this is extremely rare and commands high prices.

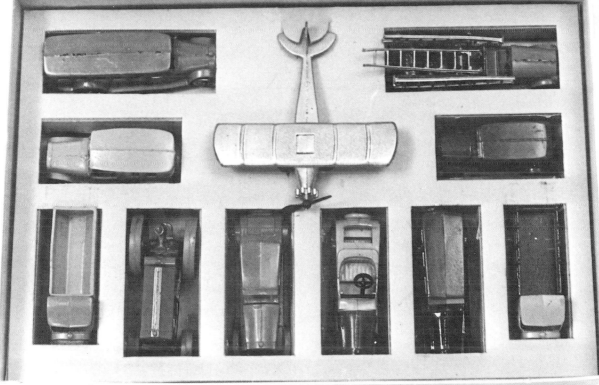

A

B

A very rare model of
a self-propelled gun,
made by S.R. of
France *c*.1910. One of
the earliest diecast
toys to be made, it
has considerable
detail even though it
is only 2in (5cm) long.

C

C

Another rare diecast
toy by S.R., this
model of an aeroplane
is not based on any
specific prototype –
indeed, it seems
unlikely that such an
aircraft could fly.

B

A

During the 1930s
there was a vogue for
model cars that could
be taken apart and
re-assembled. This
racing car by Hornby
is of exceptionally
heavy construction.

A

were made to the standard 2in (5cm) size. Detailed and attractive, they were far removed from full-sized objects that could fly or be fired with safety, rather they were visions of an improbable future, like the more recent space vehicles.

Being a cheap method of producing visually striking toys, diecasting attracted many of the major manufacturers, including Märklin, especially after the change of material from a lead to a zinc-based alloy, known as zamak or mazak, which also included magnesium, aluminium and copper. While mazak was lighter and harder than the lead alloy, it tended, over a period, to become very brittle and to crack. This weakness, mainly caused by impurities in manufacture, is aggravated by humidity, and it can lead to the virtual destruction of a toy.

Being one of the first on the scene, Tootsietoy, a Chicago-based company, dominated the world market until the 1930s. Its range was vast, from aeroplanes and cars to cooking stoves to dolls' houses, and it worked mainly from American

D

The realism of the Hornby Dublo locomotives and rolling stock was achieved by diecasting. This 0-6-0 tank engine was made in the 1950s and is in British Railways, post-nationalization livery.

prototypes. The company was responsible for most of the technical innovations in production methods, introducing in 1928, for example, a separately cast radiator grille, nickel-plated for greater realism. It pioneered the use of mazak, and was the first to make a common chassis to which the bodies of different models were attached. From the mid-1920s Tootsietoy normally recessed the lines around the doors and the engine compartment, while its European competitors continued to use unrealistic raised lines for another 30 years.

During the first third of the 20th century, diecast toys in Great Britain were produced chiefly by the makers of soldiers, as adjuncts to their main business, and they provided little serious threat to the imported Tootsietoys. In the early 1930s Hornby, which had largely captured the domestic model railway market, began to produce lead figures of people, to add realism to the layouts, and then went logically to the production of road vehicles in scale with its railways. Originally sold as Hornby Modelled Miniatures, the name was changed in

Diecast Toys

A

A traffic jam of Dinky Toys and a few Lesney Models of Yesteryear. All were made in the 1950s and later. The vehicles in the Models of Yesteryear range are extremely popular with collectors, for they are handsome, well-detailed models; the first of the series appeared in 1956.

1934, first to Meccano Miniatures and then to Meccano Dinky Toys. Their success was immediate, partly because they were the product of an already successful company, but mainly because they were the first to be based on purely British prototypes.

Dinky retained its predominant position in the market in Great Britain until the late 1950s, although not without competition in the post-war years from Wells-Brimtoy, Mettoy and Chad Valley, all of which made diecasts as an addition to their tinplate ranges. One of the more interesting of the Chad Valley products was a range of models of Rootes Group vehicles. They were sold as promotional aids – in the manner of André Citröen – in Rootes garages as well as toy shops.

The company that eventually superseded Dinky as market leader was Lesney, founded in 1947. Originally it produced castings for other

B

Meccano Ltd, the company established by Frank Hornby, originally concentrated on the production of metal construction sets. In 1931, however, it introduced Modelled Miniatures, a series of cast metal accessories intended to complement Hornby train sets. The earliest sets in the series, numbers 1 to 21, were of station figures, railside furniture and even agricultural equipment. Set 22, which is illustrated here and which was announced in *Meccano Magazine* for December 1933, consisted of six diecast vehicles: a motor truck, a delivery van, a tractor, a tank and two cars, a sports car and a sports coupé. These toys were cast in a lead alloy and their comparative fragility has resulted in great rarity.

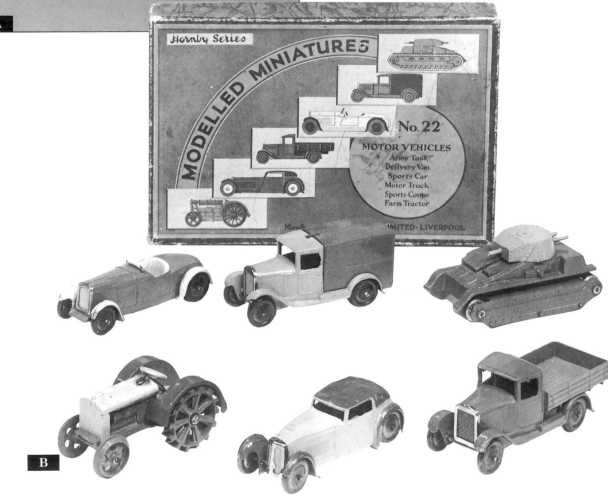

companies, but in the early 1950s it began to make its own models under the Matchbox label. By 1960 it was the strongest of the British manufacturers in the home market, and had achieved a similar position in the United States, producing 75 new models a year. Of a smaller size than their predecessors (reverting to the 2in (5cm) standard), they captured the imagination of children with their representations of both current and early prototypes. So successful were they that the size again became an industry standard.

In 1956, Lesney's Models of Yesteryear made their appearance prompted by the already burgeoning interest in the nostalgic. Priced identically to other toys in the range, they

appealed to both children and adults, and were the first to create, almost accidentally, a new market for toys for the collector, which has continued to grow until the present day. They were also the first of the diecast toys to show a significant increase in value over the short term, and were probably instrumental in creating the interest in the collecting of diecasts in general.

Although Lesney had captured a large section of the market in the 1950s, Dinky retained a strong following because of the larger size of its models. In the same year that the Models of Yesteryear were launched, however, an attack on Dinky's primacy in the larger scale was made by Mettoy's introduction of its Corgi

By early 1936 some 200 types of Dinky Toy had been manufactured in Liverpool, and additional items were also made in the Meccano factory in France. Some of the French Dinky Toys were marketed in the UK, and many collectors believe that the style and finish of the French-made pieces are superior to those made in the UK. Although the toys illustrated here were made in France, only the Panhard bus, the Citroën car and the motorcycle delivery vehicle are based on French prototypes.

A

A group of Dinky Supertoys in mint condition. Made in the early 1960s, the same basic chassis was used with several different bodies, a system that allowed Hornby to increase the range economically.

B

These boxed sets of Dinky Toys from the post-war period are based on World War II prototypes. At the back is a large model of a howitzer by Britains; it ejects the shell-case after firing the projectile.

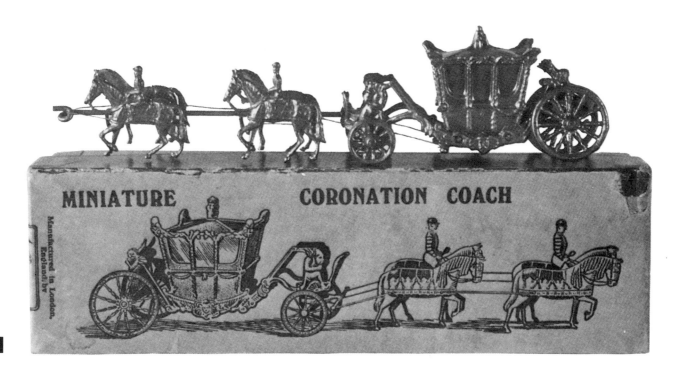

C

The earliest of the diecast toys made by Lesney was a miniature coronation coach. The most famous state coach in toy collecting is the large Lesney coach, which is about 12in (30cm) long. It was first made in 1952 and achieved a degree of notoriety when an advertisement in *The Times* offered £100 ($175) for an example. In the years that followed, however, the large Lesney coach rarely achieved more than about £20 ($35) at auction. Nevertheless, the small Lesney coach, which is about 4½in (11cm) long, continues to attract attention among toy collectors.

range. The models were more up-to-date than Dinky's and were made more realistic by the inclusion of features such as treaded tyres, aluminium hub caps and plastic windows, something not previously seen on diecasts, but quite common on tinplate toys such as Triang's Minic series. The toys were well produced and made a severe impact on the dominance previously held by Hornby. Despite many vicissitudes, the Corgi name continues, and while the company aims mainly at the toy market, it produces a special range for collectors.

Triang, a firm that included in its catalogues almost every kind of toy, could not ignore diecasts. It entered the arena in 1959 with its own Spot-On label. The venture was fairly short-lived, being abandoned in 1968, when Hornby, the makers of Dinky Toys, was acquired. The Spot-On toys had little impact on the market, as the models were, in the main, less well detailed than their rivals and lacked features that were becoming commonplace, such as opening doors and bonnets, which, although adding realism, weakened the structure.

During the 1960s the British market was hit by an American range of small-scale cars, known as Hot Wheels. Fitted with low-friction bearings and extremely thin axles, they were able to travel faster and further than other models, and all the other makers were forced to follow the trend, with names such as Superfast, Speedwheels and Whizzwheels. By this stage, the interior of the vehicles had become almost as important as the exterior, having such fittings as vacuum-moulded plastic seats and metal engine blocks.

European manufacturers made little effort at penetrating overseas markets, even though Märklin produced some diecasts and was, in fact, the first to use a tinplate base plate,

A

These two Dinky delivery vans are distinguished only by the transfers. Both were made c.1935, and such vehicles are now rare, the type of transfer causing great variation in price.

B

This group of post-war Dinky Toys indicates something of the range available to collectors. The military vehicles are now a specialist collecting subject in their own right, while all the aircraft are of great interest, especially the Heinkel bomber at the bottom left.

A

on which the name of the model was stamped. The method was almost immediately followed by other manufacturers throughout the world. At its French factory Hornby produced a series of models based on French prototypes, as did Solido, which was the major force in that market.

The diecast collector has a large choice of themes open to him, as most manufacturers tried to cover transport of every conceivable type. Some specialize in military models, which were among the earliest to be produced; others concentrate on individual manufacturers or models based on a particular prototype, such as the Jaguar car. There were also models associated with films, such as the James Bond series, or television, with the Thunderbirds.

Large-scale sets of lorries and vans are also popular, and some of the good examples, such as Corgi's Chipperfield Circus, which included a Land Rover, crane, trailers and giraffes, are interesting and attractive toys that command substantial prices. In addition to road transport, there are aeroplanes, space vehicles and waterline models of ships, all of which have strong followings.

As with any toys, condition is of paramount importance, and in sales the highest prices are always paid for examples that can be called 'mint and boxed', although there is interest in items that are playworn if they are unusual models. The main enemies of diecasts are sunlight, which can lead to the fading of paint and applied logos, and excessive humidity, which can accelerate the

onset of metal fatigue. Some collectors attempt to overcome this by sealing all openings and joints with superglue, but this procedure is of doubtful value, since the decay, once started, is irreversible. There are now many spare parts available, especially tyres, for most models, and some collectors undertake quite extensive restoration, even though a restored vehicle does not command the same price as one in its original condition.

Because of the wide choice and the small size of the models, they have attracted a considerable following, and there are many specialized shows or swap-meets for the devotees. Easy to display and inherently less fragile than tinplate, and a good and interesting collection can be formed with little difficulty.

A

B

Major Manufacturers of Dolls and Automata

ABT & FRANKE HANOVER, GERMANY

Founded in 1865, by the 1890s it was advertising dressed dolls, celluloid bathing dolls and 'leather dolls with celluloid heads'.

ADAMS, EMMA E. OSWEGO, NEW YORK, USA

In 1891 Emma and her sister Marietta Adams began to make fabric dolls filled with cotton and sawdust. The dolls, in a range of sizes and types, were distributed by Marshall Field and were stamped *Columbian Doll/Emma E. Adams/Oswego N.Y.*

ALEXANDER DOLL CO. NEW YORK CITY, USA

The dolls of Beatrice Alexander Behrman and the Alexander Doll Company are among the most keenly collected of all US dolls, although they are rarely seen in Europe. The first rag dolls were made in the 1920s, and over the next two decades the company issued a range of character dolls.

ALT, BECK & GOTTSCHALCK NAUENDORF, GERMANY

Established in 1854, this company is known to have made a wide range of bisque heads and all-bisque dolls. It provided heads for Grace Storey Putnam's Bye-Lo in the 1920s and also made appealing character dolls of its own.

AMBERG, LOUIS, & SON CINCINATTI AND NEW YORK CITY, USA

When Amberg established his company in 1878 he was a doll importer and dealer, but after 1903 the company began to manufacture composition dolls for the US market as well as continuing to import from Europe. When supplies from Europe were interrupted during World War I, Amberg advertised his dolls with the slogans 'American Dolls for Americans' and 'The American Standard'.

AMERICAN CHARACTER DOLL CO. NEW YORK CITY, USA

In the early 1920s a series of composition character dolls was produced under the tradename *Petite*. The company produced a composition based on wood fibres, and dolls made of this were marked *Aceedee-dee Doll.* the trademarks used in the 1930s included a distinctive horseshoe.

ARNOLD, MAX OSCAR NEUSTADT, GERMANY

Founded in 1877, the factory made mechanical dolls, including talking dolls. It also produced bisque heads and was the first company to use pourable papier mâché.

ARNOLD PRINT WORKS NORTH ADAMS, MASSACHUSETTS, USA

A prints and dress fabrics manufacturer, founded in 1876, which produced printed doll patterns to be cut out, stitched and stuffed at home.

ARRANBEE DOLL CO. NEW YORK CITY, USA

Established in 1922, the company imported doll parts, which it assembled, and dolls. In 1924 it offered My Dream Babies, with bisque heads made by Marseille (q.v.) in direct competition with the Bye-Lo Babies of Grace Storey Putnam (q.v.). Other dolls registered included Kurly Head and Nancy (both 1930) and Little Angel (1940).

ART FABRIC MILLS NEW YORK CITY, USA

The major competitor of Arnold Print Works (q.v.), Art Fabric Mills was founded in 1899 and produced colourful printed patterns for dolls and animals for cutting out and making at home.

AU NAIN BLEU PARIS, FRANCE

Sold both French and German bisque-headed dolls in the last half of the 19th century, and, in the 1920s, S.F.B.J. dolls, which were marked *Unis France.*

BAHR & PROSCHILD OHRDRUF, GERMANY

A porcelain factory was founded in 1871 making both bisque and celluloid dolls, including the all-bisque frozen Charlottes or bathing dolls.

BELL & FRANCIS LONDON, UK

Manufactured simple printed dolls and toys on sheets for cutting out and assembling at home. Characters include Duck, Tabby Cat, Rabbit and Toy Spaniel.

BERGMANN, C.M. WALTERSHAUSEN, GERMANY

Founded in 1889, the company specialized in ball-jointed composition bodies; bisque heads were bought in from, among others, Marseille and Simon & Halbig (qq.v.). The company went bankrupt in 1931.

BISC NOVELTY MANUFACTURING CO. EAST LIVERPOOL, OHIO, USA

The company was founded by Ernst Reinhardt (q.v.) and was among the first US doll manufacturers to produce good quality bisque heads of US materials.

BONTEMS PARIS, FRANCE

Founded by Blaise Bontems in 1840; he was succeeded by his sons Charles and Alfred and by his grandson Lucien. A specialist automata manufacturer, the company was especially known for its singing birds and tableaux.

BORGFELDT, GEORGE, & CO. NEW YORK CITY, USA

A distribution company established in 1881 to import French and German dolls into the US, Borgfeldt was also responsible for commissioning Grace Storey Putnam's Bye-Lo and Rose O'Neil's Kewpie, two of the most successful dolls ever made.

BRU JNE. & CIE PARIS, FRANCE

Founded by Leon Casimir Bru in 1866, the company produced some of the most desirable dolls. It was also a pioneer of mechanical dolls and used other materials – leather, wood and papier mâché – in the creation of its dolls. Bru was a founder member of the S.F.B.J.

BUTLER BROTHERS SONNEBERG, GERMANY

A doll manufacturer and distributor founded in 1877, the company's catalogue included a wide range of wax, china, French bisque and kid-bodied dolls. It became one of the largest doll distributors to the US, with a main office in New York City. One of its most important suppliers was Cuno & Otto Dressel (q.v.).

BUTTON & LOENIG FRANKFURT-AM-MAIN, GERMANY

The company produced printed fabric figures c.1900; the dolls appear to have been assembled by the factory before sale.

CAMEO DOLL CO. NEW YORK CITY AND PORT ALLEGANY, PENNSYLVANIA, USA

Joseph Kallus, a successful designer, founded the company in 1922 to manufacture wooden and composition dolls, including Rose O'Neill's Kewpies (1922), Grace Storey Putnam's Bye-Lo Babies (1924) and Little Annie Rooney (1925), which Kallus designed with Jack Collins. Many of the company's dolls were distributed by Borgfeldt.

CHASE, MARTHA J. PAWTUCKET, RHODE ISLAND, USA

Martha Jenks Chase (1880–1925) made a soft, washable doll for her own children at the end of the 19th century and enjoyed unexpected commercial success with the Chase Stockinet Doll.

COX, JAMES LONDON, UK

A clockmaker, jeweller and showman James Cox (d.1788) also made automata. He is best known for the Silver Swan in Bowes Museum, County Durham, UK.

D'AUTREMONT PARIS, FRANCE

Founded in 1858, the company patented a rubber doll; its name is also found on some china-head dolls with kid bodies.

DEAN'S RAG BOOK CO. LONDON, UK

Samuel Dean began to make rag cut-out dolls for packaging in books in 1903; this soon gave way to selling doll patterns on linen sheets and then to selling pressed and stuffed dolls.

DECAMPS
PARIS, FRANCE

Established *c.*1847 by H.E. Decamps, the son of Jean Roullet, with whom he made automata. The letters *R.D.* (Roullet et Decamps) were used as a mark. Gaston Decamps (1882–1972) continued the family tradition and produced some of the company's best known work.

DIAMOND
POTTERY CO
HANLEY, UK

The company made bisque heads for UK dolls, using the mark *D.P. Co.* from 1908.

DRESSEL,
CUNO & OTTO
SONNEBERG,
GERMANY

Founded in the 1700s, this is the oldest doll-making company for which records exist. As well as making its own dolls, many of which were exported to the US, the company bought in heads from Simon & Halbig, Gebrüder Heubach and Armand Marseille (qq.v.) among others.

DROZ, PIERRE
JAQUET
SWITZERLAND

Droz (1721–90) made clocks and automata with his son, Henri Louis, and with J.F. Leschot. His name sometimes appears engraved on the musical movements of his pieces.

EDISON, THOMAS
NEW JERSEY, USA

Edison (1847–1931) patented the first phonograph doll in 1879. The commercially produced version, with a bisque head was made from 1889.

EFFANBEE
NEW YORK CITY,
USA

Founded as Fleischaker & Baum in 1910, the trademark *Effanbee* was registered in 1913, and the company is now more often known by that name. It continues to make a wide variety of dolls, although the most desirable are those made before World War II.

EICHORN,
CHRISTIAN,
& SOHNE
STEINACH,
GERMANY

Founded in 1860 by Max and Albert Eichorn, the company became known as Christian Eichorn & Söhne in 1909. It made porcelain dolls' heads, bathing dolls and doll parts until the 1930s.

FLEISCHMANN
& BLOEDEL
FURTH AND
SONNEBERG,
GERMANY

Founded in 1873, this company soon became an important supplier of dolls to France, making dolls specifically for that market. Because of its success in France, the company was a founder member of the S.F.B.J.

GAULTIER
ST MAURICE,
CHARENTON,
SEINE AND PARIS,
FRANCE

Some of the most exquisitely modelled of all bisque heads bear the mark *F.G.* in a cartouche, and although not all can be said definitely to have been made by Gaultier, a porcelain manufacturer, the fact that the company won several international competitions suggests that the company's work must have been of a high standard. Some Gesland (q.v.) bodies have Gaultier heads.

GESLAND
PARIS, FRANCE

From 1860 Gesland made wire-framed dolls with stockinet-covered bodies, some of which have heads made by Gaultier. It is possible that Gesland assembled dolls from parts bought in from other manufacturers.

GOODYEAR,
CHARLES
NEW HAVEN,
CONNECTICUT, USA

In 1851 Charles' brother Nelson patented his invention of hard rubber, and the company's rubber dolls are marked *Goodyear* or *Goodyear's Pat, May 6 1851. Ext. 1865.*

GOSS & CO.
STOKE-ON-TRENT,
UK

Primarily a manufacturer of porcelain busts in the 19th century, the company also made some bisque heads in the first decades of the 20th century.

GREINER & CO
STEINACH,
GERMANY

Founded in 1860 as a trading company, Greiner began to make leather dolls and doll parts in 1890. Borgfeldt distributed many of its dolls, which had bisque heads by Armand Marseille, Eichorn and Ernst Heubach (qq.v.).

GREINER, LUDWIG
PHILADELPHIA,
USA

From 1840 Greiner made papier mâché dolls' heads, and the company's heads are found on bodies made by Jacob Lacmann (q.v.). After 1874 the company was known as Greiner Brothers and, in 1890, was succeeded by Knell Brothers.

HANDWERCK, HEINRICH WALTERSHAUSEN, GERMANY

Founded in 1855 as a manufacturer of novelty items, from the 1880s the company produced a variety of ball-jointed dolls. In 1902 the factory was bought by Kämmer & Reinhardt (q.v.).

HEUBACH, ERNST KOPPELSDORF, GERMANY

The company was founded in 1887 to manufacture bisque dolls' heads and bathing dolls. After 1910 it specialized in character dolls. In 1919 the company merged with Armand Marseille (q.v.), the new partnership being known as the United Porcelain Factory of Köppelsdorf. The partnership ended in 1932.

HEUBACH, GEBRUDER LICHTE, GERMANY

Originally a porcelain manufacturer making figurines, this was one of the most prolific manufacturers of dolls' heads, especially for character dolls, and all-bisque dolls.

HORSMAN, E.I. & CO. NEW YORK CITY, USA

Edward Imerson Horsman began to import dolls from Europe in 1865, but by 1900 his company was manufacturing dolls, including rag dolls. He employed a number of artists, including Grace G. Drayton, Helen Trowbridge and Bernard Lipfert, to design dolls, and the company introduced character dolls such as the Campbell Kids in 1910 and the HEbees SHEbees in 1925.

JUMEAU PARIS, FRANCE

The company began to manufacture dolls in 1843 when Pierre François Jumeau, in a partnership known as Belton & Jumeau, established a doll factory. In 1873 Jumeau opened his own factory, and Emile Jumeau, Pierre's eldest son, developed the factory so that it handled all aspects of production, including the clothing and glass eyes. Jumeau dolls, with their charming facial expressions and beautiful 'paperweight' eyes, are world famous.

KAMMER & REINHARDT WALTERSHAUSEN, GERMANY

The partnership was founded in 1886 and established lasting fame through its successful range of character dolls. After 1902 all Kämmer & Reinhardt dolls have heads made by Simon & Halbig (q.v.), which were made specifically for the Waltershausen company. In 1920 Kämmer & Reinhardt bought Simon & Halbig, although the two companies continued to operate independently.

KESTNER, J.D. WALTERSHAUSEN, GERMANY

Johann Daniel Kestner established a papier mâché factory in 1816 and was soon making wooden doll joints. In 1863 his grandson, Adolf, took control, and the company started to produce a wide variety of bisque, porcelain, nanking and composition dolls, many of which were supplied to other German and to US companies. After 1900 the company also made celluloid dolls. The factory was closed in 1938.

KLING C.F. & CO OHRDRUF, GERMANY

A porcelain factory was founded in 1834 and began to produce dolls and dolls' heads c.1870. Kling made china and bisque heads, bathing dolls, and nanking dolls, and its dolls' heads are unusual in having not only moulded hair (usually blond) but also moulded jewellery, flowers and, around the neck, clothing. The bell trademark was introduced in 1880, and production continued until the 1940s.

KOENIG & WERNICKE WALTERSHAUSEN, GERMANY

Max Koenig and Rudolf Wernicke founded the company in 1912 to manufacture jointed dolls, character dolls, bent-limb baby dolls, hard rubber dolls and doll parts, using bisque heads supplied by Marseille, Bähr & Pröschild and Hertel, Schwab & Co. and celluloid heads from Rheinische Gummi (qq.v.). Production continued until at least 1935.

KATHE KRUSE BAD KOSEN, GERMANY

Before World War II, all Käthe Kruse dolls were made, by hand, of cheesecloth, stuffed and delicately painted. After 1945 the factory moved to Donäuworth and the dolls were mass-produced, thereafter showing a marked deterioration in quality. The company is still operating.

LACMANN, JACOB PHILADELPHIA, USA

Between 1860 and c.1883 dolls' bodies were made, with heads by Ludwig Greiner and Cuno & Otto Dressel (qq.v.).

LAMBERT, LEOPOLD
PARIS, FRANCE

Lambert originally worked for Vichy (q.v.). His automata, made between 1888 and 1923, are often marked with the letters *L.B.* on their keys.

LENCI
TURIN, ITALY

Under the tradename Lenci, Enrico Scavini made pressed-felt dolls from *c.*1920 in a wide variety of styles.

LESCHOT, JEAN FREDERIC
SWITZERLAND

Leschot (1746–1827) worked on automata with Pierre Jaquet Droz (q.v.).

MARSEILLE, ARMAND KOPPELSDORF AND NEUHAUS, GERMANY

Armand Marseille bought a toy factory in 1884 and a porcelain factory in 1885; he began to make shoulder-heads *c.*1890. Bisque heads were made both for Marseille's own company and for several other German and US companies.

MARSH, CHARLES
LONDON, UK

Poured-wax and papier mâché dolls were made from 1878 until 1894.

MEECH, HERBERT JOHN
LONDON, UK

Meech, who was the royal family's doll maker from 1865 to 1891, made both composition and wax dolls.

MERRYTHOUGHT TOYS
IRONBRIDGE, SHROPSHIRE, UK

Founded in 1930, the company produces soft toys and dolls covered in fur fabric or felt. The figures bear sewn-on labels and sometimes tags. In 1931 it registered a patent for a metal armature for soft toys.

MONTANARI
LONDON, UK

The whole family was involved in the manufacture of wax dolls from 1851 to the 1870s.

MOTSCHMANN, CHRISTOPH SONNEBERG, GERMANY

It seems likely that Motschmann was the first manufacturer to have patented a talking doll mechanism, which could be mass-produced. It was used in 1857–9.

O'NEILL, ROSE WILKES-BARRE, PENNSYLVANIA, USA

In 1912 the first Kewpie dolls appeared, and by 1914 21 companies in Germany and the USA were manufacturing them to meet the demands of George Borgfeldt & Co., which had exclusive distribution rights.

PECK, MRS LUCY
LONDON, UK

Mrs Peck made and sold dolls at her shop, The Doll's Home, from 1891 to 1921.

PIEROTTI
LONDON, UK

Finely modelled wax dolls' heads were made from *c.*1789; by 1850 papier mâché and composition dolls were being produced. Pierotti heads were combined with stuffed bodies, also made by the family.

PUTNAM, GRACE STOREY OAKLAND, CALIFORNIA, USA

Mrs Putnam's creation of a doll based on a 3-day-old baby – Bye-Lo Baby – was an immediate success and was marketed by George Borgfeldt & Co. Bisque and celluloid heads were made by a number of German companies.

RAVCA, BERNARD
PARIS, FRANCE

A maker of cloth art dolls during the 1930s and 1940s, Ravca also made dolls representing entertainers such as Mistinguette and Maurice Chevalier.

REINHARDT, ERNST PHILADELPHIA; EAST LIVERPOOL, OHIO; IRVINGTON, METUCHEN AND PERTH AMBOY, NEW JERSEY, USA

Reinhardt emigrated to the USA from Germany in 1909 and produced bisque-headed dolls with papier mâché bodies and wooden limbs. He established the short-lived Bisc Novelty Manufacturing Co. (q.v.) before manufacturing bisque dolls in several locations in New Jersey.

RHEINISCHE GUMMI- UND CELLULOID-FABRIK MANNHEIM-NECKARAU, GERMANY

Originally a rubber-goods factory founded in 1873, Rheinische Gummi eventually became the primary German manufacturer of celluloid dolls and, for other companies, dolls' heads.

ROULLET & DECAMPS PARIS, FRANCE

One of the leading manufacturers of mechanical dolls, the company was founded in 1865. Its mechanical swimming dolls were known as Ondine; the heads were made by Simon & Halbig (q.v.).

SAALFIELD PUBLISHING CO. AKRON, OHIO, USA

Produced a set of cut-out muslin doll patterns in 1907, and its output included designs based on Kate Greenaway's illustrations. In the 1930s it obtained rights to manufacture Shirley Temple paper dolls.

SCHMIDT, BRUNO WALTERSHAUSEN, GERMANY

The company was founded in 1900 to make dolls of celluloid and wood. During the early 20th century it manufactured many character dolls with bisque heads, most of which were exclusively made for it by Bähr & Pröschild, which it bought in 1918. It continued also to produce celluloid dolls.

SCHMIDT, FRANZ, & CO. GEORGENTHAL, GERMANY

Founded in 1890, this innovative company produced dolls of wood, leather, composition and bisque. Bisque heads were made to Schmidt's designs by Simon & Halbig. The company is believed to have introduced many improvements in the manufacture of character dolls, including sleeping eyes, pierced nostrils, moving tongues and universal arm joints.

SIMON & HALBIG GRAFENHEIM, GERMANY

The second largest (after Armand Marseille) manufacturer of dolls' heads in Germany. Founded as a porcelain factory in 1869, it soon turned to the production of bisque dolls' heads, both for its own use and for other companies.

STEIFF, MARGARETE GIENGEN, GERMANY

Steiff established a felt clothing factory in 1877 and began to make felt toys in 1893. The first teddy bear was made in 1903. The company also made a number of character dolls after 1911.

STEINER, JULES NICHOLAS PARIS, FRANCE

Founded in 1855, the company specialized in the manufacture of mechanical bébés.

THEROUDE, ALEXANDER NICHOLAS PARIS, FRANCE

Théroude produced automata and toys from 1842 until 1895, using the mark *A. N. Théroude, Paris*.

VAUCANSON, JAQUES DE GRENOBLE, FRANCE

Vaucanson (1709–82) was the maker of some spectacular automata, which he exhibited at fairs. He eventually sold his work in 1743.

VICHY, HENRY PARIS, FRANCE

Best known for dolls that appeared to play music or shake tambourines to the tune of a musical box hidden in the cube-shaped platform on which they stood.

VIELMETTER, PHILIP GERMANY

Working *c.*1897, Vielmetter made, apparently, just one toy, the Artist, which draws caricatures by means of interchangeable, hand-operated cams.

WELLINGS, NORA WELLINGTON, SHROPSHIRE, UK

Working from the Victoria Toy Works, Nora Wellings and her brother Leonard produced, between 1926 and 1959, a wide range of exceptionally well-sewn soft toys and dolls. The toys, made of felt, plush, velvet, fur cloth and sometimes cotton, were marked with a sew-on label.

WOLF, LOUIS, & CO. SONNEBERG, GERMANY BOSTON AND NEW YORK CITY, USA

The company, which was founded *c.*1870, distributed both German and US dolls and commissioned special designs from companies including C.M. Bergmann, Hertel, Schwab & Co. and Marseille (qq.v.). Bisque-head dolls handled exclusively by Wolf after 1916 were marked *L.W. & Co.*

Major Manufacturers of Tin Toys and Toy Soldiers

ALLGEYER FURTH, GERMANY

Established as a maker of flat toy soldiers before 1800, Johann Christian Allgeyer also made semi-flats and a few solids. The family name was signed on the base of the figures. The company ceased production in 1896, and the moulds were dispersed.

ALTHOF, BERGMANN & CO. NEW YORK, USA

Founded as a jobbers in 1867, the company entered the toy trade in 1874, commissioning toys and possibly making some. It was one of the first US companies to make carpet (floor) trains. Its trademark, *A.B.C.*, was registered in 1881.

AMERICAN FLYER CHICAGO, USA

One of the most prolific manufacturers of toy trains in both cast iron and tinplate, the company was founded in 1907. It also made the unsuccessful British Flyer for the UK market.

AMERICAN SOLDIER COMPANY GLENDALE, NEW YORK, USA

In the early 1900s made hollow-cast toy soldiers that are almost copies of the work of Britains (q.v.).

AMMON NUREMBERG, GERMANY

A master pewterer, Johann Wolfgang Ammon made flat soldiers based on the troops of the Napoleonic Wars. He was succeeded by his son, Christoph, in 1836 and by his grandson, Christian, who continued to run the company until 1921. The fine quality figures are marked *C.A.*, *C. Ammon* or *C. Ammon in Nürnberg*.

ARNOLD NUREMBERG, GERMANY

Karl Arnold founded the company in 1906 and pioneered toys with sparking flints. The company produced a wide range of novelty toys both before and after World War II.

BASSETT-LOWKE NORTHAMPTON, UK

Wenman J. Bassett-Lowke had made steam engines for his father's firm, J.T. Lowke & Son, but in 1899 he founded a company supplying high quality toys, scale models and parts for model locomotive enthusiasts by mail-order. The first retail shop was opened in 1908. Märklin, Carette and, especially, Bing supplied Bassett-Lowke, which exercised a tremendous influence on the styles of trains made by the German manufacturers. Although Bassett-Lowke himself died in 1953, the company continued to produce model trains until the late 1960s.

BERGMANN STRASBOURG, FRANCE

A.J., C.T. and Charles Bergmann produced flat toy soldiers between 1800 and 1904.

BING, GEBRUDER NUREMBERG, GERMANY

Founded in 1863 or 1865 by Ignaz and Adolf Bing, this prolific manufacturer of toys, specialized in tinplate boats, cars and trains. Many of its lines were taken over by Bub (q.v.) in 1933. The mark *G.B.N.* was used until 1919 when it was replaced by *B.W.* (*Bing Werke*).

BLONDEL & FILS PARIS, FRANCE

Made solid toy soldiers between 1839 and 1851.

BOIS, DU HANOVER, GERMANY

Established in 1830, J.E. du Bois made mostly flats, although some, now rare, solid toy soldiers were produced.

BONNET, VICTOR, & CIE PARIS, FRANCE

In 1919 Bonnet took over the original Fernand Martin (q.v.) company and continued to produce many of Martin's original toys.

BRIMTOY LTD LONDON, UK

This company was manufacturing tinplate toys from some time before 1914. Its main output consisted of cheap train sets and road vehicles, and its mark was Nelson's Colum. In 1932 it amalgamated with Wells (q.v.) to become Wells Brimtoy.

BRITAINS LTD LONDON, UK

Established in the late 1840s by William Britain (1828–1906), an ingenious toy maker, William Britain Jr (1860–1933) created the first hollow-cast toy soldiers, which appeared on the market in 1893. The company was incorporated in 1907 and became the leading producer of toy soldiers in the world. Although economics forced the company into the production of plastic soldiers in 1965, metal soldiers have been made again since 1985.

BROWN, GEORGE W., & CO.
CONNECTICUT, USA

Founded in 1856, this was the first US company known to have used clockwork mechanisms in its toys. Its output included a wide range of toys from novelty figures to boats. In 1869 it amalgamated with J. & E. Stevens to become Stevens & Brown Manufacturing Co. (q.v.).

BUB
NUREMBERG,
GERMANY

Founded in 1851 by Karl Bub, the company made a variety of tinplate toys, including trains, some of which had clockwork mechanisms. In 1933 Bub took over many of the Bing (q.v.) lines, and after World War II it worked closely with Tipp & Co, before closing in 1967.

BURNETT LTD
BIRMINGHAM AND
LONDON, UK

Founded c.1910, the company made tinplate road vehicles and was taken over by Chad Valley.

CARETTE
NUREMBERG,
GERMANY

A Frenchman, Georges Carette began producing tinplate toys in 1886, supplying both Bing and Bassett-Lowke (qq.v.). The company's peak of production was between 1905 and 1914, but the factory closed in 1917 when Carette returned to France during World War I.

CARLISLE & FINCH
CINCINATTI, OHIO,
USA

Robert S. Finch and Morton Carlisle founded the company in 1894

to make model railways and electric-powered streetcars.

CHAD VALLEY
BIRMINGHAM, UK

Established by 1820 by Anthony Bunn Johnson, the name Chad Valley was used as a trademark when the new factory near the Chad stream was opened in 1897. The company made tinplate toys, mainly cars and buses, in the 1930s and also made soft toys.

CHARBENS
LONDON, UK

Founded in the 1930s by Charles Benson, the company was among the first UK manufacturers of diecast toys. It also produced a range of hollow-cast toy soldiers and figures. It ceased production in the 1960s.

C.I.J. (COMPAGNIE
INDUSTRIELLE
DU JOUET)
PARIS, FRANCE

The company, founded c.1920, made toy quality model cars, including an Alfa Romeo P2. It took over André Citröen Toys (q.v.) in 1936.

CITROEN
BRIARE, FRANCE

Founded in 1923 as Les Jouets Citroën to make models of Citroën to make models of Citroën cars to promote the real thing; the tinplate toys were made by C.I.J. (q.v.) from 1936.

COMET METAL
PRODUCTS
NEW YORK, USA

First made toy soldiers, sold under the name Brigadier, in 1938. The figures have thick stands, and flats, semi-flats and solids were produced.

CORGI TOYS
LONDON, UK

Launched in 1955, Corgi Toys were part of the Mettoy Company (q.v.). A range of scale model automotive toys with clear plastic windows appeared, designed to compete with Disney Toys, which it did successfully by continually introducing details such as opening bonnets, opening boots with spare wheels and full suspension.

CRESCENT TOY CO.
LONDON AND
CYMCARN, UK

A company founded in 1922 to make hollow-cast toy soldiers.

DENECKE
BRUNSWICK,
GERMANY

In the early 19th century, flat toy soldiers were produced representing Napoleonic troops and Brunswick militia. In 1820 Denecke's widow sold part of the company to Wegmann; the remainder was taken over by Wollrath Denecke in 1842 and sold, in 1870, to L. Link.

DINKY TOYS
LIVERPOOL, UK

Part of the Meccano group, Dinky Toys were made from 1933 until 1979. They were launched in direct competition with Tootsietoys and by the mid-1930s were market leaders.

DISTLER, JOHANN
NUREMBERG,
GERMANY

Famed for penny toys and a range of toy cars and trains, the company, founded in 1900, was taken over by Trix (q.v.) and ceased production in 1962.

DOLL & CIE
NUREMBERG,
GERMANY

Peter Doll and J. Sondheim founded the company in 1898 to make steam engines and other novelty toys. It was taken over by Gebrüder Fleischmann (q.v.) in 1938.

DORFLER
FURTH, GERMANY

Hans Dorfler made semi-flats and solids between c.1980 and 1945. The figures were mostly based on the armies of World War I.

EBERL, HANS
NUREMBERG,
GERMANY

Founded c.1900, the company produced novelty toys and cars. Its trademark was *H.E.N.* or a clown in a circle with *Ebo Hui Hui* or *Oi Oi.*

EINFALT,
GERBRUDER
NUREMBERG,
GERMANY

Founded in 1922 by George and Johann Einfalt, the company produced a range of novelty toys and road vehicles.

FISCHER, H., & CO.
NUREMBERG,
GERMANY

Henry Fischer founded the company in 1908 to manufacture a wide range of tinplate toys, including cars and some animated toys such as the Toonerville Trolley. The trademark, which was not always used, was a fish.

FLEISCHMANN,
GEBRUDER
NUREMBERG,
GERMANY

Jean Fleischmann founded the company in 1887; it manufactured a wide range of toys – especially boats and floating toys – and, later, trains.

FRAAS
BRESLAU, POLAND

Between 1854 and 1912 Johann Carl Fraas made flats and solids, including some civilian models.

GOTTSCHALK
NUREMBERG,
GERMANY

J.W. Gottschalk produced a range of flats between 1768 and 1843. Many were marked *F.E.* for F. Eggiman, Gottschalk's most important engraver.

GREY IRON
CASTING COMPANY
MOUNT JOY,
PENNSYLVANIA,
USA

Founded c.1904, the company produced rather crudely moulded cast iron toy soldiers.

GUNTHERMANN
NUREMBERG,
GERMANY

Founded in 1877 by Siegried Günthermann, the company made a wide range of toys, including cars, aircraft and horse-drawn vehicles.

HAFFNER, JOHANN
FURTH, GERMANY

Founded in 1838, the company produced a range of toy soldiers as flats, semi-flats and solids, including representations of soldiers from the 1870 Franco-German War.

HASELBACH, J.C.
BERLIN, GERMANY

Between c.1848 and 1900 the company used 5,000–6,000 different moulds for toy soldiers representing forces of the Thirty Years' Wars and the Crusades.

HAUSSER, O. & M.
LUDWIGSBURG
AND STUTTGART,
GERMANY

Founded in 1904 by Otto and Max Hausser, who had previously traded as Muller & Freyer, the company specialized in the production of well-made tinplate vehicles and composition figures and toy soldiers, which were made of a substance known as Elastolin, the trademark found on the bases of the figures.

HEINRICHSEN,
ERNST
LUDWIGSBURG
AND STUTTGART,
GERMANY

Founded in 1830, the company produced toy soldiers, especially flats. It was taken over by Ernst's son, Wilhelm in 1869 and ceased production in 1945.

HESS
NUREMBERG,
GERMANY

Mattheus (Mathias) Hess founded the company in 1826 originally to make toy trains. He later introduced fly-wheel driven toy cars, in a range known as 'Hessmobiles', which may be identified by the starting handle used to wind up the friction mechanism. Johann L. Hess inherited the company in 1866; it ceased production in 1934.

HEYDE, GEORG
DRESDEN,
GERMANY

Established by 1870, the company made toy soldiers, producing solids, semi-flats and some hollow-cast figures. Production ceased during World War II.

HILL, JOHN, & CO.
ISLINGTON,
LONDON, UK

Founded *c.*1900 by the Wood brothers, this company is perhaps the best known UK manufacturer of hollow-cast toy soldiers after Britains, with whom it was a direct competitor. The factory closed in 1960.

HILPERT
COBURG AND
NUREMBERG,
GERMANY

The family business was active from *c.*1720 to 1822 making flat toy soldiers, which are marked *H., Hilpert* or *J.C. Hilpert.* It is thought to be the first company to manufacture model armies made up of large numbers of figures.

HORNBY
LIVERPOOL, UK

Frank Hornby founded the company in 1901. It is best known for toy trains and for Meccano. Dinky Toys were introduced in 1933, and the company produced a vast range of toy road vehicles. It had branches in the US and France.

ISSMAYER
NUREMBERG,
GERMANY

Johann Andreas Issmayer founded a company in 1861 to make novelty toys and children's cooking ranges; it later made toy trains.

IVES
PLYMOUTH,
CONNECTICUT, USA

Edward R. Ives founded the company in 1868 to manufacture good quality cast iron and tinplate toys, automata, walking figures and, later, toy trains. In 1872 it became Ives, Blakeslee & Co, but was taken over by Lionel (q.v.) in the late 1920s.

J.E.P.
PARIS, FRANCE

Founded in 1899 as S.I.F. (Société Industrielle de Ferblanterie), the company was renamed Jouets de Paris in 1928 and Jouets en Paris in 1932. It made trains, boats, submarines and cars.

KINGSBURY
NEW HAMPSHIRE,
USA

James Wilkins founded a toy factory in 1888, and this was bought by Harry Thayer Kingsbury in 1895, the name being changed to Kingsbury in 1919. In the 1920s and 1930s it was the largest manufacturer of clockwork automotive toys in the US.

KOHNSTAM
FURTH, GERMANY

Moses Kohnstam founded a toy distribution company in 1876 and eventually opened branches in London, Milan and Brussels. A merchant rather than a manufacturer, Kohnstam's vast stock came from a number of German manufacturers, including Distler and Tipp (qq.v.), which added Kohnstam's trademark *Moko* to the packaging.

LEHMANN
BRANDENBURG,
GERMANY

Ernst Paul Lehmann founded the company in 1881. It originally made metal containers but branched out into novelty tinplate toys, many of which had fly-wheel mechanisms. Johann Richter joined the firm in 1911. It was sequestered by the Russians in 1949 but re-established in Nuremberg in 1951, where it is still in production.

LINEOL
BRANDENBURG,
GERMANY

Founded by Oskar Wiederholz *c.*1906, the company originally made horse-drawn tin vehicles but turned to the production of composition toy soldiers and figures (very similar to those produced by Hausser, q.v.) and tinplate military vehicles.

LINES BROTHERS
LONDON, UK

Walter, Arthur and Williams Lines founded the company in 1919; it manufactured tinplate and pressed-steel toys, including vehicles. In 1927 it registered the trademark *Tri-ang*, and that company became an offshoot of the parent organization, producing a wide variety of wood and metal toys.

LIONEL
NEW YORK, USA

Founded by Joshua Lionel Cowan (1881–1965) in 1906, the company at first made a variety of toys but later specialized in model railways and accessories. Part of the group that bought out Ives (q.v.), Lionel went into decline in the late 1930s and was taken over by the Gilbert Cohn group.

LUCOTTE
PARIS, FRANCE

In operation at the time of the French Revolution, the company made solid toy soldiers and figures. It was taken over by Mignot (q.v.).

LUTZ
ELLWANGEN
AN DER JAGST,
GERMANY

Ludwig Lutz founded the company *c.*1846 to make high-quality tin toys, including clockwork horse-drawn carriages, boats and trains. It was taken over by Märklin (q.v.) in 1891.

McLOUGHLIN BROTHERS
NEW YORK, USA

Between 1900 and 1912 this company produced copies of Britains' hollow-cast figures.

MARKLIN
GOPPINGEN, GERMANY

Thought by many to be the greatest producers of tin toys ever, the company was founded by Theodor Friedrich Wilhelm Märklin in 1859. It originally made children's cooking ranges, but diversified into boats, planes and trains. It is still in production.

MARTIN
PARIS, FRANCE

In 1878 Fernand Martin founded a company that produced an enormous variety of hand-painted, novelty toys and figures.

MARX
NEW YORK, USA

Louis Marx founded the company that was to become the largest toy manufacturer in the world in 1920. Marx bought up many other toy makers, especially those manufacturing novelty toys. After 1950 most of the company's output was in plastic.

METTOY
LONDON, UK

When Philip Ullmann of Tipp & Co. (q.v.) fled to the UK he founded Mettoy to make tinplate toys, notably cars and aircraft, similar to those made by Tipp. In the 1930s and 1940s the trademark was *Mettoy*, but in the 1960s it was *Corgi*.

MIGNOT
PARIS, FRANCE

Founded *c*.1825, the company began to produce toy soldiers in 1838, when it used the mark *C.B.G.* (for the initials of the founders, Cuperly, Blondel and Gerbeau). Lucotte (q.v.) was incorporated at some stage, and that company's mark, *L.C.* with the Imperial bee, is found on some pieces. Mignot is still producing toy soldiers.

MORRIS & STONE
LONDON, UK

Produced good quality diecast toys, which, in the 1960s and 1970s, were marketed as Budgie Toys. Its range included more than 60 models, but it could not compete successfully with Dinky Toys and went out of business in the 1970s.

OCHEL, ALOYS
KIEL, GERMANY

Produced flats in the 1920s and 1930s, including Kilia and Oki ranges, which were aimed at collectors rather than the toy market.

PLANK
NUREMBERG, GERMANY

Ernst Plank founded the company in 1866. It originally made magic lanterns and optical toys but began to make stationary and locomotive steam engines and road vehicles in the early 1880s. Production came to an end in the 1930s.

RADIGUET
PARIS, FRANCE

The company, founded in 1872, specialized in well-made steam boats and brass toy locomotives. A partnership with Massiot was formed in 1889.

REKA LTD
LONDON, UK

Founded by Charles W. Baker *c*.1908, the company produced a wide range of hollow-cast soldiers, many based on Britains' designs. Some of the moulds were sold to Crescent (q.v.) in 1933. Figures are marked *Reka* or *Reka/C.W. Baker.*

RENVOIZE, J.
LONDON, UK

Produced hollow-cast toy soldiers between 1900 and 1914. The horses are marked *J. Renvoize* on the base.

RIECHE, GEBRUDER
HANOVER, GERMANY

Founded in 1806, the company made flats based on subjects including the Indian Mutiny, Waterloo and the Conquest of Mexico. It ceased trading in 1938.

ROCK & GRANER
BIBERACH AN DER RISS, GERMANY

Established in 1813, the company produced many tin toys, including horse-drawn vehicles and clockwork trains. Up to *c*.1860 it was probably the largest manufacturer of tin toys in Germany.

ROSSIGNOL
PARIS, FRANCE

Founded in 1868, the company made tin toys, including carpet (floor) trains, clockwork cars, buses and fire-engines, which are often marked *C.R.* (after the founder, Charles Rossignol). It is thought to have been the first company to manufacture toy motor cars.

SCHOENNER
NUREMBERG, GERMANY

Founded in 1875 by Jean Schoenner, the company made steam trains, engines, boats and clockwork toys. It ceased production *c*.1904.

SCHREYER & CO. (SCHUCO)

In 1912 Herr Schreyer and Heinrich Muller founded a company that produced a wide range of novelty toys and some soft toys. Its range of plush-covered metal toys was introduced in 1920. The company is still in production.

SCHWEIZER DIESSEN-AMERSEE, GERMANY

Founded by Adam Schweizer in 1796 to make flats, which were sold, probably unpainted, by the pound, the company still produces a wide range of flats and semi-flats of both military and civilian subjects.

STEVENS & BROWN MANUFACTURING CO. CONNECTICUT, USA

Formed by the merger of George W. Brown & Co. (q.v.) and J. & E. Stevens, makers of cast iron toys, the company made tinplate dolls' house furniture and cast iron toys and money boxes (banks).

STOCK & CO. SOLINGEN, GERMANY

Founded in 1905 by Walter Stock, the company made tinplate toys, including cars, some of which were made in the style of Lehmann (q.v.).

SUTCLIFFE PRESSINGS LTD HORSFORTH, LEEDS, UK

The company was founded in 1885 but began to make toy boats in the 1920s. Early examples had spirit-fired, water-circulatory engines, but later models were powered by clockwork.

TIPP & CO. NUREMBERG, GERMANY

Founded in 1912 by Miss Tipp and Mr Carstens, the company became a prolific manufacturer of toys, especially cars. In 1934 the proprietor Phillip Ullmann, fled from Nazi Germany and founded Mettoy (q.v.).

TOOTSIETOY CHICAGO, USA

The name Tootsietoy was given to a range of metal toys, especially dolls' house furniture, made by Dowst Manufacturing Co., which was also one of the first makers – c.1910 – of diecast toys. In the late 1930s, it was renamed Playtoys.

TRIX NUREMBERG, GERMANY

The company made construction sets and introduced 16.5mm gauge electric trains. It was founded in 1927, and a UK subsidiary was established in 1935.

UEBELACKER NUREMBERG, GERMANY

Leonhard Uebelacker founded the company c.1860; it specialized in tinplate air and water toys.

WEGMANN BRUNSWICK, GERMANY

Established before 1820 by Carl Wegmann to make flats, the company used Denecke (q.v.) moulds. Carl was succeeded by his son, Theodor, and the company was later acquired by Bernhard Borning.

WELLS & CO. LONDON, UK

Established by A. W. Wells and registered in 1923, the company made tinplate aircraft, buses, cars and so on and was a pioneer of lithography. It took over Brimtoy (q.v.) in 1932 to form Wells Brimtoy.

WEYGANG GOTTINGEN, GERMANY

Carl Weygang manufactured flats from c.1820 until his death in 1872, when his son, Victor, took over the company. It continued in production until 1919. Figures were marked *C.W.G.*, *C.W.*, *W.* or, occasionally, *Weygang*.

WRIGHT, J.L., INC. CHICAGO, USA

Trading under the name Lincoln Logs USA, the company made metal alloy figures and log forts between 1910 and 1943.

Museums and Collections to Visit

A

Britains made this fly-wheel operated Equestrienne *c*.1910. As the horse circles around, the circus girl jumps over the bar.

A

B

The bisque head of this piano-playing automaton was made by Jumeau, one of the best known of French doll manufacturers. The French manufacturer of the automaton itself is unknown. The figure turns and nods her head as three mechanical movements cause her to move. The 4½in (11cm) cylinder plays four airs, the titles of which are listed on the tune sheet on the piano.

B

DENMARK

Legoland Museum, Copenhagen

FRANCE

Musée Carnavalet, Paris
Musée des Arts Décoratifs, Paris

GERMANY

EAST
Toy Museum, Sonneberg

WEST
Bavarian National Museum, Munich
Germanic National Museum, Kornmarkt 1, Nuremberg

HOLLAND

Open Air Folk Museum, Arnhem

MONACO

Musée Nationale, Mme Gallea's Collection, Monte Carlo

SWEDEN

Swedish Museum, Djurgården, Stockholm

UNITED KINGDOM

ENGLAND
Arreton Manor, Arreton, Newport, Isle of Wight
The Bowes Museum, Barnard Castle, Co. Durham
Bath Museum of Costume, Assembly Rooms, Alfred Street, Bath
Bethnal Green Museum of Childhood, Cambridge Heath Road, London E2 9PA
Birmingham City Museums and Art Gallery, Congrave Street, Birmingham
Blaise Castle Folk Museum, Henbury, Bristol BS10 7QS
Burrows Toy Museum, The Octagon, Milsom Street, Bath
Cambridge and County Folk Museum, Castle Street, Cambridge
The Castle Museum, York
The Gallery of English Costume, Platt Hall, Rusholme, Manchester
The London Toy & Model Museum, Craven Hill, London W2
The Lost Street Museum, Ross-on-Wye, Hereford & Worcester
Museum of Childhood, Judges' Lodging, Lancaster
Pollock's Toy Museum, 1 Scala Street, London W1
Strangers' Hall Museum, Charing Cross, Norwich
Victoria & Albert Museum, South Kensington, London SW7
Warwick Doll Museum, Oken's House, Castle Street, Warwick

SCOTLAND
Museum of Childhood, 42 High Street, Edinburgh EH1 1TB

WALES
Penrhyn Castle Museum, Bangor
The Welsh Folk Museum, St Fagan's, Cardiff

UNITED STATES OF AMERICA

ARIZONA
Christine's Doll Museum, 4940 East Speedway, Tucson, AZ 85712

ARKANSAS
Gay 90's Button & Doll Museum, Route 1, Box 78, Eureka Springs, AR 72632
Geuther's Doll Museum, 188 North Main Street, Eureka Springs, AR 72632

CALIFORNIA
Anita's Doll Museum & Boutique, 6737 Vesper Avenue, Van Nuys, CA 91405
Cupid's Bow Doll Museum, 958 Cambridge Avenue, Sunnyvale, CA 94087
Helen Moe Antique Doll Museum, Hollywood 101 and Wellsona Road, Paso Robles, CA 93446

COLORADO
Cameron's Doll & Carriage Museum, 218 Becker's Lane, Manitou Springs, CO 80829

CONNECTICUT
1840 Doll House Museum, 196 Whitfield, Guilford, CT 06437
Memory Lane Doll & Toy Museum, Old Mystic Village, Mystic, CT 06355

C
Louis Marx's speciality was to produce cheap and cheerful toys. The Walking Porter, which is 7¾in (20cm) tall, was made c.1935.

D
Tidy Tim was manufactured by Louis Marx c.1935. It is 7in (18cm) tall.

Museums and Collections to Visit

FLORIDA
Dolls in Wonderland, 9 King Street, St Augustine, FL 32084
Homosassa Doll Museum, Route 5, Box 145, Homosassa, FL 32646
Museum of Collectable Dolls, 1117 South Florida Avenue, Lakeland, FL 33803

GEORGIA
Madame Alexander's Doll Museum, 711 South 3rd Avenue, Chatsworth, GA 30705
Museum of Antique Dolls, 505 East President Street, Savannah, GA 31401
Toy Museum of Atlanta, 2800 Peachtree Road, Northeast, Atlanta, GA 30305

ILLINOIS
Lolly's Doll & Toy Museum, 225 Magazine Street, Galena, IL 61036
Time Was Village Museum, Route 51, Mendota, IL 61342
University Historical Museum, Illinois State University, Normal, IL 61761

INDIANA
Poor Doll's Shop Museum, RR 2, Box 58, Syracuse, IN 46567
Children's Museum, 3000 North Meridian Street, Indianapolis, IN 46206

IOWA
Doll Museum & Trading Post, Highway 30, Legrand, IA 50142

KANSAS
Thomas County Museum, 1525 West 4th Street, Colby, KS 67701

KENTUCKY
Essie's Doll Museum, Route 16, Beech Bend Road, Bowling Green, KY 42101

LOUISIANA
Doll Cabinet & Museum, Star Route, Box 221, Ferriday, LA 71334

MASSACHUSETTS
Children's Museum, 300 Congress Street, Boston, MA 02210
Fairbanks Doll Museum, Hall Road (off route 131), Sturbridge
Fairhaven Doll Museum, 384 Alden Road, Fairhaven, MA 02719
Wenham Historical Museum, 132 Main Street, Wenham, MA 01984
Yesteryears Doll Museum, Main & Diver Streets, Sandwich, MA 02563

MICHIGAN
Alfred P. Sloan Museum, 1121 East Kearsley Street, Flint, MI 48503
Children's Museum, 67 East Kirbey, Detroit, MI 48202
Gerwecks Doll Museum, 6299 Dixon Road, Monroe, MI 48161

MISSISSIPPI
Cotonlandia Museum, PO Box 1635, Greenwood, MS 38930

MISSOURI
Society of Memories Doll Museum, 813 North 2nd Street, St Joseph, MO 64502

NEW JERSEY
Doll Castle Doll Museum, 37 Belvedere Avenue, Washington, NJ 07882
Dolls Den & Museum, 406 River Avenue, Point Pleasant, Beach, NJ 08742
Good Fairy Doll Museum, 205 Walnut Avenue, Cranford, NJ 07016
Space Farms Zoo & Museum, RFD 6, Box 135, Sussex, NJ 07460

NEW MEXICO
Playhouse Museum of Old Dolls & Toys, 1201 North 2nd Street, Las Cruces, NM 88005

A

Zip, the climbing monkey, was made in the USA by the C.E. Carter Company. The tinplate string toy is 8in (20cm) tall.

NEW YORK
Adirondack Center Museum, Court Street, Elizabeth-town, NY 12932
Aunt Lens Doll & Toy Museum, 6 Hamilton Terrace, NY 10031
Brooklyn Children's Museum, 145 Brooklyn Avenue, Brooklyn, NY 11213
Diminutive Doll Domain, Box 757, Indian Brook Road, Greene, NY 13778
Margaret Woodbury Strong Museum, 1 Manhattan Square, Rochester, NY 14607
Town of Yorktown Museum & Shop, 1974 Commerce Street, Yorktown Heights, NY 10598
Victorian Doll Museum, 4332 Buffalo Road, Route 33, Rochester, NY 14514

OKLAHOMA
Disney Dolls Museum, Grand Lake 'O the Cherokees, Disney, OK 74340
Treasure House Doll Museum, 1215 West Will Rogers, Claremore, OK 74017

OREGON
Jacksonville Doll Museum, 5th and California Street, Jacksonville, OR 97530

PHILADELPHIA
Jonaires Doll & Toy Museum, Route 4, Box 4476, Stroudsburg, PA 18360
Mary Merritt Doll Museum, Route 2, Douglassville, PA 19518

SOUTH DAKOTA
Enchanted World Doll Museum, Sioux Falls
Camp McKensie Doll Museum, Mudo, SD 57559

TEXAS
Antique Doll Museum, 1721 Broadway, Galveston
Hobby Horse Doll and Toy Museum, 5310 Junius, Dallas, TX 78214
Storybook Museum, 620 Louis Street, Kerrville, TX 78028

UTAH
McCurdy Historical Doll Museum, 246 North 100 East, Provo, UT 84601

VIRGINIA
Doll Museum at Anne Le Ceglis, 5000 Calley, Norfolk, VA 23508

WASHINGTON D.C.
Washington Dolls' House Museum, 5236 44th Street, Northwest, Washington, D.C. 20015

WISCONSIN
Heirloom Doll Hospital, Shop and Museum, 416 East Broadway, Waukesha, WI 53186

B

Among the many toys inspired by the animated films of Walt Disney, was Marx's clockwork-powered Donald Duck Duet. As the smaller Donald bangs a drum, the larger figure dances on his drum. The toy was made c.1937 and is 7in (18cm) tall.

DEALERS AND FAIRS

UNITED KINGDOM
Chelsea Lion, c/o Chenil Gallery, 181–183 Kings Road, London SW3
Granny's Goodies, PO Box 734, Forest Hill, London SE23
The London International Antique Dolls, Toys, Miniatures and Teddy Bear Fair, PO Box 734, Forest Hill, London SE23

UNITED STATES OF AMERICA
Cohen Auctions, PO Box 425, Routes 20–22, New Lebanon, NY 12125
Confederate Dollers, PO Box 24485, New Orleans, LA 70124
Helen Harten, Red Door Antiques, Prescott, AZ 86031
Jackie Kaner, 9420 Reseda Boulevard, Northridge, CA 91325
Kimport Dolls, PO Box 495, Independence, MO 64051

Bibliography and Further Reading

DOLLS AND AUTOMATA

Borger, Mona, *Chinas: Dolls for Study and Admiration*, Borger Publications, 1983

Buchholz, Shirley, *A Century of Celluloid Dolls*, Hobby House Press Inc., Maryland, 1983

Cieslik, Jürgen and Marianne, *German Doll Encyclopedia 1800–1939*, Marianne Cieslik Verlag, Jülich, 1984; Hobby House Press Inc., Maryland/White Mouse Publications, London, 1985

Coleman, Dorothy S., Elizabeth A. and Evelyn J., *The Collector's Encyclopedia of Dolls* (volume I), Crown Publishers Inc., New York, 1968; Robert Hale, London, 1970

Coleman, Dorothy S., Elizabeth A. and Evelyn J., *The Collector's Encyclopedia of Dolls* (volume II), Crown Publishers Inc., New York, 1986; Robert Hale, London, 1987

Coleman, Dorothy S., Elizabeth A. and Evelyn J., *The Collector's Book of Dolls' Clothes*, Crown Publishers Inc., New York, 1975; Robert Hale, London, 1976

Coleman, Dorothy S., *Lenci Dolls*, Hobby House Press Inc., Maryland, 1977

Eaton, Faith, *Dolls in Colour*, Blandford Press, Dorset, 1975

Foulke, Jan, *Gebrüder Heubach Dolls*, Hobby House Press Inc., Maryland, 1980

Foulke, Jan, *Kestner, King of Dollmakers*, Hobby House Press Inc., Maryland, 1982

Foulke, Jan, *Simon & Halbig Dolls, The Artful Aspect*, Hobby House Press Inc., Maryland, 1984

Gerken, Jo Elizabeth, *Wonderful Dolls of Papier Mâché*, Doll Research Associates, Lincoln, Nebraska, 1970

Goodfellow, Caroline G., *Understanding Dolls*, Antique Collectors' Club, Woodbridge, Suffolk, 1983

Hillier, Mary, *Dolls and Doll Makers*, Weidenfield & Nicolson, London/ G.P. Putnam's Sons, New York, 1968

Hillier, Mary, *Automata and Mechanical Toys: An Illustrated History*, Jupiter Books, London, 1976

Hillier, Mary (editor) and Fawdrey, M., *Pollock's Dictionary of English Dolls*, Robert Hale, London, 1982

Hillier, Mary, *The History of Wax Dolls*, Hobby House Press Inc., Maryland/ Souvenir Press, London, 1985

King, Constance Eileen, *Jumeau: Prince of Dollmakers*, Hobby House Press Inc., Maryland, 1983

Richter, Lydia, *The Beloved Käthe Kruse Dolls Yesterday and Today*, Hobby House Press Inc., Maryland, 1983

St George, Eleanor, *The Dolls of Yesterday*, Charles Scribner's Sons, New York, 1948

Seeley, Mildred and Vernon, *How to Collect French Bébé Dolls*, HP Books, Tucson, Arizona, 1985

METAL TOYS

Adburgham, Alison (ed.), *Gamage's Christmas Bazaar, 1913*, David & Charles, Newton Abbot, Devon, 1974

Ayres, William, S., *The Warner Collector's Guide to American Toys*, The Main Street Press, Warner Books Inc., New York, 1981

Barenholtz, Bernard and McClintock, Inez, *American Antique Toys*, Harry N. Abrams, New York/New Cavendish Books, London, 1980

Bartholomew, Charles, *Mechanical Toys*, Hamlyn Publishing Group, Feltham, Middlesex, 1979

Boogaerts, Pierre, *Robots Futuropolis*, Paris, 1978

Bossi, Marco, *Autohobby*, Priuli & Verlucca, Ivrea, Italy, 1975

Cieslik, Jürgen and Marianne, *Lehmann Toys*, New Cavendish Books, London, 1982

Culff, Robert, *The World of Toys*, Hamlyn Publishing Group, Feltham, Middlesex, 1969

Daiken, Leslie, *Children's Toys Throughout the Ages*, Spring Books, London, 1963

Flick, Pauline, *Discovering Toy Museums*, Shire Publications, Tring, Hertfordshire, 1971

Franklin, M.J., *British Biscuit Tins*, New Cavendish Books, London, 1979

Gardiner, Gordon and Morris, Alistair, *Metal Toys*, Salamander Books Ltd, London, 1984

Gardiner, Gordon and O'Neill, Richard, *Toy Cars*, Salamander Books Ltd, London, 1985

Griffith, David, *Decorative Printed Tins: The Golden Age of Printed Tin Packaging*, Studio Vista, London, 1979

Harley, Basil, *Toy Boats*, Shire Publications, Princes Risborough, Aylesbury, Buckinghamshire, 1987

Harrer, Kurt, *Lexicon Blech Spielzeug*, Alba Buchverlag GmbH & Co., Dusseldorf, 1982

Herscher, Georges, *L'Art et les Biscuits*, Editions du Chène, Paris, 1978

Hertz, Louis H., *The Toy Collector*, Hawthorn Books/Thomas Y. Crowell Co., 1967; Funk & Wagnalls, New York, 1969

Kelley, Dale, *Collecting the Tin Toy Car*, Schiffer Publishing Ltd, Exton, Pennsylvania, 1984

Kimball, Ward, *Toys: Delights from the Past*, Applied Arts Publishers, 1978

Marchand, F., *Motos-Jouets*, L'Automobiliste, Paris, 1985

Moran, Brian, *Battery Toys*, Schiffer Publishing Ltd, Exton, Pennsylvania, 1986

Murray, Patrick, *Toys*, Studio Vista, London 1968

Pressland, David, *The Art of the Tin Toy*, New Cavendish Books, London, 1976

Rampini, Paolo, *Encyclopedia of Toy Cars*, Rampini, Milan, 1984

Rampini, Paolo, *Le Auto-Giocattolo Italiane*, Rampini, Milan, 1986

Remise, Jac and Frederick, *Les Bateaux*, Pygmalion, Paris, 1982

Remise, Jac and Frederic, *Attelages, Automobiles et Cycles*, Edita-Vilo, Lausanne, 1985

Remise, Jac and Fondin, Jean, *The Golden Age of Toys*, Edita S.A., Lausanne, 1985

Ricci, F.M. *Androids*, Scriptar S.A., Lausanne, 1979

Richardson, S., *Minic*, Mikansue, Windsor, 1981

Société des Amis du Jouet, *Jouets*, Paris, 1984

Tempest, Jack, *Collecting Tin Toys*, William Collins, London, 1987

Weltens, Arno, *Mechanical Tin Toys in Colour*, Vitgeverij Kosmos bv, Amsterdam/Blandford Press, Poole, Dorset, 1977.

TOY TRAINS

Adams, J.H.L. and Whitehouse, P.B., *Model and Miniature Railways*, Hamlyn/New English Library, London, 1976

Alexander, Edwin P., *The Collector's Book of the Locomotive*, Clarkson N. Potter Inc., New York, 1966

Bassett-Lowke, W.J., *Model Railways* (volumes I and II), W.J. Bassett-Lowke & Co., Northampton, 1906–8

Bassett-Lowke, W.J., *The Model Railway Handbook* (volumes III-XV), W.J. Bassett-Lowke & Co., Northampton, 1910–50

Becher, Udo, *Early Tinplate Model Railways*, V.E.B. Verlag für Verkehrswesen, 1979; Argus Books, Hemel Hempstead, Hertfordshire, 1980

Carlson, Pierce, *Toy Trains: A History*, Harper & Row, New York/Victor Gollancz Ltd, London, 1986

Carstens, Harold H., *The Trains of Lionel's Standard Gauge Era*, Railroad Model Craftsman, 1964

Coluzzi, Count Giansanti, *The Trains on the Avenue de Ruminé*, New Cavendish Books, London/Editions Serge Godin, Paris, 1982

Ellis, Hamilton, *Model Railways 1838–1939*, Allen & Unwin, London, 1962

Foster, Michael, *Hornby Dublo Trains*, New Cavendish Books, London, 1980

Fraley, Donald S., *Lionel Trains, Standard of the World 1900–1943*, Train Collectors' Association, 1976

Fuller, Roland, *The Bassett-Lowke Story*, New Cavendish Books, London, 1984

Gomm, P.G., *Older Locomotives 1900–1942*, Thomas Nelson, Walton-on-Thames, 1970

Graebe, Chris and Julie, *The Hornby Gauge 0 System*, New Cavendish Books, London, 1985

Hare, Frank C., Burke, James J., Jr and Wolken, I. Stephen, *Toy Train Treasury* (volumes I and II), Iron Horse Productions, 1974

Harley, Basil, *Toyshop Steam*, Model and Allied Publications, Argus Books, Hemel Hempstead, Hertfordshire, 1978

Hertz, Louis H., *Riding the Tinplate Rails*, Model Craftsman Publishing Co., 1944

Hertz, Louis H., *Collecting Model Trains*, Mark Haber & Co., 1956

Huntingdon, Bernard, *Along Hornby Lines*, Oxford Publishing Co., Oxford 1976

Joyce, J., *Collectors' Guide to Model Railways*, Model and Allied Publications, Argus Books, Hemel Hempstead, Hertfordshire, 1977

Kowal, Case, *Toy Trains of Yesteryear*, Model Craftsman Publishing Co., 1972

Lamming, Clive, *Cents Ans de Trains Jouets en France*, La Vie du Rail, Paris 1981

Levy, Allen, *A Century of Model Trains*, New Cavendish Books, London, 1974

McCrindell, Ron, *Toy Trains*, Salamander Books Ltd, London, 1985

Randall, P.E., *Recent Locomotives 1947–1970*, Thomas Nelson, Walton-on-Thames, 1970

Reder, Gustav, *Clockwork, Steam and Electric: A History of Model Railways up to 1939*, Ian Allan, Shepperton, Middlesex, 1972

Steel, E.A. and E.H., *The Miniature World of Henry Greenly*, Model and Allied Publications, Argus Books, Hemel Hempstead, Hertfordshire, 1973

Thompson, R., *Hornby Silhouette: Whispers of Childhood* (video), Thompson, Sale, Cheshire, 1984

TOY SOLDIERS

Carman, W.Y., *Model Soldiers*, Charles Letts, London, 1973

Garrett, John G., *Model Soldiers; A Collector's Guide*, Seeley Services, London, 1965

Garratt, John G., *The World Encyclopedia of Model Soldiers*, Frederick Muller, London, 1981

Johnson, Peter, *Toy Armies*, B.T. Batsford, London, 1982

Kurtz, Henry I and Ehrlich, Burtt, *The Art of the Toy Soldier*, New Cavendish Books, London, 1979

McKenzie, Ian, *Collecting Old Toy Soldiers*, B.T. Batsford, London, 1975

Opie, James, *Toy Soldiers*, Shire Publications, Princes Risborough, Aylesbury, Buckinghamshire, 1983

Opie, James, *British Toy Soldiers: 1893 to the Present*, Arms and Armour Press Ltd, London, 1985; revised edition 1988

Opie, James, *Britains Toy Soldiers 1893–1932*, Victor Gollancz Ltd, London/Harper & Row, New York, 1985

Opie, James, *Collecting Toy Soldiers*, William Collins, London, 1987

Opie, James, *Toy Soldiers*, Boxtree Ltd, London, 1989

Richards, Len, *Old British Model Soldiers 1893–1918*, Arms and Armour Press Ltd, London, 1970

Rose, Andrew, *Toy Soldiers*, Salamander Books Ltd, London, 1985

Ruddle, John, *A Collector's Guide to Britains Model Soldiers*, Model and Allied Publications, Argus Books, Hemel Hempstead, Hertfordshire, 1980

Wells, H.G., *Little Wars*, London, 1913

JOURNALS AND PUBLICATIONS

Antique Toy World, published
monthly, by subscription only: Dale
Kelley, Box 34509, Chicago, IL
60634, USA (tel: 312-725-0633)

British Doll Artists' Directory: c/o
Ann Parker, 67 Victoria Drive,
Bognor Regis, West Sussex, PO21
2TD, UK

*Bulletin of the British Model
Soldier Society*, J. Cox,
Membership Secretary, 6
Anderson Close, Woodley, Romsey,
Hampshire SO5 17UE, UK

Collectors' Gazette, published
monthly, on sale at swap-meets
and by subscription: Martin Weiss,
92 Kirkby Road, Sutton-in-
Ashfield, Nottingham, NG17 1GH,
UK (tel: 0623-515574)

Doll Talk, Kimport Dolls, PO Box 495,
Independence, Missouri 64071,
USA

Granny' Goodies International Club –
Doll World Information Service:
PO Box 734, Forest Hill, London
SE23, UK (send stamped,
addressed envelope for reply)

Military Hobbies, A.E. Morgan
Publications Ltd, Stanley House, 9
West Street, Epsom, Surrey KT18
9RL, UK

Old Toy Soldier Newsletter, 209
North Lombard, Oak Park, Illinois
60302, USA

The Plastic Warrior, 65 Walton
Court, Woking, Surrey GU21 5EE,
UK

Toy Soldier Review, 1127 74th
Street, North Bergen, New Jersey
07047, USA.

Index

Italic page numbers refer to illustrations or their captions

NB Further information relating to manufacturers can be found at the end of the book.

PICTURE CREDITS

r = right, l = left, c = centre, t = top, b = bottom

Arundel Toy and Model Museum: p164. **Mr and Mrs Austin Smith Collection:** p134b. **Atwater Kent Museum, Philadelphia, Pennsylvania:** p186b. **Bethnal Green Museum of Childhood:** pp19; 76/77; 79; 80l; 80/81c; 82; 83; 144/145. **Bowes Museum, Barnard Castle, Durham:** p125. **Burrows Toy Museum, Bath:** pp147b; 164t; 165b. **Caleco, Inc:** pp96/97. **Pierce Carlson:** pp8/9t; 96/97; 151; 153; 156/157; 167; 168. **Chelsea Lion, London:** pp100; 135t, **Christies, South Kensington, London:** pp7; 9; 14; 126; 136/137b; 146/147t; 162; 163; 175; 178b; 179; 181t; 186/187b; 188; 189b; 191; 192; 193t; 194r; 197; 210/211; 213t; 214b; 217b; 219t; 221tr; 26t; 231; 244; 246. **Christies East, New York:** p161b. **Claude Detave Collection:** p66b. **Brenda Gerwat-Clarke Collection:** pp16/17c; 20; 23tl; 22/23b; 24/25b; 26; 29; 32; 34; 35; 36/37; 38/39b; 40; 41; 42; 43; 45; 46; 48; 55; 59; 58t; 60b; 78; 84/85; 86; 90; 91; 94; 95; 120c; 128; 135b. **Leona Gerwat-Clarke Collection:** pp30; 58b; 88/89. **Naomi Gerwat-Clarke Collection:** pp49; 54l; 80bl; 88/89; 92b. **Germanisches National-Museum, Nuremburg:** pp154; 155; 208t. **Granny's Goodies, London:** pp22t; 25r; 28; 47; 54r; 56/57; 61br; 61l; 64b; 66; 67; 70t; 72tl; 72b; 74l; 81. **Betty Harvey-Jones Collection:** p44. **Constance King Collection:** pp129t; 133b; 136; 139; 140t; 145; 224tr; 224tl. **The London Toy and Model Museum:** pp35bl; 141; 142; 143; 147b. **The Long Gallery, Chequers, Buckingham:** p24tl. **Lost Street Museum, Ross-on-Wye:** pp12; 178b; 185t; 190b; 191t; 193b; 194l; 196; 199b; 200; 201; 204; 209; 212/213b; 214; 221br; 219b; 220; 221tl; 224b; 225. **Eric Morgan Collection:** p183. **Musee d'Art et d'Histoire, Neuchtel:** pp105; 106; 107. **Museum of London:** pp208b. **Courtesy New Cavendish Books:** pp216; 217t; 218. **Phillips of London:** pp149bl; 158. **David Pressland Collection:** pp8b; 124. **Mildred D Seeley Collection:** pp69; 70b; 72tr. **Sotheby's, Billinghurst:** pp10; 148b; 149t; 161c; 23; 226b; 227. **Sotheby's, Chester:** p230. **Sotheby's, London:** pp11; 13t; 50/51c; 64; 68; 102; 104; 110; 111; 112; 117; 118; 119l; 120; 122; 123; 129b; 130; 131; 132; 174; 176t; 176bl; 177; 180; 181b; 182; 189t; 190t; 199t; 245; 247. **Sotheby's, New York:** pp103; 109; 113; 114/115; 119r; 172/173c; 244; 246b. **Tolson Memorial Museum, Huddersfield:** p18. **Jane Vandell Picture Library:** pp15; 121c; 121tr; 138t; 150; 152; 159; 160; 166; 187t; 198; 202; 203; 206; 228; 229. **Welsh Folk Museum, Cardiff:** p140b. **Margaret Woodbury Strong Museum, NY:** p53; 60t; 86tr; 92; 93; 132; 133; 165b.